Guide to the National Parks
Alaska

Moose antler tree

Guide to the National Parks
Alaska

N1451X

National Geographic
Washington, D.C.

ARCTIC

Point Barrow

CHUKCHI
SEA

NORTH SLOPE

Prudhoe
Deadhor

BROOKS RANGE

Cape
Lisburne

Alaska
Maritime
N.W.R.

Colville

Noatak
National Preserve

GATES OF THE ARCTIC
NATIONAL PARK
AND PRESERVE

ARCTIC CIRCLE

Cape Krusenstern
Nat. Mon.

Noatak

Kotzebue Sound

RUSSIA Bering Strait

C. Prince of Wales

KOBUK
VALLEY
N.P.

Kobuk

Kotzebue Sound

James
Dalton
Hwy.

Koyukuk

U.S.

Bering Land Bridge
National Preserve

Seward
Peninsula

ALASKA

Yukon

Norton
Sound

St. Lawrence
Island

N

Yukon

DENALI
NATIONAL PARK
AND PRESERVE

St. Mathew
Island

Kuskokwim

Dena
State Pa

Independent
Mine S.H.

Nunivak
Island

LAKE CLARK
N.P. AND
PRESERVE

Anchorage

Kenai
N.W.R.

Cook Inlet

Sewa

Wood-
Tikchik
State
Park

Kachemak Bay S.P.

BERING SEA

Kachemak Bay S.W.P.

McNeil River
S.G.S.

KATMAI
N.P. & PRES.

KENAI
FJORDS
N.P.

Pribilof
Islands

Bristol
Bay

Shelikof Strait

KODIAK
ARCHIPELAGO

Kodiak
Island

| miles | 200 |
| kilometers | 300 |

0

0

ALASKA PENINSULA

ALEUTIAN ISLANDS

Fox Islands

Alaska Maritime N.W.R.

Attu I.

ALEUT

Near Islands

Buldir I.

Rat Islands

Alaska Maritime N.W.R.

Same scale as main map

O C E A N
BEAUFORT SEA

Arctic National Wildlife Refuge

Chandalar

Porcupine

ARCTIC CIRCLE

CANADA
U.S.

White Mts. N.R.A.

Chena River S.R.A.

Fairbanks

Tanana

Charley

Yukon-Charley Rivers Nat. Pres.

Denali to Wrangell- St. Elias Drive

Yukon

A N G E

Delta W. & S.R.

Richardson Hwy.

sitna

Tetlin N.W.R.

Glennallen
Glenn Hwy.

Copper

Chugach S.P.

Valdez

Thompson Pass

WRANGELL- ST. ELIAS N.P. & PRES.

MAP KEY

☐ National Park

▨ Excursion Site

hugach N.F.

yard y.

Caines Head S.R.A.
Fox Island

Prince William Sound

Klondike Gold Rush N.H.P.

Alaska Chilkat Bald Eagle Pres.

Chilkat S.P.

Mendenhall Glacier

Juneau

Kootznoowoo Wilderness

GLACIER BAY N.P. & PRES.

Lituya Bay

Point Adolphus

Admiralty Island Nat. Mon.

Tracey Arm-Fords Terror Wilderness

G u l f   o f   A l a s k a

P A C I F I C   O C E A N

BERING SEA

Islands of Four Mountains

N   I S L A N D S

Andreanof Islands

Alaska Maritime N.W.R.

PACIFIC OCEAN

Contents

Opposite: Moose calf
Cover: Cruising Johns Hopkins Inlet, Glacier Bay National Park and Preserve
Pages 2–3: Mount McKinley flight-seeing, Denali National Park

Into the Wilds

*Scale and diversity foil all who try to simplify Alaska. Its immense
and ceaseless grandeur numbs the mind, glazes the eye, and plagues
the writer who would describe it.*
—William E. Brown
This Last Treasure: Alaska's National Parklands

THERE'S NO DOUBT ABOUT IT. ALASKA IS BIG—*REALLY* BIG. In fact,
365-million-acres big. As one resident points out, "If you were to
explore a thousand acres a day, 365 days of the year, it would take
you a thousand years to uncover all of Alaska."

It's also remarkably diverse. An Italian geographer who visited the
University of Alaska to observe the designing of the state's regional
atlases declared, "Alaska is like six different countries in Europe all
under the same flag."

Indeed, from the treeless tundra in the north, where the Arctic
Ocean freezes in winter, Alaska stretches 1,500 miles south to a
temperate coastal rain forest whose mountains rise abruptly from the
sea. From the Coast Mountains to Attu Island, Alaska is nearly as wide
as the lower 48 states. And with the tip of its Aleutian chain crossing
the International Date Line, Alaska is at once the most northern, the
most western, and the most eastern state in the Union.

In 1867 Secretary of State William Seward bought all this from
Russia for two cents an acre, and the public dubbed the seemingly
vast and empty land Seward's Folly. Today, it is this same spectacular
vastness and wildness (which is anything but empty) that draws
visitors by the thousands to Alaska's parks and preserves.

Eight national parks and six preserves, each one unique, protect
46.4 million acres of natural treasures. Katmai and Lake Clark lie
along the Pacific Ring of Fire, a region of active volcanoes, earthquakes, giant brown bears, and salmon. Whales, sea lions, and flocks
of seabirds seek out the cold, bountiful waters of Glacier Bay—a
mountainous refuge from the last ice age and the most visited of
Alaska's national parks—and Kenai Fjords, a favorite among sea
kayakers. Wrangell-St. Elias (at 13.2 million acres, the largest park and
preserve in the National Park Service) is a jumble of mountains and
glaciers so rugged and hard to reach that many remain unnamed and
unvisited by humans.

Above the Arctic Circle, Gates of the Arctic and Kobuk Valley
protect the tundra and migrant herds of caribou. Contained within the
fastness of Kobuk Valley, too, are a desert of sand dunes and a major

Curious bear, Katmai National Park

archaeological site. By comparison, Denali (one of the oldest parks in the U.S. and the keeper of the continent's tallest peak, Mount McKinley) seems positively civilized with its nearby railroad and hotels, yet the abundance and accessibility of the wildlife here has earned the park its characterization as a "subarctic Serengeti."

Except for Kenai Fjords and Kobuk Valley, Alaska's national parks adjoin national preserves—that is, wilderness lands where hunting is permitted and the construction of roads and buildings is prohibited. These preserves also protect native-owned lands that still are used for traditional subsistence activities just as they have been for thousands of years.

Most of the state's national parks are accessible only by plane or boat, but you can drive to Denali and Wrangell-St. Elias and to the borders of Kenai Fjords and Gates of the Arctic.

With so many spectacular parks and such diversity, how do you choose? A good strategy is to pick a geographic region—southeast, south central, southeast, the interior, or the Arctic—to explore in depth and then factor in accessibility and activities.

"Alaska," said one resident, "is so awesome, so much more extreme than anywhere else—higher, deeper, colder, lighter longer. Yet instead of making you feel puny, it encourages you to be more of who you are." In many ways, you have to live up to the landscape here. You also have to respect it: Travel wisely, be prepared, and know your limits.

If Alaska's parks are rugged, they are also fragile. Remember always to tread lightly. And wherever you decide to go, know that you are experiencing one of the planet's last great wilderness treasures.

HOW TO USE THIS GUIDE

Using the Guide

Welcome to the eight scenic national parks of Alaska. Whether you are a regular visitor or a first-timer, you have a great treat in store. Each of the parks offers you fun, adventure, and—usually—enthralling splendor. What you experience will depend on where you go and what you do. But exploring an unknown land is best done with a guide such as the one you now hold in your hand.

This book offers detailed strategies and practical information for visiting Alaska's parks. Itineraries guide you to the major sights within each park and highlight outstanding walks and hikes, kayak and canoe routes, and river runs, with estimates of time and distance to help you plan your trip. You'll also find suggestions for scenic drives and excursions to worthwhile sites near each park, from state parks and wildlife refuges to historical and archaeological sites to museums and cultural centers.

Our coverage of each park begins with a portrait of its natural wonders, ecological setting, history, and, often, its struggles against such environmental threats as pollution, erosion, and development. You'll see why a single step off a trail can harm fragile plants, and why visitors are detoured from certain areas that shelter wildlife.

Remote as Alaska parks are, some have already suffered from the impact of tourism. Be sure to leave all items—plants, rocks, artifacts—where you find them. Each park introduction is followed by the following blocks of practical advice to help in planning your visit.

How to Get There Getting around in Alaska can be challenging, due to the lack of roads. Boats and planes are sometimes the only option. The regional map in the front of the book shows the parks in relation to one another, in case you want to try to include more than one in a single trip. These parks definitely do not lie alongside interstates; where they exist, park roads are usually rugged.

When to Go The parks of Alaska are mainly summer parks. Summer days are long and temperatures cool. Weather is unpredictable; August and September can be wet. Be prepared for mosquitoes, particularly in June and July.

How to Visit Give yourself plenty of time to savor the beauty. Each park's How to Visit section recommends a plan for visits of one-half, one, two, or more days. Guidebook writers devised the plans and trekked the tours, but in most Alaska parks, you will want or need to hire guides or

MAP KEY and ABBREVIATIONS

□ National Park Service system

□ National and State Forest Service system

▣ National Wildlife Refuge system

▣ State and Provincial Park systems

State or Provincial Highway
—(33)—(1)—   Other Road

Scenic Byway   Unpaved Road

Trail   Railroad

Ferry   Inside Passage

Pipeline   Continental Divide

Wilderness Area   National Wild & Scenic River

Alaskan Maritime Nat. Wildlife Res.

National boundary   State boundary

POPULATION

- **Anchorage**   50,000 to 500,000
- Juneau   10,000 to 50,000
- Haines   under 10,000

SYMBOLS

⊛ State capital

⌂ Ranger Station/ Visitor Center/ Park Headquarters

□ Point of Interest

△ Campground

⛱ Picnic Area

ᴗ Overlook / Viewpoint

+ Elevation

≍ Pass

⤙ Falls

}···{ Tunnel

ABBREVIATIONS

Cr.	Creek
DR.	Drive
Fk.	Fork
Gl.	Glacier
Hdqrs.	Headquarters
HWY.	Highway
I.-s.	Islands
L.	Lake
Mt.-s.	Mount-ain-s
NAT.	National
N.F.	National Forest
Nat. Mon.	National Monument
N.H.P.	National Historical Park
N.H.T.	National Historic Trail
N.W. & S.R.	National Wild & Scenic River
N.P.	National Park
N.R.A.	National Recreation Area
N.W.R.	National Wildlife Refuge
Pen.	Peninsula
Pk.	Peak
Pres.	Preserve
Pt.	Point
R.	River
RD.	Road
Res.	Reserve
R.R.	Railroad
R.S.	Ranger Station
S.G.R.	State Game Refuge
S.G.S.	State Game Sanctuary
S.H.P.	State Historical Park
S.R.S.	State Recreation Site
S.W.P.	State Wilderness Park
S.W.S.	State Wildlife Sanctuary
S.P.	State Park
S.R.A.	State Recreation Area
U.S.F.S.	United States Forest Service

outfitters. The park chapters and the resources section at the back of the guide *(pp. 244–49)* offer suggestions of licensed companies that offer their services throughout the state.

Other Features of the Guide:

Excursions The excursions at the end of each park entry take you to other natural areas in the region if you have time to explore further. The distances noted at the start of each excursion are approximate and intended only to help in planning your trip.

Maps The park maps and the regional map are also intended to help in planning. For more detail on hiking trails and other facilities inside a park, contact the Park Service, phone the park itself, or visit the website. Get in touch with the individual excursions sites for more information about them. Always use a road map when traveling and make sure you carry detailed hiking maps when walking into the backcountry.

The maps note specially designated areas within park borders: Wilderness areas are managed to retain their primeval quality. Roads, buildings, and vehicles are not allowed in them. National preserves may allow hunting.

The following abbreviations are used for federal and state lands:

NP   National Park
NRA   National Recreation Area
NF   National Forest
NM   National Monument
NWR National Wildlife Refuge
BLM   Bureau of Land Management
SP   State Park

Information & Activities This section, which follows each park entry, offers detailed visitor information. Call or write the park, or visit the park's website to learn more. Brochures are usually available free of charge from the parks. For a small fee you can buy a copy of the "National Park System Map and Guide" by writing or calling the Consumer Information Center, P.O. Box 100, Pueblo, CO 81002; or phoning 719-948-3334. Visit the Park Service website at: http://www.nps.gov.

Entrance Fees Most of Alaska's national parks charge no fees at all. For national parks in general, how-

ever, in addition to a single vehicle entry fee, you can buy a National Parks Pass, which is good for a year and admits all occupants of a private vehicle to all national parks. The pass does not cover parking fees where applicable. For an additional $15 you can purchase a Golden Eagle hologram to affix to the pass for unlimited admission to U.S. Fish and Wildlife Service, Forest Service, and Bureau of Land Management sites. This is good until your parks pass expires.

People over 62 can obtain a lifetime Golden Age Passport for $10, and blind and disabled people are entitled to a lifetime Golden Access Passport for free, both of which admit all occupants of a private vehicle to all national parks and other federal sites and a discount on usage fees. These documents are available at any Park Service facility that charges entrance fees.

For further information on purchasing park passes, call 888-467-2757 or visit http://buy.nationalparks.org.

Pets Generally they're not allowed on trails, in buildings, or in the backcountry. Elsewhere, they must be leashed. Specific rules are noted.

Facilities for Disabled This section of the guide explains which parts of each park, including visitor centers and trails, are accessible to visitors with disabilities.

Special Advisories

■ Do not take chances. People are killed or badly injured every year in national parks. Most casualties are caused by recklessness or inattention to clearly posted warnings. Alaska requires special caution in getting around because weather can be so unpredictable. If it looks dicey, don't go flight-seeing or boating or take an air taxi. And beware of unlicensed bush pilots and charter-boat operators. Insist on inspecting their credentials.

■ Stay away from wild animals. Do not feed them. Do not try to touch them, not even raccoons or chipmunks (which can transmit diseases). Try not to surprise a bear and do not let one approach you. If one does, scare it off by yelling, clapping your hands, or banging pots. Store all your food in bear-proof containers (often available at parks); keep it out of sight in your vehicle, with windows closed and doors locked. Or suspend it at least 15 feet above ground, and 10 feet out from a post or tree trunk.

■ Guard your health. If you are not fit, don't overtax your body. Boil water that doesn't come from a park's drinking-water tap. Chemical treatment of water will not kill *Giardia,* a protozoan that causes severe diarrhea and lurks even in crystal clear streams. Heed park warnings about hypothermia. Take precautions to prevent Hantavirus pulmonary syndrome, a potentially fatal airborne virus transmitted by deer mice. And in Alaska, remember the mosquitoes can be wicked. Come prepared.

Campgrounds The National Parks Reservation System (NPRS) handles reservations for campgrounds at only one national park in Alaska, Katmai. You can reserve up to five months in advance by calling 800-365-CAMP (2267), or visiting the NPSR website at http://reservations.nps.gov. Pay by credit card over the phone or Internet. Or, write to NPRS, 3 Commerce Dr., Cumberland, Md. 21502.

Hotels, Motels, & Inns The guide lists accommodations as a service to readers. The lists are by no means comprehensive, and listing does not imply endorsement by the National Geographic. The information can change without notice. Many parks keep full lists of accommodations in their areas, which they will send you on request. You can also contact local chambers of commerce and tourist offices for other suggestions of places to stay.

Resources The back pages of this guide list additional resources that can be helpful: federal and state agencies, hotel and motel chains, and a select list of outfitters, guides, and activities.

Enjoy your explorations!

Denali

On any summer day in Denali, Alaska's most popular national park and preserve, visitors witness breathtaking moments in the wild: a golden eagle soaring off the cliffs at Polychrome Pass or a herd of Dall's sheep resting on a green shoulder of Primrose Ridge. Perhaps a grizzly rambling over the tundra at Sable Pass or a loon calling across Wonder Lake. Or clouds parting to unveil the massif of Mount McKinley, also called Denali, at 20,320 feet the roof of North America.

The ever changing drama plays endlessly. To experience it you need only follow the 85 miles of park road. The farther you travel, the more you'll see; the subarctic landscape opens up as big as the sky and Denali's creatures move through it with the grace of wild, ancient poetry.

In 1907–08, Charles Sheldon, a wealthy Easterner and friend of Theodore Roosevelt, overwintered in a cabin on the Toklat River. He fell in love with the region, which inspired the writing of his 1930 classic, *The Wilderness of Denali*. Dedicated to protecting the region, Sheldon spent nine years lobbying for legislation to create Alaska's first national park.

Finally, on February 26, 1917, President Woodrow Wilson signed the bill creating Mount McKinley National Park, named for President William McKinley. In 1980 it was renamed Denali—an Athapaskan name for the mountain meaning "the high one."

Expanded three times (the last in 1980 when the original park was designated as wilderness), Denali National Park and Preserve protects an intact subarctic ecosystem shared by about 40 species of mammals and (in summer) some 160 species of birds.

With only one dead-end, mostly gravel road slicing to its center, this "accessible wilderness" offers the rare chance to view Alaska's marquee wildlife in a truly stupendous landscape.

- South-central Alaska

- 6.03 million acres

- Established 1917

- Best months late May–mid-Sept.

- Camping, hiking, kayaking, cross-country skiing, wildlife viewing

- Information: 907-683-2294 www.nps.gov/dena

Mount McKinley reflected in kettle lake, Denali National Park and Preserve

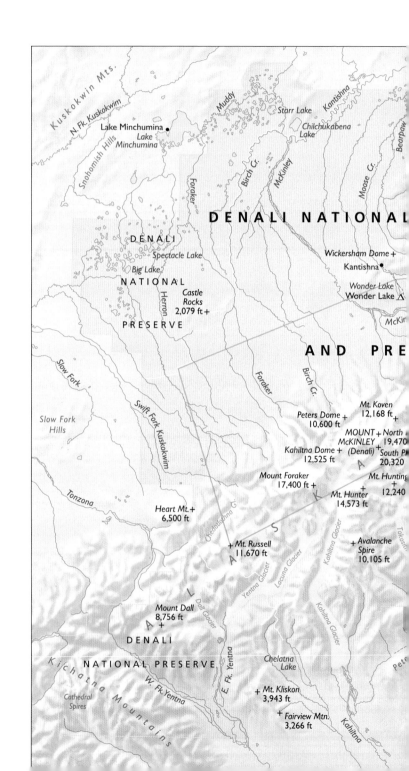

Kuskokwin Mts.

N. Fk. Kuskokwim

Lake Minchumina •
Lake
Minchumina

Snohomish Hills

Muddy

Starr Lake

Chilchukabena
Lake

Kantishna

Bearpaw

McKinley

Birch Cr.

Moose Cr.

Foraker

DENALI NATIONAL

DENALI

Spectacle Lake

Big Lake

NATIONAL

Castle
Rocks
2,079 ft +

Herron

Wickersham Dome +
Kantishna •

Wonder Lake
Wonder Lake ⋀

PRESERVE

McKin

Slow Fork

Swift Fork Kuskokwim

Foraker

Birch Cr.

AND   PRE

Slow Fork
Hills

Mt. Koven
12,168 ft +
Peters Dome +
10,600 ft

MOUNT + North
McKINLEY 19,470
Kahiltna Dome + (Denali) + South P
12,525 ft   20,320

Tonzona

Heart Mt.+
6,500 ft

Chedotlothna Gl.

Mount Foraker
17,400 ft +

A

Mt. Hunting
+
Mt. Hunter 12,240
14,573 ft

+ Mt. Russell
11,670 ft

Kahiltna Glacier

S

A

Lacuna Glacier

+ Avalanche
Spire
10,105 ft

Tokosit

L

Dall Glacier

Yentna Glacier

Kahitna Glacier

Mount Dall
8,756 ft
+

A
+

DENALI

Kichatna

NATIONAL PRESERVE

Cathedral
Spires

Mountains

W. Fk. Yentna

E. Fk. Yentna

Chelatna
Lake

Pet

+ Mt. Kliskon
3,943 ft

+ Fairview Mtn.
3,266 ft

Kahiltna

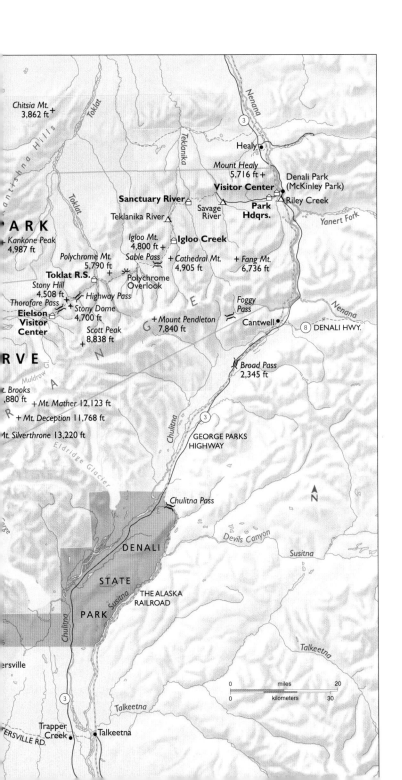

Chitsia Mt.
3,862 ft +

Kantishna Hills

Toklat

Teklanika

Nenana

3

Healy •

Mount Healy
5,716 ft +

Visitor Center

Denali Park
(McKinley Park)

Sanctuary River

Savage
River

△ Riley Creek

**Park
Hdqrs.**

Teklanika River △

Yanert Fork

P A R K

Kankone Peak
4,987 ft

Toklat

Igloo Mt.
4,800 ft +

△ **Igloo Creek**

Polychrome Mt.
5,790 ft

Sable Pass

+ Cathedral Mt.
4,905 ft

+ Fang Mt.
6,736 ft

Toklat R.S.

Polychrome
Overlook

Stony Hill
4,508 ft

Highway Pass

Thorofare Pass

Stony Dome
4,700 ft

Foggy
Pass

Nenana

**Eielson
Visitor
Center**

Scott Peak
8,838 ft

+ Mount Pendleton
7,840 ft

Cantwell •

8 DENALI HWY.

R V E

Muldrow

Broad Pass
2,345 ft

t. Brooks
,880 ft

+ Mt. Mather 12,123 ft

+ Mt. Deception 11,768 ft

3

Chulitna

Mt. Silverthrone 13,220 ft

Eldridge Glacier

GEORGE PARKS
HIGHWAY

Chulitna Pass

N

DENALI

Devils Canyon

Susitna

STATE

THE ALASKA
RAILROAD

Susitna

PARK

Chulitna

Talkeetna

ersville

0   miles   20

0   kilometers   30

3

Talkeetna

Trapper
Creek •

ERSVILLE RD.

• Talkeetna

How to Get There

From Anchorage, take Alas. 1 (Glenn Hwy.) 35 miles north to Alas. 3 (George Parks Hwy.). Go north 205 miles. From Fairbanks, take Alas. 3 west and south 120 miles. In summer, the Alaska Railroad runs between Anchorage and Fairbanks and stops daily at the Denali railroad station. In winter, the train runs on weekends only. Air service available in summer to nearby airstrips from Anchorage, Fairbanks, and Talkeetna.

When to Go

In summer, expect up to 21 hours of sunlight. The park road is open from late May through mid-September. July and August are the busiest months.

Autumn colors the tundra in late August or early September. In winter, visitors can travel 3 miles by road to park head-quarters and cross-country ski, snowshoe, or dogsled from there.

May and early June are the best times to climb Mount McKinley; after June, avalanches and crevasses threaten.

How to Visit

Plan on at least 2 days. The park is undergoing major mod-ifications to manage increased traffic; ask in advance about road and trail changes.

What Not to Miss

- Scenic, 11-hour bus trip to Wonder Lake with wildlife viewing
- Flight-seeing over the park
- Bear-watching at Sable Pass
- Caribou spotting at Stony Hill Overlook
- Walking Horseshoe Lake Trail around oxbow lake

If you have a camping permit, you can drive on the **park road** as far as Savage River Check Station *(Mile 14)*. Shuttle and tour buses run day and evening, late May through mid-September; schedules vary.

The shuttle-bus trip along the 85-mile park road to **Wonder Lake** takes 11 hours round-trip, including many stops to view wildlife; other buses offer shorter trips. Take a jacket, binoculars, and lunch *(food available only near visitor center or outside park)*.

If you want to get off and hike, buses will stop almost anywhere. To reboard, just flag one down; you may have to wait if buses are full.

Park campgrounds and buses fill up quickly. Plan to stay a night or two in a hotel or nearby private campground while waiting for reservations.

Where the Wild Things Are

In a land renowned for its wildlife, many people are both surprised and disappointed by how little they see. In truth, wild critters can be anywhere but often are not obvious due to forest or ground cover. Many animals, such as ptarmigan, sport colorations that offer excellent camouflage. You'll improve your chances considerably by looking in early morning or late evening.

If you are hoping to see a particular animal, make sure you look in the right season. Some migratory birds head south as early as August. Moose are most visible during the September rutting season. Caribou migrate spring and fall, sometimes startling visitors by crossing major highways. Bears wander salmon streams in midsummer.

Use your vehicle as a blind. Find a good vantage point, turn off the engine, and wait quietly. Many animals are not afraid of vehicles, but will fly or run if you get out. In the backcountry, sit still and scan carefully with binoculars. This strategy reveals far more wildlife than if you dash about the tundra.

Finally, look not for whole animals but for pieces of them—the flick of an ear, the tine of an antler, a color or shape that does not quite blend in with the rest of its surroundings.

Even on the tundra, don't expect to see animals as they appear on the cover of National Geographic magazine. Some willow and alder thickets are so tall they are able to obscure even a standing moose.

Brown bear

EXPLORING THE PARK

Park Road by Bus: 85 miles one way; 11 hours round-trip

Your bus journey begins at the visitor center *(Mile 0.7)*, surrounded by the spruce forest, or taiga. Within minutes you will see the railroad station used by the Alaska Railroad, and you pass park headquarters, where sled dogs are kept for winter patrols and summer demonstrations.

You soon begin climbing out of the taiga and into the treeless expanse of the tundra. Magnificent vistas open up; on a clear day (early morning or evening is best), Mount McKinley can be seen 70 miles to the southwest. As the bus crosses the **Savage River Bridge** *(Mile 14.8)*, note how the gentle, glacier-sculpted topography to the south meets the rugged river-cut canyon to the north; this spot marks the farthest advance of a glacier that flowed north out of the Alaska Range and across the valley thousands of years ago.

The road winds along **Primrose Ridge** before dropping into a marshy flat where spruce trees lean haphazardly. This "drunken forest" forms as permafrost thaws and the land slumps gradually downhill, tilting the trees. Watch for moose here and in other spruce forests, especially in areas with willow, their favorite browse.

Just beyond Teklanika River Campground *(Mile 29)* is the **Teklanika River Bridge**. Like other rivers in Denali, the Teklanika is braided by channels. Its Athapaskan name means "middle water." The road passes Igloo Creek Campground and cuts between **Igloo** and **Cathedral Mountains**, haunts of Dall's sheep, the world's only species of wild white sheep. Watch for them on the upper slopes.

If you want to see grizzly bears, a good place is just up the road at **Sable Pass** (3,895 feet). The grizzlies feed primarily on roots, berries, and other plant materials, and occasionally on arctic ground squirrels, moose calves, injured or infirm caribou, and carrion. To protect the bears' habitat, the Sable Pass area is closed to foot traffic, except on the road.

About 5 miles farther, the road climbs a steep slope to **Polychrome Pass,** where golden eagles nest in the multihued cliffs and a spectacular view of the Alaska Range opens to the south. Below see the **Plains of Murie,** where fast running water has created alluvial terraces. At Mile 53.1, the **Toklat River** has special significance, for it was here *(5 miles N of where bridge crosses river today)* that the naturalist Charles Sheldon built a cabin and spent the winter of 1907–08.

The road reaches its highest elevation at **Highway Pass** (3,980 feet) before descending to cross Stony Creek and climbing again to the **Stony Hill Overlook,** where, weather permitting, Mount McKinley looms into view 40 miles away. Watch for caribou as they funnel through the Stony Hill area. Although the total Denali herd numbers about 2,700, the caribou usually move in small groups. They can appear almost any time of day anywhere in the lowlands between the park road and the Alaska Range.

Eielson Visitor Center *(Mile 66)* is a scenic rest stop 33 miles from Mount McKinley. Arctic ground squirrels scamper about, begging for handouts they don't need—and shouldn't have. Wildflowers splash the tundra with reds and yellows, and sometimes you'll see a grizzly on a distant ridge or on the road.

Continuing west, the road cuts along a steep cliff, then enters more gentle terrain as it comes within a mile of the dark, gravel-covered snout of the **Muldrow Glacier** to the south. Beginning just below the summit of Mount McKinley, the Muldrow flows 35 miles through a granite gorge and across the tundra to its terminus. Twice in the last hundred years, for reasons not fully understood, the Muldrow has surged forward, most recently in the winter of 1956–57, when it advanced 5 miles.

You'll pass several ponds frequented by beaver, moose, and waterfowl, before finally arriving at Wonder Lake Campground.

World's Tallest Mountain?

Quick—what's the tallest mountain in the world? If you answered Mount Everest, you're correct. Yet an equally acceptable answer is Mount McKinley. How can this be?

It's all in the way you take the measure of a mountain. Mount Everest, situated in the Himalaya on the border of Nepal and Tibet, boasts the highest absolute summit—29,035 feet above sea level—in the world. When measured from its base (which is high on the Himalayan plateau) to its peak, however, mighty Everest stands a paltry 12,000 feet.

Mount McKinley, by contrast, soars to 20,320 feet from a plateau of only 2,000 feet. Measured from its base to its summit, then, McKinley looms thousands of feet taller than Everest.

Flight-seeing, Mount McKinley

Here the bus turns around for the 5.5-hour return trip, which includes plenty of time for exploring and picture-taking.

Twenty-seven miles to the south looms Mount McKinley. Its north face, the **Wickersham Wall,** rises more than 14,000 feet in a single precipice, one of the greatest mountain walls in the world. Just north of the campground lies **Wonder Lake** (2.6 miles long and 280 feet deep), home to lake trout, burbot, and moose, which occasionally wade in belly deep to feed on aquatic vegetation. Loons, grebes, and mergansers also visit the lake.

Hikes

The hiking opportunities in Denali, which is larger than New Hampshire, are endless; however, the only maintained trails are in the front country. They begin at the visitor center and at the railroad station near the park entrance.

The **Horseshoe Lake Trail** winds gently through a forest of aspen and spruce to **Horseshoe Lake,** an old oxbow of the Nenana River. The 1.25-mile-long walk takes about 1 hour round-trip.

Branching off this trail, just past the stream crossing, is the **Mount Healy Overlook Trail.** A more strenuous hike, it climbs 1,700 feet in less than 3 miles (one way), breaks above timberline, and ends at the overlook, where wildflowers, rock outcrops, arctic ground squirrels, and pikas await. If the weather is clear, you'll see Mount McKinley more than 80 miles to the southwest. A new accessible quarter-mile trail begins at the Savage Cabin Campground and leads to **Savage Cabin,** where demonstrations are held in summer.

For those seeking a moderate hike, the 3-mile **Triple Lakes Trail** offers excellent views of Mount Fellows, Pyramid Mountain, and other peaks in the Alaska Range.

In the backcountry, you can hike wherever you like—down a drainage, up a ridge, across a valley. Always stay on a durable surface to protect the delicate tundra. The rule of thumb is: Spread out, tread lightly, and leave nothing but footprints behind you.

Popular backcountry hiking areas (without trails) include Primrose Ridge, Mount Wright, Igloo Mountain, Cathedral Mountain, Calico Creek, Tattler Creek, the Polychrome Cliffs Loop, Stony Dome and Stony Hill, the Stony Creek Loop, the Sunrise Glacier Loop, Sunset Glacier, Eielson Visitor Center Ridge, and around Wonder Lake. Some of these hikes take an hour or more, others several days.

Campers must check at the visitor center before heading out. Management units sometimes restrict or temporarily close backcountry areas to protect habitats or because of animal activity.

Tundra and Taiga

"Tundra" derives from a Finnish word meaning "barren or treeless land." Dry or alpine tundra, found on ridges from 2,000 to 4,000 feet high, has sparse ground cover with plants that seldom grow more than a few inches tall. (Above 4,500 feet, it harbors only a few flowering plants.) Wet tundra is dominated by a low-growing plant community with a nearly continuous cover of sedges, grasses, and woody and flowering plants. Both types of tundra, usually found in the Arctic, are common in the foothills of the Alaska Range. "Taiga," a Russian word meaning "land of little sticks," refers to the boreal forest—a mosaic of thickets and muskeg. The apt name for this great circumpolar forest comes from Boreas, Greek god of the north wind.

INFORMATION & ACTIVITIES

Headquarters
P.O. Box 9, Denali, AK 99755
907-683-2294
www.nps.gov/dena

Seasons & Accessibility
Park open year-round. Park
road open, weather permitting, Memorial Day to mid-
September. Car travel to Savage
River, 15 miles into the park,
restricted to persons with
camping permits. During snow
season, park road is not plowed
beyond headquarters (Mile 3.1),
which limits access to skiers,
snowshoers, and dogsledders.

Visitor & Information Centers
Visitor center at east border of
park open daily late April to
late September. Eielson Visitor
Center open early June to
mid-September. Talkeetna
Ranger Station open daily
mid-April to Labor Day;
Monday through Friday rest
of year. Off-season information
available at headquarters,
open daily all year.

Entrance Fees
$10 per person per week; $20
per family; $40 annual fee.

Shuttle Bus Transportation
From the visitor center, buses
operate regularly from 5:00 a.m.
to 3:00 p.m. between late May

and mid-September. Reserve in
person. Fees range from $2 to
$33, depending on destination.
To make reservations, call
907-272-7275 or 800-622-7275.
Trips are not narrated, but
buses stop for wildlife viewing.
Campers' buses make twice-
daily runs.

Additional tours include the
Tundra Wilderness ($74) and
Natural History ($40). Reserva-
tions required; call 907-276-
7234 or 800-276-7234.

Facilities for Disabled
Most buildings accessible to
wheelchairs, as are some buses.
Please advise staff of need
when making reservations.

Things to Do
Free ranger-led activities:
nature walks, children's programs, sled-dog demonstrations, talks, slide shows, and
films. Also, narrated bus tours,
hiking, fishing, rafting, horseback riding, cross-country
skiing, and dogsledding.

Overnight Backpacking
Backcountry is divided into
units with limits on number
of campers (2 to 12). Permits
required; available free at
visitor center *(summer)* and
park headquarters *(winter)*,
first-come, first-served. Must

Bearberry in autumn colors

carry bear-proof containers. Backpacker shuttle fee $23.

Campgrounds

Four campgrounds (294 sites). 14-day limit from mid-May to mid-September; other times, 30-day limit. **Riley Creek** open all year; others late spring to early fall. Fees $6-16. RV sites available, except at **Sanctuary** and **Wonder Lake**; no hookups. In summer, reservations strongly recommended; call 907-272-7275 or 800-622-7275. Buses transport campers to Sanctuary, **Igloo Creek**, Wonder Lake, and elsewhere. Reservations required for **Savage River Group Campground**, contact headquarters.

Hotels, Motels, & Inns

(Unless otherwise noted, rates are for two persons in a double room, high season.)

INSIDE THE PARK:

■ **Camp Denali and North Face Lodge** P.O. Box 67, Denali NP, AK 99755. 907-683-2290. **Camp Denali:** 17 cabins, central showers. **North Face Lodge:** 15 rooms. $400 per person, all inclusive. 3- and 4-night stays only. Early June to mid-September.

■ **Denali Backcountry Lodge** 410 Denali St., Anchorage, AK 99501. 800-841-0692. 30 units. $340 per person, all inclusive. June to September.

OUTSIDE THE PARK:

■ **Denali Cabins** (8 miles south) P.O. Box 229, Denali NP, AK 99755. 907-683-2643. 42 cabins. $159. Restaurant. Mid-May to mid-September.

■ **Denali Princess Wilderness-Lodge** (half mile north) 2815 Second Ave, Ste. 400, Seattle, WA 98121. 800-426-0500. 352 units. $179-$249. Restaurant. Mid-May to mid-September.

■ **McKinley Chalet Resort** (1 mile north) 241 W. Ship Creek Ave., Anchorage, AK 99501. 800-276-7234. 345 units. $190-$240. Pool, restaurant. Mid-May to mid-September.

■ **McKinley Village Lodge** (7 miles south) 241 W. Ship Creek Ave. Anchorage, AK 99501. 800-276-7234. 150 units. $175-$220. Restaurant. Late May to early September.

Excursions from Denali

Denali State Park

| 75 miles southwest of Denali |

Wedged between the Talkeetna Mountains to the east and the spectacular Alaska Range and Mount McKinley to the west is Denali State Park, Alaska's third largest. Down the middle of the park runs **George Parks Highway,** the main link between Anchorage and Fairbanks.

A little exploration reveals a shifting panorama of wetlands and small lakes to forest to alpine tundra. The **Curry** and **Kesugi Ridges** (35 miles long and running north to south) form the backbone of the eastern half of the park, where alpine plants predominate. Marking the western section is the swift-running **Chulitna River.**

Expanded to its present size in 1976, Denali State Park shares a boundary with its larger neighbor, Denali National Park and Preserve, assuring protection for this intact ecosystem.

Although the park's mixed habitat supports a variety of wildlife, including common loons, moose, black and brown bears, beavers, and marten, don't expect to see many animals because of the thick vegetation (*see p. 19*). Denali State Park encompasses forests of cottonwood, white spruce, and paper birch with an understory of alder, cow parsnip, tall grasses, currants, and spiny devil's club. Dense thickets of birch and alder clog open areas. In summer, the landscape sprouts wild geraniums, lupine, fireweed, dogwood, and prickly rose.

Characterized by a cool and rainy climate fanned by southerly winds, Denali State Park's short summer averages temperatures in the mid-60s, with lows in the 40s. Moderated by the relatively warm coastal climate, winter temperatures generally range from 30° F to zero, but they can dip below minus 25° F. Annually, the average 30 inches of precipitation brings 180 inches of snow. First snows dust the park in early October; snow cover can last into July at elevations above 2,500 feet. The deep, persistent snowpack is a big draw for avid cross-country skiers.

What to See and Do

This primitive preserve shares the natural wonders, but not the crowds, of its neighboring park. If you're just passing through and the weather is clear, be sure to pull off at any of the numerous vantage points along the Parks Highway. The views of the heart of the Alaska Range are breathtaking.

Denali Viewpoint South (*Mile 135.2*) arguably boasts the finest

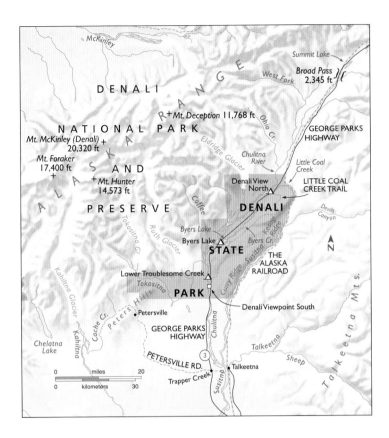

view anywhere of the Alaska Range and Mount McKinley. On fine days, even the most jaded of highway travelers pause here. The pristine panorama includes distant Ruth Glacier Valley and the Chulitna River. An interpretive display at the site identifies the peaks and other natural landmarks.

Continue on to Mile 147.1, where you enter the park. The small **visitor center** here has natural history displays along with maps, books, and bug spray for sale.

Camping

The park has four campgrounds from which to choose: Lower Troublesome Creek, Byers Lake, Byers Lake Lakeshore, and Denali Viewpoint North.

Lower Troublesome Creek, with 20 campsites, lies just off the Parks Highway *(Mile 137.2)*.

Byers Lake, the busiest campground and main attraction, has 68 wooded drive-in and walk-in campsites near the lake. You'll also find a boat launch, picnic areas, day-use parking, well water, and park trailheads. (*Caution: Black bears wander through the campground. Bear-country camping rules are strictly enforced; ask a ranger for information.*)

Two public-use lakeside cabins are available with advance reservations (*in writing or in person only*). One, a rustic log structure with a sod roof, is accessible by car. The second has a great view of the mountains and can be accessed on the southwest bay by canoe or by a short, half-mile walk.

A short canoe ride or a 1.8-mile hike gets you to beautiful **Byers Lake Lakeshore Campground.** The six sites here offer the best of forest and lake, with wondrous views of Mount McKinley and surrounding spires. Try an invigorating swim from the clean granite sandbars at the inlet stream.

If the sky is clear, stay a night at the **Denali Viewpoint North Campground** (*Mile 162.7*). This 23-site wayside offers superlative vistas, picnic tables, outdoor exhibits, a paved and fully accessible

View of Mount McKinley from Denali North Campground, Denali SP

botany loop trail, and a memorial to the World War II aircrew that crashed on Mount Deception in 1944. In high season, the campground may be noisy; however, the walk-in tent sites offer some seclusion—and a chance to wake to the sight of the mountains painted with alpenglow.

Hiking

Even drive-through visitors should stop at the **Lower Troublesome Creek Trailhead** and take the 10-minute walk (0.6 mile) to the Chulitna River for superb mountain views. Deer fern, locally called fiddleheads, carpets the forest. Watch for beaver cuttings and look for salmon at the creek mouth. Among the variety of red berries here is the poisonous baneberry; to be on the safe side, don't eat *any* berries around here.

Upper Troublesome Creek Trail begins just north of the highway bridge *(Mile 137.6)*. If you hike the entire 15 miles to **Byers Lake,** you'll follow the creek for the first 8.3 miles before climbing Kesugi Ridge and eventually descending to the lake.

For a more challenging hike, continue on the trail from Byers to **Little Coal Creek,** another 21 miles. Plan to spend at least a night or two in the backcountry. All overnight hikers are urged to use bear-resistant food containers. *(Caution: Trail closed mid-July–Sept. when bears come to feed on salmon. Heed warnings; people have been seriously injured here.)*

If these long treks don't appeal, you can take the 4.2-mile hike that begins at **Byers Lake Campground Trailhead** and leads to the alpine zone via **Tarn Point Trail**. The hike becomes rigorous near the end as you ascend Kesugi Ridge, but you're rewarded on top with 360-degree views from Broad Pass to the Talkeetna Mountains.

Backpackers and day-hikers access Kesugi and Curry Ridges from several trailheads. The most northerly, **Little Coal Creek Trail** *(Mile 163.9)*, gains only 715 feet and offers the easiest access to the alpine zone. Along with unobstructed views of the Denali massif, you'll see kettle ponds and glacial erratics, some as large as a house, left by long-vanished glaciers. Blueberries, lichens, and wildflowers such as lupine and fireweed abound in season.

Watch for bears and other wildlife (and report any sightings of elusive mountain goats) as you traverse Curry Ridge. Nearly 5,000-feet high, the ridge is one of several longitudinal faults that parallel the Alaska Range.

Savvy Salmon

The salmon is a remarkable creature. Born and reared in fresh water, the fish migrates to salt water, where it spends most of its life. Then, somewhere thousands of miles out in the ocean, an internal biological alarm summons it home again. Swimming nearly nonstop (sometimes from 2,000 miles out in its ocean pastures), the salmon navigates back to the very river of its origin.

Male sockeye salmon

Upon entering fresh water, the salmon fights the current and limited time to find its way back to its native stream, to the very gravel bar where it was born. There it spawns—and ten days later, dies.

Salmon runs are precisely timed; they typically occur within one or two days of last year's run. Why? We don't know. Nor do we understand how salmon find their way back home or manage to time the journey so exactly.

Some scientists believe that salmon make their way through the ocean by using celestial navigation or magnetic orientation, or by recognizing underwater landmarks. Once this extraordinary fish reaches its river of origin, its sense of smell guides it upstream to its home (each river has a unique chemical composition, and therefore, a unique odor).

A salmon's journey is filled with hazards and predators, none more efficient than man. Of the 4,000 eggs a sockeye salmon lays, for example, only four will survive to maturity. Of these, only two will make it back upriver to spawn. The modern salmon fishery in Alaska is so efficient that almost all salmon entering a major river system could be caught if no limits were imposed. That means an entire generation of salmon could be wiped out in a single season.

Forecasting when and where to close the fishery and how many salmon should be allowed "to escape" the nets of fishermen is an inexact and often controversial science. Sometimes it borders on an art form—with intuition and luck thrown in. But the goal remains simple: to allow enough salmon up the rivers to spawn so that the salmon will always return.

Backcountry Hiking

For rugged adventurers and orienteers, a cross-country hike into the **Peters Hills** in the western end of the park provides an escape from the summer crowds. There are no trails here so the area sees far fewer visitors than elsewhere. The summits of the Peters Hills offer dramatic views across the Tokositna River to Mounts McKinley, Foraker, and Hunter.

You can access the area from the end of the 40-mile-long, gravel-surfaced Petersville Road, which intersects the Parks Highway at Trapper Creek *(Mile 114.9)*. *(Caution: Beware of seasonal flooding and potholes. Beyond Forks Roadhouse, Mile 19 Petersville Rd., 4WDs recommended)*.

This scenic route, with good views of the mountains from various locations, leads through homesteads and areas of pristine forest to the historic **Cache Creek/Petersville mining district.** Backpackers use some of the abandoned vehicle trails at the very end of the road as routes into the hills. Watch for bears, and always let a ranger know when you're venturing into the interior of the park—and when you plan to return.

Boating

Outboard motors are prohibited on Byers Lake, but you can launch your own canoe or rent one. Common loons and trumpeter swans frequent the lake—but take care not to disturb nesting birds. Several outfitters offer float trips on the Chulitna, as well as on other area rivers.

Fishing

Byers Lake supports red salmon, arctic grayling, lake trout, and burbot, but fishing is poor. Most successful fishermen troll deep for lakers. Rules prohibit fishing for salmon on Byers Creek upstream from the Parks Highway bridge. At high water the creek can be floated, but it's tricky and must be finessed.

▓ **325,240 acres** ▓ **North of Anchorage, Mile 131.7 to 169.2 on George Parks Highway** ▓ **Year-round** ▓ **Camping, hiking, backpacking, orienteering, white-water kayaking, canoeing, fishing, mountain biking, cross-country skiing, snowshoeing, wildlife viewing** ▓ **Contact the park, HC 32, Box 6706, Wasilla, AK 99654; 907-745-3975. www.dnr.state.ak.us/parks/units/denali1.htm**

Denali to Wrangell–St. Elias Drive

360 miles, 2–3 days The interior is Alaska's frontier.
Most of Alaska's great heartland can be reached only
by bush plane, if at all, but this drive gives you a
sampling of the state's magnificent, if harsh, interior: tundra and
muskeg, the continent's highest peaks, glaciers, forests, wild rivers,
and lonely expanses inhabited only by moose, grizzlies, foxes,
wolves, and a wealth of birds. Other attractions en route include
inland Alaska's only city, some colorful backcountry lodges, an
exceptional museum, river-rafting opportunities, Alaska's most
popular national park, and the country's largest national park.

*At entrance
to Denali*

From Denali National Park and Preserve drive north on the
George Parks Highway. The road negotiates the steep **Nenana River
Canyon.** Phyllite, a lustrous rock containing small particles of mica,
gives the canyon walls their luminous quality. This region is rich
in coal, evidenced by the dark seams that stripe the eastern bluffs
between Miles 247 and 251. The **Usibelli Coal Mine** east of Healy
is Alaska's top producer. Look for the giant dragline (weight
4,276,000 pounds) digging for coal seams here.

The highway plays tag with the silt-laden **Nenana River** for about
55 miles, rejoining it at its confluence with the 440-mile-long
Tanana River, one of Alaska's few commercially navigable inland
waterways. This major river crossroads spawned the port town of
Nenana (*Visitor center, George Parks Hwy. and A St. 907-832-5435.
Mem. Day–Labor Day),* which began as a construction camp for
the Alaskan Railroad, and a native mission school. The site at
which President Warren G. Harding drove the golden spike in 1923
lies just across the Tanana. To learn the story of the railroad, visit
the **Alaska Railroad Museum** (*Front and A Sts. 907-832-5272. Mem.
Day–Labor Day*) in the historic depot.

Evidence of the town's past as a river port lingers. Behind the
visitor center sits the *Taku Chief,* an old tug that once pushed
barges along the Tanana. In summer, barges loaded with supplies
for remote communities along the Tanana and Yukon Rivers churn
the muddy waters in much the same way that stern-wheelers once
served the rivers' isolated mining camps and villages.

Years ago travelers might have boarded a stern-wheeler for
Fairbanks, but you can continue along the highway for the 50-mile
drive, which is particularly beautiful in autumn when birch and
aspen burnish the rolling hills.

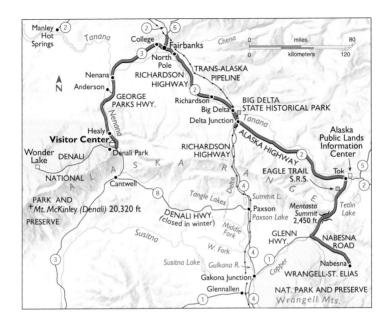

Just north of town, the Parks Highway crosses the Tanana. North of the span, on the left side of the road, is a pullout from which you can view the river, barges and tugs, the 1923 railroad trestle, and Athapaskan fish wheels set for king and chum salmon. As you drive the next half mile, look to the left and you'll see more fish wheels.

Depending on the season, you'll catch some of the best autumn colors about 4 miles north of town on the ridges above the Alaska Railroad crossing. Keep your eyes open for spruce grouse pecking for gravel along the roadside.

Between Nenana and Fairbanks, far horizons suggest the scale of Alaskan terrain. A double-ended pullout around Mile 319 overlooks the pristine forest and wetlands of the **Minto Flats State Game Refuge,** an important area for subsistence fishing, hunting, and trapping. This habitat nurtures mallard, shovelers, pintail, goldeneyes, and scaup as well as moose and black bears. You may also hear the cacaphonous cries of migrating sandhill cranes and Canada geese.

Another pullout at Mile 324.5 **(Purvis Lookout)** offers great views of rolling hills, the Tanana River, and the distant snowcapped peaks of the Alaska Range. If it's clear, Mount McKinley is visible

Sunset along the drive

to the east. As you proceed along this stretch of road known as **Skyline Drive,** watch for woodchucks (the groundhogs familiar to residents in the eastern United States), which are closely related to the Alaskan marmot and the hoary marmot.

Just shy of Mile 340 is an unmarked 1-mile loop road with views of 13,300-acre **Bonanza Creek Experimental Forest.** Bonanza Creek has been leased to the Forest Service for research until 2018. Studies indicate that the northern (boreal) forests soak up vast quantities of carbon dioxide, helping to reduce the greenhouse effect.

The Parks Highway ends near downtown **Fairbanks** (*Visitor Center 907-456-5774 or 800-327-5774*), at the junction of Alas. 2. This city of some 33,000 lies in the heart of Alaska's interior and serves as its hub. Not bad for a place that was founded by accident.

In 1901, fortune hunter and con man extraordinaire E.T. Barnette set off by stern-wheeler to Tanana Crossing. He planned

to set up a trading post midway along the Valdez Eagle Trail. The site was a busy crossroads for miners traveling to and from the goldfields. As the boat turned up the Chena River, however, it ran into trouble navigating the shallow waters. The captain dumped Barnette and all of his goods on the riverbank, leaving him no choice but to set up his post in the middle of nowhere.

But he got lucky. A year later gold was discovered nearby and the fast-talking Barnette drew miners and regional government offices to his town. His trading post exploded into a boomtown and he got rich. Eventually, though, his previous sins—grand larceny for one—caught up with him and he was run out of town.

A facet of Fairbanks's gold-mining history comes to life at **Gold Dredge Number 8** (*Mile 9, 1755 Old Steese Hwy. 907-457-6058. Mem. Day–Labor Day; adm. fee*). One of a small fleet of big dredges that extracted gold from creek beds around Fairbanks, the

5-story, 250-foot-long Number 8 operated from 1928 to 1959. You
can tour the dredge, visit the museum, and even pan for gold.

Alaska's gold rush and other historic eras come to life at
Pioneer Park *(Airport Way and Peger Rd. 907-459-1087. Schedules
and fees vary.)*. Yes, it's a theme park, but you'll find a number of
worthwhile sites here, including several museums.

The **Alaska Native Village Museum** showcases Athapaskan culture
through artifacts, arts and crafts, and native performances, while
the **Pioneer Museum** focuses on the early settlement period, particularly the Klondike and subsequent Fairbanks gold stampedes.

Visitors can also tour the *S.S. Nenana,* a grand old wooden

Giant cabbage

stern-wheeler that plied the Yukon River from 1935 to 1957.

You can experience the real thing just a few miles away. The stern-wheeler *Discovery III (1975 Discovery Dr. 907-479-6673. Mid-May–mid-Sept.; fare)* takes passengers on a 4-hour cruise along the Chena and Tanana Rivers, with stops for presentations on dogsledding and native culture.

At the nationally recognized **Georgeson Botanical Garden** (*W. Tanana Dr. 907-474-1944. May-Sept.; fee for guided tour on Fri. evenings*), the hemisphere's northernmost botanical garden, you'll discover the diversity of native and introduced plants growing under the midnight sun. The garden began in 1906 as the Horticultural Demonstration Garden. Early work at this experiment station emphasized cultivation of grains, grasses, and potatoes, but there were always plots of vegetables, flowers, fruits, and landscape ornamentals available for public viewing. From the start, the purpose of the station was to learn which crops would grow best, to develop techniques for crop production, and to share that knowledge with local residents. That tradition has continued without interruption for nearly a century.

As the tourism industry expanded during the pipeline construction boom, the demonstration flower garden became a main attraction for visitors to Fairbanks. In 1991, this garden, now part of the University of Alaska Fairbanks Agricultural and Forestry Experiment Station, became the Georgeson Botanical Garden. The 5-acre site features flowers, fruits, trees, herbs, and, after mid-July, some of the state's fabled giant vegetables, the byproduct of the long summer hours of sunlight.

Take a guided tour to learn how plants cope with the harsh winters, cultivation techniques for some of the world's hardiest plants, and other fascinating facts. The garden currently is being expanded to address its new mission as a center for education and research in subarctic horticulture.

To see a microcosm of Alaska's interior without leaving Fairbanks' city limits, visit **Creamer's Field Migratory Waterfowl Refuge** (*see pp. 40–42; 1300 College Rd. 907-459-7307. Guided tours summer only*). Bird-watching is a major draw at this 1,800-acre refuge, but you may also see snowshoe hares, wood frogs, and moose. Pleasant nature trails weave through the seasonal wetlands and boreal forest, habitats that give you a taste of what the Alaskan interior looks like.

From Fairbanks, continue by driving southeast on the **Richardson Highway** *(see pp. 230-35)*. You'll be tracking the mighty Tanana River, whose multi-channel bed at times measures more than a mile across.

About 90 miles down the road in the small farm town of **Big Delta,** take in the impressive view of the **trans-Alaska pipeline** where it crosses the Tanana. Just across the river, in **Big Delta State Historical Park,** you'll find **Rika's Roadhouse** *(907-895-4201)*. Built in 1910, it was one of a number of roadhouses that served travelers between Valdez and the goldfields around Fairbanks. Nicely renovated, it's been reincarnated as a gift shop. The grounds include a barnyard full of animals, the old telegraph station, and a small but well-stocked historical museum in a sod-roof log cabin. Note the monstrous bear trap and the wolf mittens.

Set in the woods a few miles from nearby Delta Junction is the **Alaska Homestead and Historical Museum** *(S on Dorshorst Rd. at Mile 141.5 Alaska Hwy. 907-895-4431. June–Aug.; adm. fee)*. A tour of this sprawling old homestead includes a range of items, from salmon-drying racks and a sled-dog team to antique farm equipment and an operating sawmill.

As you proceed southeast on Alas. 2, you're tracing a storied road in the state's history: the **Alaska Highway.** After Pearl Harbor was bombed, the U.S. military feared that Japan would invade Alaska—which did occur in June 1942, when Japanese troops landed in the Aleutian Islands. Knowing that military operations in Alaska would require an overland link between Alaska and the lower 48 states, the government in early 1942 sent soldiers and civilians to begin construction of a 1,422-mile-long highway between Delta Junction and Dawson Creek, British Columbia.

It was a daunting mission. The ground was so soggy in places that tractors got hopelessly mired and the road had to be built right over them. Despite the hardships, though, the thousands of workers managed to persevere and complete the vital link by November of that year. The road is pocked with potholes so be vigilant en route.

Continue a little more than 100 miles through this big-sky country and you'll come to the town of **Tok,** a tenuous beachhead in the interior wilderness—and a dogsledding hub. Stop by the attractive new **Mainstreet Visitor Center** *(Jct. Alaska Hwy. and Tok Cutoff. 907-883-5775. May–Sept.)* where locals give talks *(no*

Foxtail grass

charge) on everything from dog mushing to subsistence living. The center houses a variety of natural history exhibits, including a startlingly realistic taxidermic display of two wolves chasing a Dall's sheep.

Across the room are more natural history displays at the **Alaska Public Lands Information Center** *(907-883-5666. Closed weekends mid-Sept.–mid-May).* Here you can learn about salmon, grizzlies, and lynx—and find out why the locals prefer to trim their hoods and parkas with wolverine fur. (Frost doesn't accumulate on wolverine guard hairs). There are also exhibits on the Great Tok Fire (including a photo of one man on his roof trying to douse the encroaching flames with a garden hose) and on the things people hate most about Alaska (mosquitoes and those ankle-breaking tussocks, for starters).

Continue south on Alas. 1, also known as the Tok Cut-off. About 16 miles out of Tok, **Eagle Trail State Recreation Site** *(907-451-2695)* offers a mile-long nature trail as well as a 2.5-mile-long overlook trail that rewards with big views of the **Tok River Valley.** There are also lovely campgrounds available.

From here until **Mentasta Summit,** about 30 miles southwest, watch for wildlife, particularly moose in the ponds, bears along the rivers, and Dall's sheep on the mountain slopes.

About 20 miles past the summit is the turnoff for the **Nabesna Road** *(see pp. 219–20)* which penetrates the heart of America's largest national park and preserve, 13.2 million-acre **Wrangell–St. Elias** *(see pp. 212–223; 907-822-5235. Ranger station Memorial Day–Sept.).* One of the most expansive, rugged, and roadless mountain areas in the world, in 1980 it was designated a World Heritage site by the United Nations.

You can turn back here and retrace your route. If you decide to drive into the park on the Nabesna Road, stop first at the ranger station just off the highway to inquire about recent bear activity, road conditions (usually fine until Mile 29), potentially mucky trails, and the weather (the park spans three climate zones).

Why bother with such a troublesome side trip? Because you may see bears, moose, caribou, and even wolves in the lowland tundra along the way. Because you can pull into simple campsites that look out on small lakes sprinkled with waterfowl. Because you're surrounded by the muscular peaks of the Wrangell and Mentasta Mountains. Because it's about as wild and unpeopled a place as can be reached by car.

■ 360 miles long ■ 2-3 days ■ Late May–mid-Sept. ■ Nature walks, wildlife viewing, museums in Fairbanks ■ If driving off season, be sure to check road conditions.

Creamer's Field Migratory Waterfowl Refuge

90 miles northeast of Denali Located in the heart of Fairbanks on the site of a former dairy, aptly named Creamer's Field provides a sanctuary for large flocks of migratory birds in spring. Seasonal ponds and plowed fields strewn with tons of grain attract a variety of waterfowl and shorebirds.

Each year Canada geese begin arriving in mid-April, followed by sandhill cranes, pintail, mallard, shovelers, and other migrants such as American golden-plover. Cranes have migrated through this area for an estimated nine million years. "Their annual return," wrote biologist Aldo Leopold in *A Sand County Almanac,* "is the

Trumpeter swan

ticking of the geologic clock."

Observation platforms and easy access make for excellent bird-watching. Most of the waterfowl that stop here to feed and rest from their long journey soon move on. The refuge's mosaic of forest and open fields, however, provides seasonal habitat for a variety of songbirds, including swallows, robins, and Savannah sparrows, as well as northern harriers and some nesting ducks.

While dozens of species flock seasonally to the refuge to nest and rear their young, only a handful reside here year-round. In winter you may observe 30 resident species, including boreal chickadees, gray jays, redpolls, ravens, spruce grouse, willow ptarmigan, downy hairy woodpeckers, and even great horned owls.

As an added bonus, along the refuge's three trails you might also see a moose, a bounding snowshoe hare, or a red fox hunting voles.

The **Seasonal Wetland Trail** (*wheelchair accessible in summer*) and the **Farm Road Trail** provide access to marshes and open fields.

The easy, mile-long **Boreal Forest Trail** wends through open fields, along marshes, and through thick woods. At the trailhead *(beyond visitor center)*, pick up an interpretive brochure keyed to numbered observation points. *(Be sure to carry insect repellent in early summer.)* Along the path, you can see where hare and moose have nibbled plants, listen to ducks calling from the marsh, and watch swallows swooping after insects.

About midway along the trail stands a viewing tower from which you can see the transition zone between birch forest and black spruce bog. This ecotone attracts a variety of wildlife. Look and listen for Savannah and Lincoln sparrows, alder flycatchers, and orange-crowned warblers.

Continue your walk though black spruce bog where cotton grass, bearberry, blueberry, and cranberry proliferate. Wild rose and bluebells punctuate forested areas. That chattering you may hear from a spruce limb is likely a red squirrel. Watch for the dramatically revegetated area where a forest fire swept through in the 1950s.

Belle and Charles Hinckley started their dairy here in the early 1900s. In 1928 they sold it to Anna and Charles Creamer. Financial problems forced the Creamers to close the dairy in 1966. Because large numbers of migrating waterfowl had already discovered the farm's open grain fields, the community decided to purchase the land. Today the Creamers' old farmhouse functions as the visitor center for the refuge.

Friends of Creamer's Field *(907-452-5162)*, a nonprofit group, offers guided nature walks and seasonal events. Don't miss the annual **Crane Festival,** which runs from late August through early September. Headquartered here is the **Alaska Bird Observatory** *(907-451-7059)*, where visitors can watch songbird-banding demonstrations and generally learn about things avian.

■ 1,800 acres ■ Fairbanks ■ Year-round ■ Hiking, bird-watching ■ College Road; 907-459-7307. www.wildlife.alaska.gov/index.cfm

What Else to See & Do Around Fairbanks

Begin your interior adventures at the **Alaska Public Lands Information Center** *(250 Cushman St., Suite 1A, Fairbanks, AK 99701; 907-456-0527)*, a joint project of eight state and federal agencies.

Many trips into the interior require transport by air. If you have time to kill while waiting for a flight, take a walk on the **Fairbanks**

Musk-ox, Large Animal Research Station

International Airport Nature Trail *(W of rental-car parking lot).*

University of Alaska Museum
One of Alaska's top ten attractions, the University of Alaska Museum (*907 Yukon Dr. 907-474-7505. Adm. fee*) is a must-see. Here you can tour displays of Alaska native culture, mining, and the gold rush, as well as natural history. You can also view the aurora borealis in the museum theater and have your photo taken with Otto, the 8-foot-9-inch-tall stuffed brown bear that greets vistors at the entrance.

Among all the fossils, dinosaur bones, and the state's largest display of gold, look for Blue Babe, a 36,000-year-old steppe bison found preserved in permafrost near Fairbanks. The Boulder Patch exhibit shows how an underwater garden of kelp, sea anemones, sea stars, clams, and other plant and animal species exists at the otherwise lifeless zone at the bottom of the Beaufort Sea.

Twice daily in summer, Northern Inua athletes perform traditional native games and dances. Outdoor exhibits include totems and a restored Russian blockhouse.

Large Animal Research Station
The University of Alaska operates the **Large Animal Research Station (LARS)** (*Yankovich Rd., 1.7 miles off Ballaine Rd. 907-474-7207. Guided tours June–Aug. Tues., Thurs., and Sat., Sat. only in Sept.; viewing platforms open year-round; fee for tour*). Known as the "musk-ox farm," this research facility provides platforms from which visitors can get a close-up view of reindeer, caribou, and musk oxen. LARS scientists study the ways in which these animals have adapted to the rigors of Arctic life. The informative tour is recommended.

Chena River State Recreation Area

| 120 miles northeast of Denali |

Not 35 miles from Fairbanks lies the Chena River State Recreation Area, its rolling hills and domes dividing the Tanana and Yukon River drainages. The crystal waters and quiet forests of the upper Chena River contrast sharply with the river's lower reaches, a muddy meander through downtown Fairbanks. In the Chena River State Recreation Area, deep sphagnum mosses and black spruce cover north-facing slopes, while aspen, birch, and some white spruce blanket well-drained south-facing slopes. Pleasant campgrounds, waysides, river-access points, and trails lure summer visitors. At road's end try a soak at **Chena Hot Springs Resort** *(907-452-7881)*.

What to See and Do

If you have only a day, enjoy the 56-mile drive to the end of **Chena Hot Springs Road** *(off Alas. 6)*. The state recreation area begins at Mile 26 and enfolds the next 25 miles of the road. In summer you'll likely see grouse and moose as you drive along; take time out for a short hike or a picnic along a river sandbar.

Campgrounds include Rosehip, Granite Tors, and Red Squirrel, each with a slightly different setting *(all first-come first-served)*. Also available are six off-road public-use cabins *(contact Alaska State Parks at 907-451-2705)*, by reservation only. Year-round **Twin Bears Camp** on Twin Bears Lake is a state park facility operated by a community nonprofit organization *(907-451-2753)* promoting outdoor and environmental education.

Hikes in the Chena River SRA range from leisurely to strenuous. For a short hike take the **Rosehip Campground Nature Trail.** Numbered trail markers explain vegetation types, forest succession, evidence of wildlife activity, and river erosion. You might even see a moose, beaver, or wood frog.

Two other popular hiking routes are the Granite Tors Trail and Angel Rocks Trail. Both lead to exposed pinnacles of rock, called tors. Around 80 million to 60 million years ago, pieces of magma slowly drifted to the surface through metamorphic rock. Weathering and erosion of the surrounding earth sculpted these pinnacles into the strange shapes that loom today.

Day-hikers, rock climbers, and overnight backpackers access the **Granite Tors Trail** at Mile 39.5 of Chena Hot Springs Road. This 15-mile loop, considered moderate to strenuous, passes through forest

Chena Hot Springs Resort

of birch and aspen and out into open tundra. The trail forks after about a mile. Head east along the more developed trail. Its gradual ascent grows steeper (and the path less developed) as you continue clockwise around the loop. The middle portion of the loop traverses the **Plain of Monuments,** with grand vistas of the Alaska Range and close-ups of the tors. Rock cairns and wooden tripods mark alpine trail sections and lead to a shelter cabin about halfway around the loop.

Beginning at Mile 48.9 of Chena Hot Springs Road, the 3.5-mile **Angel Rocks Trail** leads to large granitic outcroppings near the north boundary of the recreation area. Though this loop trail gains 900 feet, it is considered an easy day hike, the tors being less than 2 miles from the trailhead (you can watch rock climbers scale them on summer days). For the physically fit, an 8.3-mile spur, the Angels Rocks to **Chena Hot Springs Trail,** leads to excellent views of the Alaska Range, Granite Tors, Chena Dome, and Far Mountain.

Other less visited trails offer quiet places where you can camp in solitude. The strenuous 29-mile loop of the **Chena Dome Trail** tops out at 4,421 feet, the highest point in the area.

The **Chena River** attracts canoers, kayakers, and rafters. Alaska State Parks provides a free guide to the river (*available on park's website*). Although the Chena is considered easy to navigate, storms often muddy the water, hiding obstacles that can capsize your boat. Logjams and sweepers (trees or logs overhanging the river) also are hazards. The narrow, upper portions of this Class II water are more challenging than the wider segments downstream.

Numerous river-access points and three bridge crossings offer several trip options. An easy float from first bridge *(Mile 37.8)* to Rosehip Campground *(Mile 27)* takes 3.5 to 6 hours. Chena Hot Springs Resort rents canoes and provides shuttle service between put-in and take-out points. Alaska Fishing and Raft Adventures *(907-388-4193)* stages guided trips. Fishing for arctic grayling is strictly catch-and-release.

■ **250,000 acres** ■ **Northeast of Fairbanks on Chena Hot Springs Rd.**
■ **Year-round access** ■ **Camping, canoeing, cross-country skiing, dog-sledding, fishing, hiking, rafting, rock climbing** ■ **Camping fee** ■ **Contact Alaska State Parks, 3700 Airport Way, Fairbanks, AK 99709; 907-451-2695. www.alaskastateparks.org**

White Mountains National Recreation Area

115 miles northeast of Denali Jagged limestone spires muscle above rolling hills, ice-cold streams, forests, and alpine tundra in this "accessible wilderness," as local land managers have dubbed it. **Beaver Creek National Wild and Scenic River** traverses the heart of White Mountains National Recreation Area, the largest national recreation area in the nation.

This region springs from vastly varied geologic origins. Because of compression along low thrust faults, patches of older rock now counterintuitively lie above younger rock. Mineral fragments of both volcanic and metamorphic character litter the surface.

The White Mountains themselves are sequences of limestone deposits. Forty-foot **Windy Arch,** one of the many area caves and arches, was formed from the continuous freezing and thawing of the fragile and easily eroded limestone. A careful traverse of the White Mountains will turn up marine fossils from ancient reefs ten million years old.

Four glacial advances spanning several hundred thousand years are evident here as well. Today, however, this vast wilderness is completely free of the glaciers that once burdened the slopes of its limestone peaks.

What to See and Do

Summer road access into White Mountains National Recreation Area begins at Mile 57 of the Steese Highway. Here, turn onto US Creek Road and drive 6 miles to Nome Creek Road. Go right, and continue 4 miles to the 13-site **Mount Prindle Campground.** Located near the 16-mile-long **Quartz Creek Trail**—one of more than 40 miles of summer trails in the NRA—this staging point provides ideal access to alpine meadows and views of Mount Prindle.

Return to the intersection with US Creek Road and travel 12 miles west on Nome Creek Road to reach the forested Ophir Creek Campground (19 sites), near the put-in for Beaver Creek National Wild and Scenic River.

Nome Creek Valley, the site of mining activity in the early 1900s, provides catch-and-release fishing and recreational gold panning in specified areas. Several ridges lead north to the high country around **Lime Peak,** offering spectacular views of alpine tundra, granite tors, and limestone cliffs. Off-trail hiking can be a challenge so be prepared.

At the Mile 57 turnoff from Steese Highway you'll see the **Davidson Ditch,** an 83-mile series of troughs and pipes that once carried water to the gold dredges of Fox and Chatanika. Capable of channeling 56,100 gallons per minute, the Davidson Ditch was an engineering marvel in 1929. Just up the road at Mile 60 of the Steese Highway is Cripple Creek Campground. It has 12 campsites *(2 are wheelchair accessible)* and a short **hiking trail** that winds through tall white spruce along the Chatanika River.

Wet and muddy trail conditions make the ten public-use cabins in the NRA accessible mostly in winter, when they are highly sought after. The 10-by-12-foot cabins sleep four, while the 12-by-16-foot cabins have a loft and sleep four to eight. Amenities are minimal, so you must provide your own firewood, as well as white gas for the lantern and cook stove. The Fred Blixt Cabin at Mile 62.5 of the Elliott Highway, is wheelchair accessible. Reservations for all cabins *(907-474-2251 or 800-437-7021)* may be made up to 30 days in advance.

Hikers and off-road vehicles share some trails: For example, both use 16-mile **Quartz Creek Trail.** Three research natural areas are closed year-round to motorized use. You can access two popular hiking trails—the 20-mile-long **Wickersham Creek Trail** and the 20-mile **Summit Trail** *(closed to vehicles)*—from Mile 28 of the

South view of Alaska Range from Wickersham Dome

Elliott Highway. At 3,207 feet, **Wickersham Dome** provides an easy 4-hour round-trip hike from the highway.

The BLM maintains more than 200 miles of **winter trails** groomed for both motorized and nonmotorized use. Call ahead *(907-474-2372)* for conditions. These trails access all the public-use cabins, spaced about a day apart for cross-country skiers, as well as the surrounding country. Special events here include skijoring races, in which dogs pull cross-country skiers. A 5-mile **cross-country ski loop** offering views of the Alaska Range and Mount McKinley begins and ends at the Wickersham Dome Trailhead.

Beaver Creek Boating

A clear-water, Class I river, **Beaver Creek National Wild and Scenic River** *(BLM NFO, 1150 University Ave., Fairbanks, AK 99709. 907-474-2200)* flows past the jagged peaks of the White Mountains and through part of **Yukon Flats National Wildlife Refuge** before joining the Yukon River. From Nome Creek Road to the Dalton Highway Bridge across the Yukon, a distance of about 360 miles, this may be the longest road-to-road float in North America. If you're not going all the way to the Yukon (a 3-week trip), arrange to be airlifted from a gravel bar near Victoria Creek, a good 110 miles downriver.

Put-in is at the lower end of the Nome Creek Road at the Ophir Creek Campground, where a small, long-term parking area provides a place to organize and prepare. Motorboats launching in the Nome Creek Valley have a 15-horsepower limit. You'll be on Nome Creek for 3 miles before joining Beaver Creek. Be prepared to line—that is, to tow the boat from shore or while wading— through shallow water and around sweepers before the paddling improves at Mile 7.

The river slows again in Yukon Flats National Wildlife Refuge. (A small boat motor will get you through.) Gravel bars make perfect camping spots to watch for wildlife and enjoy the solitude. Fishing excels for pike, Arctic grayling, burbot, and whitefish.

■ 1 million acres ■ 25 miles north of Fairbanks, between Elliott and Steese Hwys. ■ Year-round ■ Camping, hiking, boating, fishing, hunting, cross-country skiing, gold panning ■ Camping fee; cabin-use fee ■ Contact Northern Field Office, Bureau of Land Management, 1150 University Ave., Fairbanks, AK 99709; 907-474-2200. aurora.ak.blm.gov

Delta Wild & Scenic River

150 miles southeast of Denali

Flowing through the scenic Amphitheater Mountains and the foothills of the Alaska Range, the Delta River offers views of tundra, boreal forest, distant glaciers, and 13,832-foot Mount Hayes. River runners often see waterfowl such as pintail, mallard, and goldeneyes. They may also glimpse red foxes, beavers, moose, caribou, bears, and ptarmigan. Bald eagles nest along the river, and northern harriers fly over the tundra and wetlands.

Because of road access at both ends, experienced boaters enjoy this 2- to 3-day trip. Experience is a must: The Delta River is not for novices. On the upper stretches you'll have to run Class II to IV rapids and portage around hazards that include boulders, jagged rocks, waterfalls, and downed trees. Even experienced boaters should take precautions such as scouting the rapids below portages and at the river's confluence with **Eureka Creek.**

Begin at Tangle Lakes Campground at Mile 21 on the Denali Highway, west of Paxson. Here you will find a boat launch as well as lodging.

The first 9 miles of the trip pass north through three of the placid **Tangle Lakes,** which are connected by shallow channels of clear, slow-moving water. At low water you might need to line your boat through the channels for short distances.

The Delta River flows north out of **Lower Tangle Lake** and continues 20 miles from the outlet to the take-out point. The first shallow 1.25 miles are rocky and rated Class II to III. Following this first segment, and before you reach Wildhorse Creek, the river enters a wide canyon where you'll have to portage around unnavigable waterfalls. Watch the right-hand bank for the sign marking the portage. Here, a half-mile maintained trail takes you over steep, rocky terrain.

Below the falls, the river narrows and speed increases. Boaters must have white-water experience to float the next mile of rocky, Class II to III rapids. If you're lacking the experience, line this section. Below the rapids you'll find 12 miles of slow, meandering Class I water.

At its confluence with Eureka Creek, the Delta becomes cold, silty glacial water. At high water or after storms, strong cross-currents can tip a canoe. The last 7 miles to the take-out point are often shallow and braided with numerous channels and gravel bars. The water is swift and generally Class II. Most floaters take out near **Phelan Creek** *(Mile 212.5 on Richardson Hwy.),* a river distance of 29 miles from the put-in. Watch for the take-out sign on the right bank. By road it is 49 miles back to Tangle Lakes.

While it's possible to travel from Tangle Lakes to the town of Delta Junction, the river becomes very swift with high-standing waves and powerful hydraulics. Only experts should attempt Black Rapids, rated Class III to IV.

■ 62 miles long, including 20 miles wild, 24 miles scenic, 18 miles recreational ■ Alaska Range ■ Best months mid-June–mid-Sept. ■ Camping, hiking, white-water rafting and kayaking, canoeing, fishing, wildlife viewing ■ Contact Glennallen Field Office, Bureau of Land Management, P.O. Box 147, Glennallen, AK 99588; 907-822-3217. www.glennallen.ak.blm.gov

Yukon-Charley Rivers National Preserve

300 miles northeast of Denali

Sprawling westward from the Alaska-Canada border, Yukon-Charley Rivers National Preserve guards a variety of natural, cultural, and paleontological sites within its river valleys, rolling hills, and sawtooth cliffs. This massive but subtly beautiful and unscarred wilderness protects 115 miles of the Yukon River, as well as the entire 1.1-million-acre pristine Charley River watershed, which is half the size of Yellowstone National Park. Born of spring runoff, this national wild and scenic river tumbles 108 miles before its clear waters merge with those of the murky Yukon.

In the preserve, the Yukon River, silt-laden and confined, slices through a deep fault, grinding away ancient rock on its ineluctable surge to the Bering Sea. The Tintina Fault stretches east-west through the preserve and is known by geologists for its role in the Klondike gold rush. Look at a map and you'll notice that gold discoveries in Yukon-Charley have occurred only on the Yukon's south bank. Millions of years ago two crustal plates shifted along

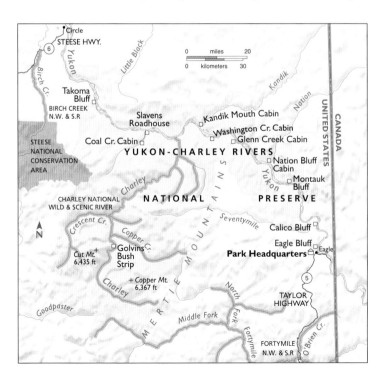

Moose

the Tintina Fault, carrying gold and silica (which later became quartz) toward the surface. Erosion then separated the gold from the quartz and washed it into mountain streams, where it gradually settled to the bottom. Since 1898, miners have used gold pans, sluice boxes, and dredges to separate this treasure from its trough.

Interior Alaska's transition from summer to winter—a long, dark season of prolonged cold snaps—is swift and sometimes sudden. Ice begins flowing in the Yukon River in October, and freeze-up comes by mid-November. As tributaries dry out and ice over, the Yukon runs clear beneath almost 6 feet of ice. In the wake of such an extreme deep freeze, breaking up is hard to do: Ice-out does not occur until early May.

The preserve shelters wolves, moose, black bears, and lynx, as well as the calving grounds of the Fortymile caribou herd. Designated in part to protect its abundant peregrine falcons, the preserve hosts 20 percent of the state's population of those raptors. Ravaged by DDT, only 50 to 100 pairs of American peregrine falcons still nested in Alaska by the early 1970s. Their comeback is well under way; 400 pairs now nest in the state.

Rocky palisades above the Charley River provide numerous nesting sites. You might also see a peregrine on Eagle Bluff near town or atop one of the 1,000-foot-high bluffs downstream, such as the Calico, Montauk, or Takoma. Although the birds summer in this remote land, they fly more than 5,000 miles to Central and

South America to spend the north's winter months.

Migrants in a different medium, king and chum salmon power up the Yukon and through the preserve. Some chum travel as far as 2,000 miles to reach their Canadian spawning grounds. As they have for millennia, native Athapaskan people, the land's original inhabitants, await their coming.

Long gone are the gold seekers of yore with their dreams of sudden riches. Their decaying log cabins are now the only evidence of their presence here.

What to See and Do

Yukon-Charley Rivers National Preserve has no direct road access. The 162-mile Steese Highway (Alas. 6) from Fairbanks terminates at Circle, 17 miles northwest (downstream) of the preserve, while the 161-mile Taylor Highway (Alas. 5) from Tetlin Junction ends at Eagle, 12 miles south (upstream) of the preserve. Taylor Highway is usually passable from late April to mid-October, or until snow closes the road.

Flowing from Eagle to Circle, the **Yukon River** is the principal means of access to the preserve. Free of rapids, this brawny river is ideal for rafts, canoes, and motorboats. The lower portions of the Yukon's major tributaries—the **Nation, Kandik,** and Charley Rivers —beg to be explored. Exposed geological features, historical relics, magnificent scenery, and varied wildlife are highlights of each day's travel. Most of the clear-water side streams also provide excellent fishing for arctic grayling, northern pike, and whitefish. The 158-mile-long **Eagle-to-Circle float** takes paddlers 5 to 10 days (contact Eagle Canoe Rentals 907-547-2203).

Small campgrounds are located in or near Eagle and Circle. Seven public-use cabins lie within the preserve, all of them along the Yukon River corridor. Coal Creek Cabin, Slaven's Roadhouse, and Nation Bluff Cabin were all built in the 1930s. Glenn Creek Cabin, Washington Creek Cabin, Kandik Mouth Cabin, and Slaven's Public Use Cabin followed over the next six decades. Use is on a first-come, first-served basis, with a limit of 7 days per cabin in any 30-day period.

The **Eagle Ranger Station** contains cultural and natural history exhibits; it also dispenses up-to-date information. Don't miss the summer tour of Eagle and nearby Fort Egbert led by town residents (contact historical society 907-547-2325).

You can also access the Yukon River at **Dawson City** in Canada's Yukon Territory, approximately 100 miles upriver from Eagle. Even on a fast float, you'll see a lot of wildlife, as well as remnants of the Klondike gold rush and the downriver stampede to Alaska's gold. The river segment from Dawson City to Circle (allow 8 to 15 days) may be the most scenic, safe river traverse in North America.

If you'd like to experience a part of Klondike history, take the cruise between Dawson City and Eagle aboard the paddle wheeler *Yukon Queen II.*

For a much more rugged paddling experience *(novices should not attempt this river on their own),* try the swift **Charley River.** Plunging from 4,000 feet above sea level at its source to 700 feet at its mouth, the Charley hurtles past spectacular upland cliffs, over rapids, and out onto a flat plain, where it slowly meanders to the Yukon River. Dall's sheep, usually at home on mountain slopes, often scale riverside scarps.

Aircraft access necessitates the use of inflatable watercraft. Put in at the gravel airstrip located in the upper portion of the Charley just above Copper Creek. Helicopters can also drop off trekkers and floaters. Two reputable air taxis are run by Tatonduk Flying Service *(P.O. Box 55, Eagle, AK 99738. 907-450-2350)* and 40-Mile Air *(Box 539, Tok, AK 99780. 907-883-5191).*

Boating season on this Class II to Class IV river usually lasts from June until water levels drop in late August. The average float time for the 75 miles from the airstrip to the Yukon River is 6 days.

You can arrange for a powerboat or a floatplane to pick you up at the mouth of the Charley River—or for that matter anywhere along the Yukon. Plan on at least 3 or 4 more days to float the 70 miles to Circle.

This journey requires top-notch backcountry skills, white-water experience, and thorough preparation. Once you leave the well-traveled Yukon River corridor, you are completely on your own. Contact the rangers in Eagle for further information.

Guided river trips are available through Pristine Adventures *(P.O. Box 83909, Fairbanks, AK 99707. 877-716-4366).*

There are no maintained trails here, just a few game trails and miners' paths. Open mountain ridges provide the best hiking. Explorers with good backcountry skills blaze trails through dense thickets to reach the highlands along the rivers, boldly going where few wafflestompers have gone before. Those who forge into Yukon-Charley could be sorely tested at times, but the rewards will be deep and abiding.

■ **2.5 million acres** ■ **About 150 miles east of Fairbanks** ■ **Best months June–Sept. Access by boat or aircraft only** ■ **Camping, hiking, boating, fishing, wildlife viewing, float trips** ■ **Contact the preserve, 201 First Ave., Fairbanks, AK 99701; 907-457-5752; or the preserve field office, P.O. Box 167, Eagle, AK 99738; 907-547-2234. www.nps.gov/yuch/s**

Floating the Yukon River on a homemade raft

Gates of the Arctic

"The view from the top gave us an excellent idea of the jagged country toward which we were heading. The main Brooks Range divide was entirely covered with snow. Close at hand, only about ten miles to the north, was a precipitous pair of mountains, one on each side of the North Fork. I bestowed the name Gates of the Arctic on them."

It was the early 1930s, and Robert Marshall had found his wilderness home, an unpeopled, uncluttered source of inspiration that would make him one of America's greatest conservationists. Gates of the Arctic was the ultimate North American wilderness. Congress created the park to keep it that way.

Climb practically any ridge in the heart of the park and you'll see a dozen glacial cirques side by side; serrated mountains that scythe the sky; and storms that snap out of dark, brooding clouds. Six national wild and scenic rivers—Alatna, John, Kobuk, Noatak, North Fork Koyukuk, and Tinayguk—tumble out of high alpine valleys into forested lowlands. The park lies entirely above the Arctic Circle, straddling the Brooks Range, one of the world's northernmost mountain chains.

With Kobuk Valley National Park and Noatak National Preserve, Gates of the Arctic National Park and Preserve protects much of the habitat of the western arctic caribou. Grizzlies, wolves, wolverines, and foxes also roam over the land in search of food. Ptarmigan nibble on willow, and gyrfalcon dive for ptarmigan.

Shafts of cinnabar sunlight pour through the mountains at 2 a.m. in June, setting the wild land ablaze. In this mammoth mountain kingdom, the northernmost reach of the Rockies, the summer sun does not set for 30 straight days.

"No sight or sound or smell or feeling even remotely hinted of men or their creations," wrote Marshall. "It seemed as if time had dropped away a million years and we were back in a primordial world."

- Alaskan Arctic
- 8.5 million acres
- Established 1980
- Best months June–September
- Camping, hiking, rock climbing, white-water rafting and kayaking, wildlife viewing
- Information: 907-457-5752 www.nps.gov/gaar

Alatna River in Gates of the Arctic National Park

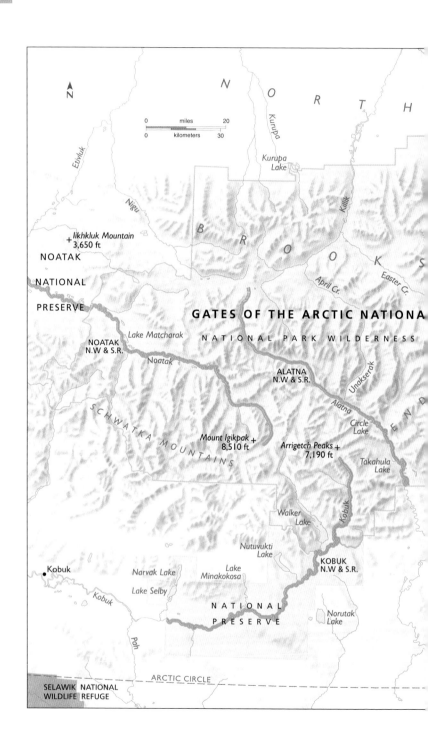

N

| 0 | miles | 20 |
| 0 | kilometers | 30 |

NORTH

Etivluk

Kurupa

Kurupa Lake

Nigu

B R O O K S

Killik

+ Iikhkluk Mountain
3,650 ft

April Cr.

Easter Cr.

NOATAK

NATIONAL

PRESERVE

GATES OF THE ARCTIC NATIONA

Lake Matcharak

N A T I O N A L   P A R K   W I L D E R N E S S

NOATAK
N.W & S.R.

Noatak

ALATNA
N.W & S.R.

Unakserak

E N D

Alatna

Circle Lake

S C H W A T K A   M O U N T A I N S

Mount Igikpak +
8,510 ft

Arrigetch Peaks +
7,190 ft

Takahula Lake

Walker Lake

Kobuk

Nutuvukti Lake

Kobuk

• Kobuk

Narvak Lake

Lake Minakokosa

KOBUK
N.W & S.R.

Lake Selby

Kobuk

N A T I O N A L
P R E S E R V E

Norutak Lake

Pah

ARCTIC CIRCLE

SELAWIK NATIONAL
WILDLIFE REFUGE

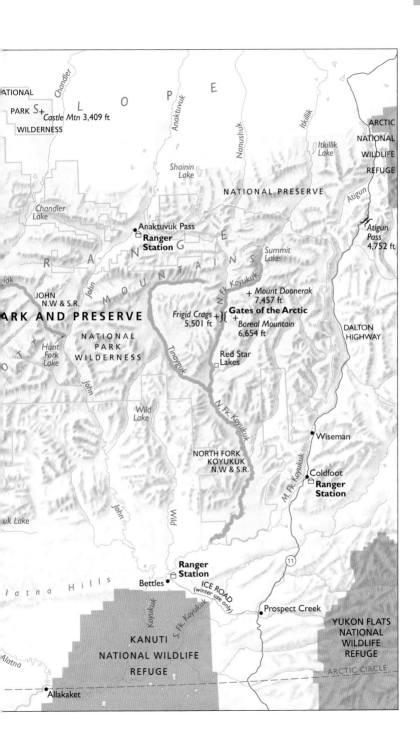

ATIONAL
PARK S+
Castle Mtn 3,409 ft
WILDERNESS

S L O P E

Chandler

Anaktuvuk

Nanushuk

Itkillik

Itkillik Lake

ARCTIC
NATIONAL
WILDLIFE
REFUGE

Shainin Lake

NATIONAL PRESERVE

Atigun

Chandler Lake

R A N G E

Anaktuvuk Pass
Ranger Station

G

Summit Lake

M O U N T A I N S

Atigun
Pass
4,752 ft

John

N. Fk. Koyukuk

idk

JOHN
N.W & S.R.

+ Mount Doonerak
7,457 ft

ARK AND PRESERVE

Frigid Crags +)(
5,501 ft

Gates of the Arctic
+
Boreal Mountain
6,654 ft

DALTON
HIGHWAY

NATIONAL
PARK
WILDERNESS

Tinayguk

Red Star
Lakes

Hunt Fork Lake

John

N. Fk. Koyukuk

Wiseman

Wild Lake

M. Fk. Koyukuk

NORTH FORK
KOYUKUK
N.W & S.R.

Coldfoot
**Ranger
Station**

uk Lake

John

Wild

**Ranger
Station**

Bettles

ICE ROAD
(winter use only)

11

latna Hills

Koyukuk

S. Fk. Koyukuk

Prospect Creek

YUKON FLATS
NATIONAL
WILDLIFE
REFUGE

KANUTI
NATIONAL WILDLIFE
REFUGE

Alatna

ARCTIC CIRCLE

Allakaket

How to Get There

Bush pilots say that where the road ends, the real Alaska begins. So it is in Gates of the Arctic. You can fly or walk in; most people fly. From Fairbanks (about 250 miles away), scheduled flights serve Anaktuvuk Pass, a Nunamiut Eskimo village within the park borders; Bettles/Evansville; and Ambler, to the west. From those points, you can air taxi into the park. Allow time for bad weather and delayed flights. From Anaktuvuk Pass, you can also hike into the park along the John River.

Or, you can drive up from Fairbanks on the unpaved James Dalton Highway (see pp. 73–80)—a pipeline haul road that's open to the public—and hike to the park from Wiseman or other points. But it's a long, hard walk into the interior.

When to Go

Summer. It is short, but days are very long and for a while temperatures may be relatively mild. Weather is highly unpredictable. Expect snow or rain in any month. August can be very wet, with freezing temperatures by mid-month. Mosquitoes and gnats are bad in late June and July. Fall colors peak in mid-August at high elevations, late August to early September at low elevations.

What Not to Miss

- Floating the Alatna River from Arctic Divide to Koyukuk River
- Flight-seeing over the park
- Dogsledding through Koyukuk Valley
- Visiting the Nunamiut Eskimo village of Anaktuvuk Pass
- Backcountry hiking in the Arrigetch Valley or the Hammond River drainage
- Combining a backcountry river-hiking trip appropriate to experience level

How to Visit

Allow time to savor the subtle beauty of this wilderness. A combination **river-hiking trip** offers the best of both. Air taxis can land on lakes and gravel bars for drop-offs and pickups.

Plan carefully and bring everything you need; there are no visitor facilities in the park. This spare, harsh land is so fragile that a hiker's step can kill lichens that take 150 years to mature. Certain areas were badly damaged by the increase in visitors after Gates of the Arctic became a park.

Contact park headquarters in Fairbanks before planning a trip to ask about areas to visit (there are no trails here) and names of air taxis, guides, and outfitters who operate in the park.

EXPLORING THE PARK

River Trips

Rivers are the main travel routes through Gates of the Arctic. Alaskan natives and caribou have followed them for centuries. Near some are lakes on which aircraft can land. Camping is good on the gravel bars, but be aware that summer rainstorms can quickly raise water levels. Most rivers are at their highest in May and June. Hiking is difficult but rewarding, especially in alpine areas. The following six rivers are only a sampling of what the park has to offer:

The **Alatna River** is ideal for a first wilderness float trip. It takes 4 to 7 days, running gently down from the treeless Arctic Divide through beautiful tundra to the forested Koyukuk River lowlands. There are put-ins at **Takahula Lake, Circle Lake,** or at a series of unnamed lakes farther upstream. Most boaters take-out at the village of Allakaket *(75 and 85 miles from Takahula and Circle Lakes, respectively)*, where the Alatna meets the Koyukuk River.

Survival Strategies

Alaska's northern exposure has sparked some fascinating adaptations. With snow on the ground for up to seven months, five animals —ptarmigan, collared lemmings, arctic foxes, weasels, and hare— change color with the seasons.

Migratory birds are best known for fleeing the winter cold, but caribou, whales, and walruses also cope by moving south. Ptarmigan, too, occasionally change ranges, alternately flying and walking.

Some animals—most famously bears—sleep the winter away, emerging with the spring thaw. During hibernation, a black bear's body temperature drops 12 degrees (to 85° F); its heart rate slows to one beat every ten seconds.

Yellow jackets and arctic ground squirrels undergo a drop in body temperature below freezing without suffering permanent damage. During hibernation, the squirrels' heart rate falls from 200 beats per minute to just 2, rendering the animals so dormant that ice crystals form in their body tissues.

The most amazing coping tactic of all belongs to the wood frog, one of Alaska's five amphibians: It freezes solid in winter, then comes to life again in spring. Scientists believe the secret to this cryogenic miracle lies in the frog's ability to convert some body fluids to sugar.

John River is a mere stream at its headwater at Anaktuvuk Pass, the permanent settlement of the Nunamiut *(contact park about guided tours)*, but it gains power and momentum as it flows south through the alpine heart of the park. **Hunt Fork Lake** is the best put-in; water levels above this point are usually too low. The John drops into lowland forest and joins the Koyukuk River just downstream of Bettles, a journey of 100 miles.

Floatplane on Takahula Lake

The **Kobuk River** begins at **Walker Lake,** a good put-in, and runs south and west through the mountains, canyons, foothills, and lowlands of Gates of the Arctic. Kobuk village, 140 river miles from Walker Lake, is a popular take-out. Or you can continue downriver to Ambler and on through **Kobuk Valley National Park** to Kiana.

The **North Fork Koyukuk** begins at **Summit Lake** and cuts between **Boreal Mountain** and **Frigid Crags**—the Gates of the Arctic—then flows past **Red-star Creek Lakes,** also a good put-in, and continues south a hundred miles to Bettles.

Creating one of the largest wilderness river basins in North America, the **Noatak** flows west 450 miles from Gates of the Arctic through **Noatak National Preserve** into the Chukchi Sea. The trip from a put-in at **Lake Matcharak** to Noatak village is 350 miles. The river, a major thoroughfare in a trackless realm, demands minimal boating skills but maximal planning. Give yourself a month for the trip.

The seldom visited **Tinayguk** flows through a broad, glacier-cut valley before joining the Koyukuk below Boreal Mountain and Frigid Crags. Put in after landing on a gravel bar along the Tinayguk, 35 miles north of where it joins the Koyukuk. *(Consult local maps and outfitters for the exact location.)* Float down to the Koyukuk, then continue on for another 80 miles to Bettles.

INFORMATION & ACTIVITIES

Headquarters
201 First Ave., Doyon Bldg.
Fairbanks, AK 99701
907-457-5752
www.nps.gov/gaar

Seasons & Accessibility
Park open year-round. Access
by air or foot; there are no
roads to the park (except
Dalton Highway, an unpaved
pipeline haul road that's parallel to park's east boundary).
There are no roads in the park.
Contact park headquarters
before planning a visit.

Visitor & Information Centers
There are no visitor centers or
facilities of any kind within the
park. The only ranger stations
are located in Bettles and Anaktuvuk Pass. An interagency
visitor center is staffed in
Coldfoot during the summer.
For visitor information, write
Gates of the Arctic NP, P.O. Box
26030, Bettles, AK 99726.

Entrance Fee
None.

Pets
Only pack dogs allowed.

Facilities for Disabled
Bettles and Anaktuvuk Pass
Ranger Stations and Coldfoot
Visitor Center are accessible.

Things to Do
Hiking (no established trails),
backpacking, canoeing, kayaking and rafting, fishing (license
required), hunting (in preserve
only, with license), rock and
mountain climbing, wildlife
watching. In winter: cross-
country skiing, snowshoeing,
dogsledding, skiing. Contact
park for a list of licensed
guides and outfitters.

Special Advisories
■ Bring supplies with you
(Fairbanks has a full selection);
few items are available in the
communities of Bettles and
Anaktuvuk Pass, which are
not accessible by road. Gas
stations on the Dalton Highway at Mile 56 (just N of the
Yukon River) and at Coldfoot,
Mile 173.6
■ All visitors should have substantial outdoors experience
and skills; firearms may be
carried for protection.
■ Grizzly bears are unpredictable and dangerous. Visit
ranger station in Bettles or
Coldfoot for advice on preventing an encounter.
■ Eskimos and other native
Alaskans use the park for
subsistence fishing and hunting
activities; respect them and
their property.
■ From mid-June through July,

be prepared for plenty of mosquitoes and gnats; bring insect repellent, a head net, and an insect-proof tent.

■ Swift currents and freezing water can make river crossings particularly hazardous.

Overnight Backpacking

No permit required, but get up-to-date information about bear activity from ranger station. An orientation is available at ranger stations. Food, stoves, and all equipment must be carried in. Camp on gravel bars to avoid damaging fragile tundra. Bear barrels are recommended; purchase or rent in advance.

Campgrounds

None; backcountry camping only.

Hotels, Motels, & Inns

(Unless otherwise noted, rates for two persons in a double room, high season.)

INSIDE THE PARK:

■ **Gates of the Arctic Wilderness Cabins** (part of Iniakuk Lake Wilderness Lodge, see below) P.O. Box 80424, Fairbanks, AK 99708. 907-479-6354 or 877-479-6354.

■ **Alatna Wilderness Cabin** (on headwaters of the Alatna River) 1 cabin, 6 beds. $4,150 per person for 3 days. Open July to early September.

■ **Nahtuk Wilderness Cabin** (on the Alatna River near Arrigetch Peaks) 1 cabin, 4 beds. $2,950 per person for 3 nights. Open mid-June–early Sept. Rates for both cabins are all-inclusive, with air transport from Fairbanks. www.gofarnorth.com

■ **Peace of Selby Wilderness Lodge** (only lodge in the national preserve, on headwaters of the Kobuk River) P.O. Box 86, Manley Hot Springs, AK 99756. 907-672-3206. 1 lodge and 5 remote, self-service cabins. Lodge: sleeps 5 in private loft, $400 per person, including meals. Cabins: sleep 4, $200 per person. Rates exclusive of airfare. Open March–Sept. www.alaska wilderness.net

OUTSIDE THE PARK:

■ **Iniakuk Lake Wilderness Lodge** (on Iniakuk Lake) P.O. Box 80424, Fairbanks, AK 99708. 907-479-6354 or 877-479-6354. 6 rooms, central bath. $3,500 per person for 3 nights, all-inclusive with air transport from Fairbanks. Mid-June–mid-Sept.www.gofarnorth.com

In Coldfoot, AK 99701:

■ **Slate Creek Inn** Mile 175, Dalton Hwy. 907-474-3500 or 800-474-3500. 52 units. $145. Restaurant, saloon, gift shop, post office. Open year-round.

Excursions from Gates of the Artic

Arctic National Wildlife Refuge

50 miles northeast of Gates

Roadless and undeveloped, America's largest national wildlife refuge stretches from the subarctic forests of interior Alaska to the frozen shores of the Beaufort Sea. The refuge encompasses a 200-mile-long east-to-west segment of the Brooks Range, which reaches its broadest sprawl—more than 110 miles north to south—within the sanctuary.

Arctic National Wildlife Refuge's greatest claim to fame, of course, is not crags but creatures: The refuge boasts the greatest animal variety of any protected area in the circumpolar north. Six distinct habitats—marine, coastal lagoons, Arctic lowland tundra, alpine, taiga, and boreal forests—support 180 species of birds, nine marine mammals, and 37 land mammals, including all three North American bears: grizzly, black, and polar. The latter sometimes wander in off the ice to den on land.

Birds, too, take pains to reside here. The American golden-plover, for example, spends the North American winters on the pampas of Argentina, then flies nearly 10,000 miles to nest on the dry tundra uplands of the reserve. By protecting a vast swath of migration routes and calving grounds, the refuge provides a safe haven for Alaska's 130,000-strong Porcupine caribou herd.

Finally, Arctic NWR takes pride in its musk-ox population; reintroduced in 1969, about 250 of the shaggy animals now wander the refuge's northern plain.

Of the 18 rivers flowing through the refuge, three have been officially designated as "wild": the Ivishak, the Wind, and the Sheenjek. Although the three merit that distinction, there are others here—among them, the Hulahula, the Coleen, and the Canning—that arguably are as beautiful and pristine and undefiled.

There are few large lakes within the refuge. Two of them, the moraine-dammed Lake Schrader and Lake Peters (the latter lies at the foot of 9,020-foot-high Mount Chamberlin), are striking for their quiet, austere beauty.

Winters here are long and severe. Some lakes do not thaw until mid-July, only to freeze up again in early September. Snow is possible at any time during this abbreviated summer. On south-flowing rivers, fall colors appear in late August or early September. On the North Slope the change takes place even earlier, with tundra plants turning red in early August.

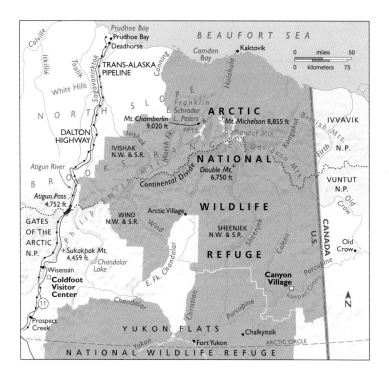

Invoking the goal of energy independence in 1973, oil companies, politicians, and unions called for oil extraction to begin on a 110-mile-long section of Arctic NWR's coastal plain. Conservationists opposed the move, predicting damage to the land and its occupants. "Opening this last protected area to oil and gas development," warned Interior Secretary Bruce Babbitt in 1999, will "lead to serious threats to the native wildlife, including the Porcupine caribou herd, and the native peoples who depend on the herd to live and maintain their traditional lifestyle." He went on to say that breaking the government's traditional aegis over the refuge would "shatter the balance of land and life into a thousand fragments."

What to See and Do

After making a visit here in 1953, biologist Lowell Sumner wrote, "This wilderness is big enough and wild enough to make you feel like one of the old-time explorers, knowing that each camp you place, each mountain climbed, each adventure with the boats is in untouched country."

This country remains untouched today: There are no lodges, campgrounds, roads, or trails anywhere within the refuge. This means that visitors are completely on their own. In addition to being well equipped, you must be well prepared, both mentally and physically, for the unique challenges the refuge presents. Experience, not high-tech gear, is critical for traveling across this country. Don't overestimate your tolerance for being swarmed by mosquitoes. The insects drive caribou to distraction during peak insect season in July, and they are just as likely to assail a hot and sweating backpacker.

Fishing the Dietrich River, Arctic National Wildlife Refuge

Getting There

Most of Arctic National Wildlife Refuge is accessible only by costly air charter, usually from one of three villages: Kaktovik on the north coast, and Arctic Village and Fort Yukon farther south. It's possible to fly directly to the refuge from Bettles, Deadhorse, or Fairbanks, but the fare may be prohibitive.

In addition, the region's limited number of air taxis *(a list of authorized air-charter services available from refuge staff)* require that flights be arranged far in advance. When making your plans, allow for several days of waiting out fog and other weather.

Complicating the already difficult access is the limited number of landing areas. Many are nothing more than glorified gravel bars scattered around the refuge. Expect that your visit to this little-visited corner of the world is likely to begin and end in a rather rough-and-ready fashion.

Hiking

The western boundary of the Arctic NWR lies 3 miles downstream from **Atigun River Crossing no. 2** (*not* no. 1!) at Mile 270 on the **Dalton Highway** *(see pp. 73–80).*

For a challenging hike, from the road follow the north bank of the river downstream along the **Atigun Gorge** for 10 or 11 miles to the river's confluence with the headwater streams of the **Sag (Sagavanirktok) River.** The tussocks can make the going difficult, but for your efforts you may be rewarded with glimpses of falcons on the cliffs and Dall's sheep, grizzlies, or wolves on the hillsides.

The mountains offer the best hiking and backpacking in the refuge. Dry ridges and riverbanks provide the best routes. With the aid of your

Keep on Truckin'

Alaska supports nearly one million caribou in about 30 separate herds. (A herd is defined by its regular and exclusive use of a calving area.) The largest group of all, some 500,000 strong, is the Western Arctic herd, which roams from Barrow to the Seward Peninsula. The caribou you're likely to spot along the Dalton Highway, as well as those you may see wandering the oil fields near Prudhoe Bay, belong to the Central Arctic herd.

The Porcupine herd, which calves in Arctic NWR in late May, is named for the Porcupine River, the major watercourse in the herd's range.

In summer, caribou eat a wide variety of plants; in winter they are limited to lichens, which they locate under the snow by smell.

You can't tell a caribou by its horns: These creatures are the only members of the deer family in which both sexes grow antlers. In general, however, the rack of a mature bull is much larger than that of a cow. Bulls shed their antlers in October and begin growing new ones in April. Pregnant cows keep their antlers all winter, using them to defend feeding sites from larger and stronger, but antlerless, bulls.

In late May, cows give birth to a single 10- to 15-pound calf. By the time they're two weeks old, calves can outrun their main predators: wolves and bears.

The survival of this species hinges on its seasonal migrations between winter and summer ranges. In June and July, large caribou herds drift north toward the cool, windswept Arctic coast, a respite from heat and mosquitoes. In August they head south again, bound for their wintering grounds on the taiga in the eastern and north-central Yukon.

One radio-collared animal in the Porcupine herd made a 3,000-mile round-trip in one year, the longest measured movement of any land mammal.

Caribou in fog

charter pilot, you may be able to be dropped off on one river and hike through a pass to a strip on another drainage. You can study maps and design your own itinerary; however, it's a good idea to check the feasibility with refuge staff and your pilot. Once you leave your drop-off site, you can go for days, or even weeks, without seeing anyone.

Hikers prepared for cool weather and icy winds can trek and camp on the bluffs and beaches along the Arctic coast. For guided backpacking trips in the refuge, contact the refuge and ask for their list, "Authorized Recreational Guiding Services."

Climbing

Climbing in Arctic NWR is just catching on. Mountaineers tackle the ice fields and spires of two peaks in the northern portion of the refuge, 9,020-foot-high **Mount Chamberlin** and 8,855-foot **Mount Michelson,** in addition to other unnamed pinnacles. Alaska Wildtrek *(907-235-6463)* offers guided climbing trips.

River Running

Most of the rivers in Arctic National Wildlife Refuge, especially those on the north side, are swift, strewn with boulders, and braided—that is, split into many channels that repeatedly rejoin and redivide. Expect high, muddy water during spring breakup and after storms. Most rivers are open from mid-June through September, but you'll find the safest water levels in late June to early August (low water levels in August can require extensive lining).

Here, as elsewhere in the American wilderness, river ratings are subjective; each run must be evaluated according to the river's current conditions. Some Kongakut River segments that are rated Class III have powerful hydraulics at higher water levels.

A hazard unique to northern rivers is thick layers of overflow ice, some more than a mile long, that persist into late summer on certain rivers. During the spring breakup, a river may carve a chute through one of these *aufeis* fields, as they are called, forcing boaters to scout the ice before floating through; if not, they may make the unpleasant (and dangerous) discovery downstream that the river suddenly flows under the ice or through a walled tunnel. These channels are usually open by late June.

If you really want to see the refuge's hidden gems, sign up for a guided backpacking trip or a combination backpack and float trip.

Guided trips may seem expensive, but they include the air-charter fees to this refuge, which can cost hundreds of dollars for two people. And with a guide on hand, you won't have to worry about developing ace wilderness skills on the spot (*ABEC's Alaska Adventures 907-457-8907; Wilderness Alaska 907-345-3567; Equinox Expeditions 907-274-9087*).

Many visitors access the refuge by floating one of three north-flowing rivers—the Kongakut, the Hulahula, or the Canning:

The **Kongakut River** rises in the Davidson Mountains at the eastern extent of the Brooks Range and flows across the coastal plain to reach the Beaufort Sea. Most trips on this river end before it exits the mountains. Because a float on this river may offer the opportunity to see caribou herds, the Kongakut is the most trafficked river in the refuge. At the peak of the season in June, as many as 30 tents from several different groups may be pitched at the Caribou Pass pickup airstrip.

From high in the Brooks Range, the **Hulahula River** flows north through steep-walled glacial valleys, then threads the coastal plain to the sea. Superb scenery combined with easy access makes the Hulahula the second most-floated river in the refuge. Though mostly Class I and II, occasional stretches of Class III rapids promise a challenging descent. A narrow pass across the Continental Divide, used by hikers and pilots, connects the headwaters of the Hulahula with those of the Chandalar River.

The longest north-flowing river in the refuge, the **Canning River** (and its tributary, the **Marsh Fork)** offers good access for aircraft. While the Canning is relatively placid, the Marsh Fork offers short segments of white water. Both run through scenic valleys gouged out by glaciers thousands of years ago.

There are other runs as well. Marginal aircraft access and typically shallow water affect river trips on two of the Arctic NWR's three wild and scenic rivers, the **Ivishak** and the **Wind**. The glacier-fed **Sheenjek River,** by contrast, takes rafters through diverse mountain and forest habitats as it drains the south side of the highest mountains in the Brooks Range. Most of the river is Class I, with a few brief sections of Class II white water (*watch for sweepers, or low-hanging branches, downstream*). The Sheenjek can be accessed at various points, the most common of which are Last Lake, the gravel bars below Double Mountain, or other sites as water levels and pilot experience allow. Grizzlies, moose, beavers, waterfowl, and picturesque spires may all be part of the scenery. With the refuge designed to offer visitors a true wilderness experience, the choice of good camping and hiking sites is completely up to you. The entire river is open to fishing.

What really distinguishes the Sheenjek, though, is its historical import: In the 1950s, conservationists Olaus and Margaret Murie made several visits to Last Lake on the Sheenjek's upper reaches. So taken were they with the region, they lobbied to have the eastern Brooks Range set aside as a wildlife refuge. It was thanks to their efforts, as well as those of Supreme Court Justice William O. Douglas, that the Arctic National Wildlife Refuge was established in 1960.

■ **19.6 million acres, including 8 million acres designated wilderness** ■ **Northeast Alaska** ■ **Best months mid-June–late Aug.** ■ **Camping, hiking, wildlife viewing, float trips** ■ **Contact the refuge, 101 12th Ave., Room 236, Box 20, Fairbanks, AK 99701; 907-456-0250. www.arctic.fws.gov**

James Dalton Highway

Passes just east of Gates of the Arctic

416 miles one way; 8–10 days round-trip America's most unusual road, the Dalton Highway, built to provide construction access to the trans-Alaska pipeline, runs from Livengood to Deadhorse, scaling the spectacular Brooks Range en route and paralleling the pipeline the entire way.

By the time the first stretch was begun in April 1974, the Dalton Highway had survived numerous legal challenges decrying the impact it would have on the area's fragile environment and native land ownership. Five months and three million man-hours later, the road stretched from the Yukon River to the Beaufort Sea. The completion of the Yukon River Bridge in 1975 connected Alaska's high Arctic to the country's continental road system for the first time.

Connected, but not cloned: This is a rough gravel road whose surface ranges from dusty to muddy, where drivers should expect broken headlights, cracked windshields, and flat tires. Travel services are extremely limited. Gas and lodging are available only at the Yukon River, Coldfoot, and Deadhorse. No emergency medical facilities are found along the way.

Obviously, then, travelers must prepare for mishaps and delays. Carry extra gasoline, two spare tires (each mounted on a rim), extra belts and headlights, radiator coolant, common tools,

Driver's view of the Dalton Highway

and a CB radio. Towing can cost $5 per mile. Take plenty of clothing, sleeping bags, extra food, water, and insect repellent.

As you've gathered, this rugged road isn't for everyone. Still, a stiff dose of common sense should stave off most disasters: Drive slowly, with your headlights on at all times. Give trucks the right of way; they kick up rocks and dust that pose significant hazards. Pull over and stop for oncoming or passing vehicles. Finally, stay off the road in winter.

If you'd like to reach the Arctic Circle but don't want to drive there, the following companies offer single-day or multiday trips to Prudhoe Bay: Alaskan Arctic Turtle Tours *(907-457-1798)*, Northern Alaska Tour Company *(907-474-8600)*, Trans Arctic Circle Treks *(907-479-5451)*.

The Bureau of Land Management (BLM) manages the land on either side of the Dalton Highway from the Yukon River to about Mile 300; the state of Alaska manages the terrain from there to Prudhoe Bay. From the highway, you'll find near limitless opportunities for camping, fishing, bird-watching, wildlife viewing, photography, and hiking.

Logging six hours a day in good weather, it takes about four to five days to drive the entire Dalton Highway from its start 4 miles west of Livengood (Mile 73.1 on the Elliott Hwy.) to its end a few miles shy of Prudhoe Bay. Along the way you'll rattle over timbered ridges and pass through untouched valleys, traversing several distinct habitats (such as tundra) that give you excellent chances of spotting unique mammals and birds.

What to See and Do

As you drive north from Livengood, you soon enter the woods below the Yukon River. Keep your eyes open here for spruce grouse, varied thrushes, and white-winged crossbills (some birders tally more than a hundred species during this section of the drive). For guided bird-watching, contact *NatureAlaska Tours (907-488-3746).*

For the first 50 miles or so, you'll be driving over discontinuous permafrost. The trans-Alaska pipeline's **Pump Station Six,** at Mile 54, was installed on a refrigerated foundation to keep it from thawing out the frozen substrate.

At Mile 55.6, you rumble over the 2,995-foot-long **Yukon River Bridge.** Traveler services (the last you'll see for 120 miles) are available on the northwest riverbank. Across the highway is the BLM's **Yukon Crossing Visitor Contact Station** *(open daily summer).*

North of the Yukon

Near **Five-mile Camp,** look for an undeveloped campground with an artesian well and an RV dump station. The boreal forest here is good habitat for black bears, which are sometimes seen crossing the road early or late in the day.

From the pullout at Mile 70, there's a great view of the **Ray Mountains** to the west. From Mile 86.5, look south to the **Fort Hamlin Hills.** East of this point stretches the vast, roadless **Yukon Flats National Wildlife Refuge** *(800-531-0676).* Its wetlands host about one to two million breeding ducks and 20,000 loons.

Picturesque **Finger Mountain Wayside** *(Mile 98)* has an outhouse, good off-road parking, and a short nature trail. The prominent tor nearby was a landmark for early aviators. To the north are **Olson Lake** and the **Kanuti River Flats.** Hikers should feel free to venture into the surrounding uplands. On a tundra walk near the granite tors to the northeast, you'll see wildflowers in season, and the occasional horned lark, whimbrel, or American golden-plover.

Numerous thermokarst lakes pockmark the Kanuti flats near Mile 102. These bodies of water formed when the ground ice in permafrost melted. Although wildlife sightings are never guaranteed, be on the lookout for grizzlies in this area.

Just after passing 3,179-foot-high **Caribou Mountain** on your left, the Dalton Highway crosses the **Kanuti River** at Mile 105.8. Both greater white-fronted and Canada geese nest at **Kanuti National Wildlife Refuge** *(907-456-0329)* downstream. More than one-third of the refuge has burned since 1990, creating a patchwork of habitats that support a variety of wildlife.

North of the Arctic Circle

The **Arctic Circle Wayside** *(Mile 115.3)*—the only place in Alaska where you can cross the Arctic Circle by car—marks north latitude 66° 33' N. Here, in theory, the sun stays above the horizon for one full day at the summer solstice. In reality, however, mountains to the north block the sun as it dips to the horizon on that day; to see the midnight sun, you must drive 17 miles farther north to the **Gobblers Knob pullout** *(Mile 132)*. There, too, you'll get your first good views of the Brooks Range, Prospect Creek, and Jim River drainages.

In January 1971, at a pipeline camp on **Prospect Creek** *(Mile 135)*, the mercury plunged to an Alaska record of minus 80° F. A rough side road leads to a pond where you can see beaver, waterfowl, and (sometimes) moose.

Jim River *(Mile 140)* supports grayling, burbot (a delicious freshwater cod), and that grizzly magnet, salmon. Undeveloped campsites dot this area. Salmon fishing is not allowed on the Jim River, which also strictly limits grayling.

At Mile 156.3 you'll cross the **South Fork** of the **Koyukuk River**, entering the Arctic mountains and leaving the Alaskan interior behind. There is a slim chance you'll find placer gold (flakes and nuggets dislodged from bedrock and deposited along watercourses) within a mile of the road here. All federally managed streams south of Atigun Pass in the Brooks Range are open to recreational mining. A BLM brochure, "Dalton Highway Recreational Mineral Collection" *(907-474-2250)*, details the sites and the rules governing them. Other good spots include **Nugget Creek** *(Mile 196)* and **Gold Creek** *(Mile 197.2)*.

About 20 miles past the South Fork is **Coldfoot**, established in 1899 as one of Alaska's northernmost gold-mining camps. It was deserted in 1912 when miners rushed to the Nolan Creek strike near Wiseman. A wealth of information is available at the interagency **Cold-foot Visitor Center** *(907-678-5209. Late May–early Sept.)*.

Autumn along the Dalton Highway

Five miles up the road is the Marion Creek Campground *(fee)*. From here to Prudhoe Bay, you'll have occasional views of the oil pipeline.

Turn left just past the Middle Fork Koyukuk River bridge *(Mile 189)* for the side road to **Wiseman.** From this community, 60 miles north of the Arctic Circle, you can hike into Gates of the Arctic National Park and Preserve. One walk leads from Wiseman toward the 1912 Nolan camp along a rough dirt mining road that also furnishes access to both the Hammond and Glacier Rivers.

The marble roots of spectacular **Sukakpak Mountain** *(Mile 203.5)* were deposited 380 million years ago. The small spruce in this area have been canted at irregular angles by the upheaval of ice-core mounds known as *palsas*. From here you can set out for the base of Sukakpak, though there is no established trail. The climb to the 4,459-foot-high summit is arduous—good hikers will need 5 to 8 hours to complete it—but rewarding: Stunning views of the Brooks Range await at the top.

From here on, you'll want to pull over often to savor the views. A stream crossing at Mile 216, for example, offers a fine panorama of the mountains and the Koyukuk and Dietrich River Valleys.

The stand of white spruce (some are 200 years old) at Mile 237 marks the northern limit of tree line along the highway. The road

On a Slippery Slope

In 1968, America's largest oil reserve was discovered at Prudhoe Bay, forever changing the face of Arctic Alaska. Two years later the state leased the fields for 900 million dollars, and by 1977 oil was flowing south through the 48-inch-diameter trans-Alaska pipeline. Running 800 miles from Prudhoe Bay to the ice-free port of Valdez on the Gulf of Alaska, the pipeline crosses two mountain ranges and 350 rivers and streams en route.

Although permafrost requires more than half the pipeline to run above ground, certain segments have been buried for wildlife corridors or highway crossings. These are refrigerated to keep them from thawing out the soil (the crude is a piping-hot 120° F when it leaves Prudhoe Bay and a still tepid 85° F by the time it reaches Valdez). For the same reason, five of the seven pump stations north of Fairbanks sit on refrigerated foundations.

Arctic Alaska's hyperactive geomorphology forced the pipeline's North Slope section to be built in a zigzag pattern. This translates the contraction and expansion caused by earthquakes and temperature extremes into lateral movement, preventing ruptures in the pipe.

All these safeguards could not keep the tanker *Exxon Valdez* from running aground in Prince William Sound in 1989, spilling 11.3 million gallons of crude oil that polluted 1,500 miles of coast and killed 390,000 birds and countless mammals. As officials debated opening the Arctic National Wildlife Refuge to oil exploration in 2001, Alaskan oil remained a combustible issue.

Alaska pipeline at Mile 146 of Dalton Highway

soon begins a long climb up a 10 percent grade to the **Chandalar Shelf** *(Mile 241)*, a large valley draining southeast into the Yukon.

At Mile 244 the highway crosses the Arctic Continental Divide through 4,732-foot-high **Atigun Pass** (actually it's a saddle in the range). On the north side begins a steep descent into a U-shaped glacial valley, scoured and deepened by successive Pleistocene glaciers. Watch for Dall's sheep, soaring golden eagles, and grizzlies.

Glittering **Galbraith Lake** lies 30 miles north of Atigun. Follow the airstrip spur road on the left 3 miles to an undeveloped campground. Look for Dall's sheep and caribou.

From Mile 280 to 288, you'll pass through the **Toolik Lake Area of Critical Environmental Concern/Research Natural Area.** Recreational camping is banned within these 82,000 acres so that scientists can conduct their investigations in a near-pristine landscape. From here to the coast, watch for rare Baird's sandpipers, bar-tailed godwits, wheatears, gyrfalcons, bluethroats, and Smith's longspurs.

Onto the North Slope

At **Slope Mountain** *(Mile 302)*, home to Dall's sheep, raptors, and grizzlies, you enter the foothills, which then flatten into the Arctic Coastal Plain. The road picks up the **Sagavanirktok (Sag) River** and tails it all the way to Prudhoe Bay. Musk-oxen and caribou may appear from here to Franklin Bluffs.

An excellent place to look for peregrine falcons and gyrfalcons is the **Ice Cut** at Mile 326. From here to the coast is a visual feast of such typical Arctic features as cotton-grass tussocks and thaw ponds.

From **Pump Station Two,** 500 feet above sea level at Mile 360, the road begins a slow descent to Prudhoe Bay, now just 70 miles to the north. This spot also marks the northern extent of dwarf birch.

Freezing of subsurface water can raise the ground into mounds, called pingos, several hundred feet high. One of these looms over the tundra flats in the west at Mile 376. Arctic foxes—known to carry rabies, by the way—commonly den on pingos.

Beyond **Franklin Bluffs,** the farthest inland point reached by John Franklin of the Royal Navy in 1827, shallow thaw lakes and frost polygons dominate the tundra, and oil-field facilities loom into view. Watch for Pacific and red-throated loons.

The Dalton Highway ends at **Deadhorse.** Oil-field roads to the Arctic Ocean are closed to the public, but tours can be arranged by calling 907-659-2368. Commercial services here are limited.

Once the Last Frontier's last frontier, the North Slope is now marred by a sprawling industrial complex the size of Rhode Island. The landscape does not invite lingering, but birders should have a look around for king and spectacled eiders, tundra swans, and snow buntings.

Off the Dalton Highway: Porcupine River Float Trip

From Canada's Ogilvie Mountains, the Porcupine River flows 500 miles to join the Yukon River 2 miles north of Fort Yukon, threading a corner of the **Arctic National Wildlife Refuge** *(see pp. 66–73).* The Porcupine, safe for novice floaters with good wilderness skills, is ideal for families with older children. Canoes and kayaks are best; oxbows and upriver winds make rafts a second choice.

From the put-in at Old Crow, the only inhabited village on the river, it's a 300-mile, 10- to 14-day paddle to Fort Yukon. The banks of the upper Porcupine contain archaeological sites and Pleistocene mammal remains. *Removing anything from these sites is illegal.*

This normally slow-moving, Class I river picks up speed at the Alaska-Yukon border, where it flows for about 40 miles through the colorful, steep-walled **Upper Rampart Canyon.** All along the river you will pass remnants of abandoned cabins, such as those at Burnt Paw. Gwich'in Indians still fish and hunt along the river, so you'll also see the occasional new cabin or powerboat, especially during the fall moose and caribou season.

Below defunct Canyon Village, the Porcupine meanders through low, rolling hills before reaching its confluence with the Coleen River. A few miles below this point, you'll float past the limestone cliffs of **Lower Rampart Canyon,** followed by the forested wetlands of **Yukon Flats National Wildlife Refuge.** Rafting this slow portion can try the patience of even the most poised paddler.

Just before the Porcupine joins the Yukon, the Sucker River enters it from the left; you can paddle 3 miles up to a road-accessible landing or float all the way to the Yukon, where you'll wind up 2 miles downstream from Fort Yukon. Here you'll need to find the local customs agent before boarding a flight to Fairbanks.

■ **416 miles long** ■ **4–5 days** ■ **Northeast Alaska** ■ **Best months June–late Aug.** ■ **Camping, hiking, fishing, wildlife viewing, gold panning, float trips** ■ **Contact Bureau of Land Management, 1150 University Ave., Fairbanks, AK 99709; 907-474-2250**

The Lynx and the Hare

A snowshoe hare—also called a varying hare for its seasonal color change from brown to white—possesses huge hind feet. Like snowshoes, these support the hare atop deep snow in which most pursuers flounder.

Although you'll spot at least a few of these creatures as you drive the roads of subarctic and Arctic Alaska, their abundance may occasionally astonish you. Every 8 to 11 years, their population explodes and then crashes. At the peak of this cycle, when their numbers can reach 600 per square mile of range, snowshoe hare seem to bound from every thicket.

Lynx

After their dramatic crash, fewer than six hare may occupy the same area. Although the cause of the cycle has yet to be determined, its effect is unmistakable: The area's population of lynx— the hare's main predator —customarily peaks precisely one year after the population crest of the snowshoe hare. Other predators— notably coyotes, great horned owls, and goshawks—likewise benefit from this bunny boom.

If snowshoe hare are underfoot everywhere, their main adversaries often seem to be the missing lynx. That's because these 18- to 30-pound northern wildcats hunt mainly at night. Moving slowly and stealthily, they use hunting beds—that is, shallow depressions in the snow—to ambush the hare. The oversize paws of the lynx also act as snowshoes.

So closely intertwined are the two species that both suffer when either one does. On the upswing of the hare cycle, lynx grow fat and give birth to an average litter of three to four kittens; on the downswing lynx may starve, producing only one kitten—if any.

Resourcefully adaptable as predators, lynx undertake surprisingly long journeys to reach new hunting grounds. A radio-collared lynx from southern Yukon, for example, once traveled more than 400 miles to reach more hospitable terrain near Chalkyitsik, Alaska.

Glacier Bay

When Royal Navy captain James Cook sailed the Alaska coast in 1778, Glacier Bay did not exist. It lay beneath a sheet of glacial ice several miles wide and thousands of feet thick. By the time Capt. George Vancouver sailed into Icy Strait in 1794, the landscape had been transfigured: He found a bay almost 5 miles long filled with broken ice.

In 1879, when John Muir and five companions paddled their canoe into Glacier Bay, they measured its length at 48 miles. By 1916, the Grand Pacific Glacier, having receded 65 miles up the bay, was in full retreat. Since then, in one of the fastest glacial retreats on record, the ice has shrunk back to unveil new land and a new bay, now returning to life after a long winter's sleep. No glacier worldwide has ever done a faster vanishing act.

Scientists call Glacier Bay National Park and Preserve a living laboratory for the grand processes of glacial retreat, plant succession, and animal dynamics. It is an open book on the last ice age. At the southern end of the bay, where the ice departed 200 years ago, a spruce-hemlock rain forest has taken root. Farther north, in areas more recently deglaciated, the land is rugged and thinly vegetated.

The bay branches into two major arms, the west arm and Muir Inlet, which themselves branch into smaller inlets. There, on slopes deglaciated 50 to 100 years ago, alder and willow grow, while mosses, mountain avens, and dwarf fireweed pioneer areas exposed within the last two or three decades.

The new vegetation creates habitats for wolves, moose, mountain goats, black and brown bears, ptarmigan, and other wildlife, and the sea supports a food chain that includes salmon, bald eagles, harbor seals, harbor porpoises, humpback and killer whales—all in an environment less than 200 years old.

Roughly 13 tidewater glaciers still flow into the park. In part because of variations in snow accumulations, most

- Southeast Alaska, 65 miles northwest of Juneau

- 3.3 million acres

- Established 1980

- Best months May–September

- Hiking, kayaking, fishing, wildlife viewing, cruising

- Information: 907-697-2230 www.nps.gov/glba

Riggs Glacier, Glacier Bay National Park and Preserve

TONGASS

NATIONAL

FOREST

Brabazon Range

Alsek

BRITISH COLUMBIA
ALASKA

SAINT ELIAS MOUNTAINS

TATSHENSHI

PROVINCIA

Tatshenshini

Melburn Glacier

ALSE

Dry Bay
Ranger Station

Dry
Bay

GLACIER BAY
NATIONAL
PRESERVE

ALASKAN
MARITIME
N.W.R.

Grand Plateau
Glacier

Grand Pacific Glacier

Mt. Lodge +
10,530 ft

CANADA

UNITED STAT

Mt. Root
12,860 ft

Mt. Fairweather
15,320 ft +

+ Mt. Quincy Adams
13,650 ft

Johns Hopkir
Inlet

GLACIER BA

Fairweather
Glacier

Cape
Fairweather

FAIRWEATHER RANGE

Mt. Abbe +
8,750 ft

Lituya Glacier

N

ALASKAN
MARITIME
NATIONAL
WILDLIFE
RESERVE

Lituya Bay

Lituya Bay

Crillon
Lake

Mt. Crillon +
12,726 ft

AN

Laperouse Glacier

P
A
C
I
F
I
C

O
C
E
A
N

GULF OF

ALASKA

Pe

0	miles	20
0	kilometers	30

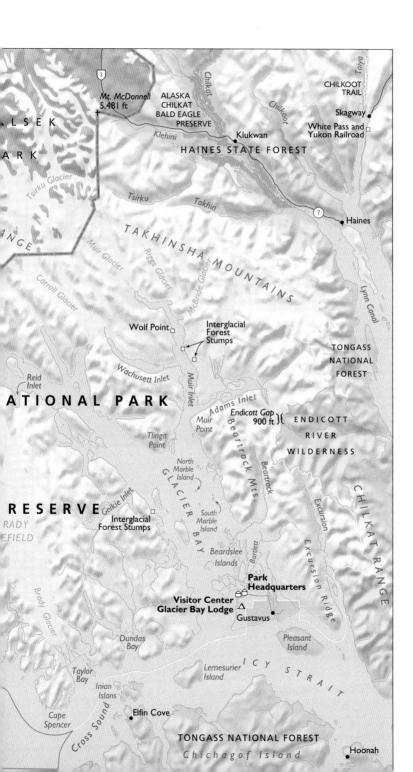

ALSEK

ARK

RANGE

Mt. McDonnell
5,481 ft

ALASKA
CHILKAT
BALD EAGLE
PRESERVE

Klehini

Klukwan

HAINES STATE FOREST

Chilkat

Chilkoot

CHILKOOT
TRAIL

Skagway

White Pass and
Yukon Railroad

Haines

Tsirku Glacier

Tsirku

Takhin

TAKHINSHA MOUNTAINS

Lynn Canal

Muir Glacier

Riggs Glacier

McBride Glacier

Carroll Glacier

Wolf Point

Interglacial
Forest
Stumps

TONGASS
NATIONAL
FOREST

Reid
Inlet

Wachusett Inlet

Muir Inlet

Adams Inlet

Endicott Gap
900 ft

ENDICOTT

ATIONAL PARK

Muir
Point

RIVER

WILDERNESS

Tlingit
Point

Beartrack

Beartrack Mts.

North
Marble
Island

GLACIER BAY

Geikie Inlet

RESERVE

Interglacial
Forest Stumps

South
Marble
Island

Excursion

CHILKAT RANGE

RADY

EFIELD

Beardslee
Islands

Bartlett

Park
Headquarters

Excursion Ridge

Visitor Center
Glacier Bay Lodge

Gustavus

Brady
Glacier

Dundas
Bay

Pleasant
Island

Taylor
Bay

Inian
Islans

Lemesurier
Island

ICY STRAIT

Cape
Spencer

Cross Sound

Elfin Cove

TONGASS NATIONAL FOREST

Chichagof Island

Hoonah

glaciers in the eastern and southwestern areas of the bay are receding, while several on its west side are advancing. The glaciers calve icebergs that hit the water with a sound like cannon shot. "White thunder," the Tlingit Indians called it, the awesome voice of glacial ice.

An iceberg's color often reveals its makeup; dense bergs are blue, while those filled with trapped air bubbles are white.

How to Get There

By boat or plane only. From Juneau, take a scheduled flight 53 miles to Gustavus. Catch the bus to Glacier Bay Lodge and Bartlett Cove Campground, 10 miles away at the park's southern end. Charter flights also service Gustavus from Juneau, Skagway, Haines, and Hoonah. The Glacier Bay Cruiseline ferry departs Monday, Wednesday, Friday, and Saturday from Juneau to Gustavus, then Bartlett Cove. Private boats can enter the bay with permits (*required June–Aug.*) obtained by phone, by mail from headquarters at Bartlett Cove, or online (*www.nps.gov/glba*).

When to Go

Late May to mid-September. Summer days are long and temperatures cool. May and June are the sunniest months, but

What Not to Miss

- **One-day or overnight cruise through Glacier Bay to view glaciers**
- **Kayaking, camping, and hiking around Muir and Adams Inlets or the bay's West Arm**
- **Hiking the three nature trails at Bartlett Cove**
- **Kayaking and wildlife-watching around the Beardslee Islands' maze of waterways**
- **Viewing sea birds and sea lions on the Marble Islands**

upper inlets can be thick with icebergs and tidewater glaciers can be less approachable. September is often rainy and windy.

How to Visit

Glacier Bay is a marine highway. Most visitors experience the park from the deck of a cruise ship, a tour boat, or a sea kayak. Many of the cruise ships that travel southeastern Alaska's Inside Passage go into the bay. Other tours offer accommodations at **Glacier Bay Lodge** (the park's center of activity) and a day or overnight boat trip to the glaciers and back. The boat will drop off campers and kayakers at one of three sites up the bay; they can be picked up later or paddle back to **Bartlett Cove.**

EXPLORING THE PARK

The Lower Bay

The lower bay reaches from Bartlett Cove north to Tlingit Point, where it separates into its two arms and continues north. If you plan to hike in Glacier Bay, the only maintained trails in the park are three short nature trails through the forest at park headquarters in Bartlett Cove.

Beginning at the Glacier Bay Lodge, the **Forest Loop Trail** is a 1-mile, 1-hour round-trip hike through the young spruce-hemlock rain forest. A boardwalk covers the first part of the trail out to **Blackwater Pond.**

For a half-day trip (and more rugged walking), the **Bartlett River Trail** begins at the roadside, a half mile from the lodge, and winds another 1.5 miles through the rain forest to the **Bartlett River**, ending in a quiet meadow. It's not unusual to see red squirrels, blue grouse, and black bears along either of these trails.

Hiking at Lamplugh Glacier, Glacier Bay National Park

Finally, the new **Beach Trail** runs 6 miles from the lodge area to park headquarters along the beachline. Especially popular among walkers and cyclists, the trail offers opportunities to see a variety of intertidal marine life. Be sure to check tide tables before setting out. Beyond these hikes, the decision is up to you.

If you want to kayak, the **Beardslee Islands,** which are located just north of Bartlett Cove, offer a maze of shorelines and waterways, and a quiet counterpoint to the buses and boats coming and going at Bartlett Cove.

Reaching across the lower bay, **Sitakaday Narrows** is a shoal that creates strong and dangerous whirlpools and currents as the tides (rising and falling an average of 15 feet in 6 hours) rush over it. Check the tide before venturing into the Narrows.

Watch for phalaropes, gulls, terns, and other birds feeding here as the swirling water flushes small fish to the surface. To the north, the **Marble Islands** rise abruptly out of the middle of the bay. Deglaciated about 1835, the islands today support breeding colonies of gulls, cormorants, puffins, and murres—and are off-limits to visitors during the summer. Watch for Steller sea lions on **South Marble Island.**

The West Arm

The bay's west arm contains the park's highest mountains and most active tidewater glaciers. Clear days afford stunning views of the **Fairweather Range,** crowned by **Mount Fairweather** at 15,320 feet; cloudy days lend a moody, rich blue cast to the tidewater faces of the **Margerie, Grand Pacific, Lamplugh,** and **Reid Glaciers.**

In **Johns Hopkins,** the wildest inlet, seven glaciers tumble down mountains, whose surrounding peaks reach 8,000 feet. While glaciers are in retreat on the bay's east and southwest sides, here on the west side several of the glaciers are advancing. Each June thousands of harbor seals give birth to their pups on icebergs in Johns Hopkins Inlet *(to protect the seals, inlet closed May–June).*

Blue Mouse Cove and the northwest corner of **Reid Inlet** are the best anchorages. Good camping sites can be found almost anywhere (except in Johns Hopkins Inlet where the terrain is generally too steep). Hiking is a matter of going where the spirit and the topography take you. Brown bears are common. This is their home and you are the visitor; be careful (see pp. 100–101).

The Glacier Bear

Look closely at every bear you see in the rain forests of southeast Alaska, because one of them might just be the state's rarest: the glacier (or blue) bear.

Both names are, in fact, misnomers. The glacier bear does not live on glaciers or ice fields, for it could not find anything to eat there. This seldom seen creature does live near glaciers, however; it is most often spotted wandering forest trails, ambling along beaches, or grazing in flower-filled meadows.

Finally, the blue bear is anything but. Its fur is black at the roots but silver at the tips, lending it an overall bluish appearance.

Muir Inlet

Reaching 25 miles into the northeast corner of the park, Muir Inlet is a mecca for kayakers. Tour boats, cruise ships, and fishing boats seldom come in here *(waters N of McBride Glacier closed to motorboats June–mid-July)*. The camping is good, and so is the hiking, if you avoid thickets of alder.

Adams Inlet branches east off lower Muir Inlet and is a favorite among kayakers; motorboats are not allowed in the inlet from May to mid-September. You can time your entry and exit by the strong tides that flow in and out through the narrow opening. To the north, **Sealers Island** was once a breeding site for arctic terns and black oystercatchers.

Nearby is **Goose Cove,** an anchorage in Muir Inlet. In contrast to the tidewater glaciers that are advancing in the west arm, most in Muir Inlet continue to retreat. The **McBride** and **Riggs Glaciers** separated from the retreating **Muir Glacier** in 1941 and 1960 respectively; since then, all three have retreated long distances.

A journey up **White Thunder Ridge** or **McConnell Ridge** rewards hikers with spectacular views of upper Muir Inlet. Both hikes are strenuous. Moreover, be prepared to struggle through thickets of alder, which takes a lot of time and energy. Each hike climbs about 1,500 feet and takes a full day.

Another hike worth considering takes you along **Wolf Creek** *(begins at S end of White Thunder Ridge),* where running water has exposed the remains of a forest buried by a glacier 4,000 to 7,000 years ago.

INFORMATION & ACTIVITIES

Headquarters
P.O. Box 140, Gustavus,
AK 99826. 907-697-2230
www.nps.gov/glba

Seasons & Accessibility
Park open year-round, but late
May to mid-September is the
main visitor season; transportation and facilities are
limited the rest of the year.
Call the park before planning
a visit during the off-season.

There are no roads to the
park; access only by airplane,
boat, or ferry. Glacier Bay
Cruiseline *(800-451-5952)*
offers ferry service between
Auke Bay *(N of Juneau)* and
Bartlett Cove. Visitors with
private boats need a permit
from June through August,
907-697-2627.

Visitor & Information Centers
Information centers located
on the dock at Bartlett Cove
and at Glacier Bay Lodge.
Call 907-697-2627 for visitor
information.

Entrance Fee
None.

Pets
Permitted on leashes on
Bartlett Cove roads only. Prohibited in backcountry; boaters
must keep pets aboard vessels.

Facilities for Disabled
Glacier Bay Lodge is accessible
to wheelchairs. Forest Loop
Trail has a stretch of boardwalk
that is also accessible.

Things to Do
Free ranger-led activities,
based at Glacier Bay Lodge,
include nature walks, films,
slide presentations, and
evening programs.

Other activities include
kayaking, crabbing and fishing
(license required), boat tours,
whale-watching, bird-watching,
hiking, berry picking, mountain and glacier climbing *(for
experienced visitors only),*
flight-seeing, and cross-
country skiing.

Kayaks can be rented from
Glacier Bay Sea Kayaks *(907-
697-2257)* in Gustavus.

For information about
ranger-guided boat tours up
the east or west arm from
Bartlett Cove, and to make
reservations, contact Gustavus
Marine Charters *(P.O. Box 81,
Gustavus, AK 99826. 907-697-
2233. www.gustavusmarine
charters.com).*

Contact park headquarters
for a list of additional authorized concessionaires offering
rental and guide services
*(www.nps.gov/glba/visit/ser
vices.htm).*

Ice on the rocks

Special Advisories

■ Do not get too close to icebergs when boating, and do not climb on glaciers unless you are experienced or accompanied by a guide.

■ Mosquitoes are vicious; bring plenty of insect repellent.

■ This is bear country; be vigilant. Obtain bear-safety guidelines from information centers or rangers.

Overnight Backpacking

Permit required. Backcountry users must go through orientation with rangers before departing. Use of Park Service food storage canisters is required.

Campgrounds

Park has one campground, Bartlett Cove. No fee, permit required. 14-day limit. Open year-round, first-come, first-served. Tent sites only. Showers at lodge (within a mile) available seasonally; warming hut on grounds.

Hotels, Motels, & Inns

(Unless otherwise noted, rates for two persons in a double room, high season.)

INSIDE THE PARK:
■ **Glacier Bay Lodge**
241 W. Ship Creek Ave., Anchorage, AK 99501. 888-229-8687. 56 units. $179. Packages that include airfare available. Restaurant, gift shop, daily boat tours of glaciers. Open mid-May to mid-September.

OUTSIDE THE PARK
In Gustavus, AK 99826:
■ **Glacier Bay Country Inn**
P.O. Box 5. 907-697-2288 or 800-628-0912. 10 units. $370, including all meals. Open mid-May to mid-September.

■ **Gustavus Inn** P.O. Box 60. 907-697-2254. 13 units, 11 with private baths. $160 per person, including all meals and some activities. Open May to early September.

■ **Salmon River Cabins**
P.O. Box 13. 907-697-2245. 10 rustic cabins with kitchenettes, 4 private baths. $350–$550 per month. Open mid-May through September.

Whale Country

Whales—enormous, mysterious creatures that travel great distances and live in all seven oceans of the world—galvanize humans. Often we see only a flash of them: a flipper, a tail fluke, a vapor plume, an arced segment of back as one swims away. The biggest whale (the blue) is larger than any creature that has ever lived on Earth—and that includes the dinosaurs. At 150 tons, the blue whale weighs as much as 33 African elephants. With seven stomachs, it can eat more than a million calories a day. Its blood vessels are so large that a person could swim right through them.

Like us, whales are mammals: They are warm blooded, breathe air into their lungs, and propagate by live births.

They have not always been revered as gentle giants, however: Whaling ships once plied the world's oceans, hunting the creatures for their oil-rich blubber, which was used to light lamps all over the globe.

Some of the leviathans earned a not-so-gentle reputation for fighting back. In fact, sailors nicknamed the gray whale "devil fish" for its tendency to turn and attack pursuing ships.

As a result of so much commercial hunting, all of the great whales (except the gray and the minke) are now on the endangered species list.

However, scientists have not reliably determined just how many whales there are. "It's a big ocean and water covers most of the planet," explains one marine biologist. "Even in whale country, you can fly for

Orcas in Prince William Sound

Breaching humpback

days and, because of bad weather or fog, you might not see one whale. There is much about whales we don't know."

Fifteen of the world's great whales swim through Alaskan waters: the sperm, gray, minke, fin, sei, blue, humpback, bowhead, right, killer, beluga, goosebeak, Bering Sea beaked, giant bottle-nose, and narwhal.

From the vantage point of a ferry, a cruise ship, or a kayak cruising the coastal waters, you are most likely to spot the black fins of orcas (killer whales) or the acrobatic displays of humpbacks. To watch one of these 35-ton leviathans breach the surface and then throw itself backward into the water with a crash is an unforgettable sight.

Every year, to the delight of residents and tourists alike, hundreds of humpback whales make an extraordinary odyssey, traveling from their winter breeding grounds off Hawaii to their rich summer feeding grounds in Alaska. Here they bulk up on schools of herring and small, shrimplike creatures known as krill.

These tiny marine creatures proliferate in the cold, northern waters. Thus do whales, the world's largest creatures, draw their sustenance from some of the planet's very smallest.

Humpbacks dive and feed in all the popular waterways of southeastern Alaska—particularly in Chatham Strait and Sitka Sound, in Icy Strait around Point Adolphus, and in Glacier Bay, Frederick Sound, and Stephens Passage, as well as offshore in the open ocean.

Excursions from Glacier Bay

Admiralty Island National Monument–Kootznoowoo Wilderness

80 miles south of Glacier Bay

To the Tlingit Indians, this forested and mountainous island has always been Kootznoohoo—"fortress of the bears." It's an apt description for one of North America's premier bear habitats. Early Russian explorers, perhaps all too aware of the proximity of the powerful animals, called it the Island of Fear. In 1794, British explorer Capt. George Vancouver named it Admiralty Island.

The Alaska National Interest Lands Conservation Act, passed by the U.S. Congress in 1980, established 14 wilderness areas in **Tongass National Forest** and designated Admiralty Island as a national monument. With 678 miles of forested coastline and 67 salmon streams, Admiralty is prime bear habitat. There are no black bears on the island, just brown bears grown to immense size on the bountiful salmon. Thanks to enlightened conservation, this island gem still supports about one brown bear for every square mile of terrain; that's about 1,700 bears, or almost three times the island's human population.

Most of the 96-mile-long, 25-mile-wide island is a mosaic of open meadow and thickets of old-growth forest, mainly western hemlock and Sitka spruce between 200 and 700 years old. Under

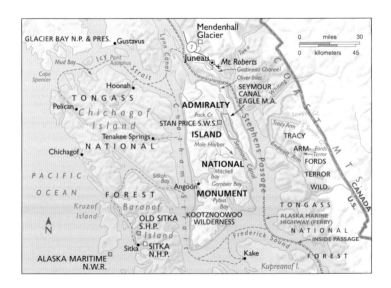

the dense canopy, the ground is covered with thick layers of sphagnum moss and brambles. Above tree line (about 1,500 to 2,000 feet) the land gives way to alpine tundra, rocky outcroppings, snow, and ice fields.

Lower down, the ebb and flow of glacial ice over thousands of years has carved out deep, U-shaped valleys. These are now covered by fjords, forests, and streams—a dynamic landscape that is constantly being reshaped by sea, wind, rain, and snow.

The island's numerous Sitka black-tailed deer can often be seen along the beach boundaries and open hillsides. Mink, land otters, marten, and beavers are common, too. Blue grouse forage in the understory, Steller's jays flit from branch to branch, and ravens and crows call from the timber. Great blue herons and oystercatchers sometimes stalk the ocean edge; on the wing farther out are common murres, marbled murrelets, surf scoters, pigeon guillemots, and gulls and kittiwakes. You'll see bald eagles everywhere.

Steller sea lions, harbor seals, harbor porpoises, minke whales, orcas, and humpback whales patrol just offshore, occasionally coming within feet of the rocky beaches. The sleek black-and-white Dall's porpoise, one of the fastest cetaceans, can frequently be seen playing in the bow wake of passing vessels.

What to See and Do

Whale-watching is popular in the waters around Admiralty, particularly on the island's south and west sides, and especially in July. Each summer, humpback whales travel here from distant wintering grounds to feed in the rich inshore waters (see pp. 92-93). Their sudden, aerial breaches will amaze you. Experienced charter boat captains know the whale-watching rules and are careful not to harass these endangered animals. Orcas also make an occasional appearance, as do sea lions, harbor seals, seabirds, and Dall's porpoises. Though Dall's porpoises usually travel in groups of 20 to 30, a group of 3,000 was once spotted in Stephens Passage. Sea otters sometimes swim off the north end of the island, but they are not common. The best way to enjoy all of these wonderful marine inhabitants is a multiday cruise that anchors each night in a different bay.

The Forest Service maintains 15 rustic public-use cabins; these are usually reserved months in advance. Some of the cabins are on salt water, others are on lakes, and a few are accessible from the Cross Admiralty Canoe Route (see p. 99). To stay in one of the cabins, you'll need all the standard camping gear except a tent. For information, call the Forest Service Information Center *(907-586-8751)*. Thayer Lake Wilderness Lodge (*P.O. Box 8897, Ketchikan, AK 99901; 907-247-8897*) on the west side of the island is the only lodge in the monument, but there is additional lodging in Angoon.

With planning and preparation, anyone can pull off a safe and exhilarating island adventure. An abundance of guides and charter services operate out of Juneau; for a list, contact the Juneau Convention and Visitors Bureau *(888-581-2201)*.

Admiralty Island has three major recreational areas: Seymour Canal, Mitchell Bay, and the Cross Admiralty Canoe Route.

Seymour Canal

Although brown bears can be seen almost everywhere on Admiralty Island, Seymour Canal is the best place to spot them. At the 60,000-acre **Stan Price State Wildlife Sanctuary** on Pack Creek, 30 or so bears regularly fish for salmon or graze in the timber or tidewater marshes. Protected since 1930, these grizzlies pay little attention to people, and no one has ever been injured at the sanctuary. Nearby **Swan Cove** and **Windfall Harbor** *(both accessible only by air or water)* also offer excellent bear-viewing opportunities. Morning and evening are the best times to watch the bears.

Access to the sanctuary is by permit only from June 1 to September 10, with a maximum stay of three days. Permits are especially hard to acquire during the peak viewing season of mid-July to mid-August. Contact the national monument for information about obtaining them.

You can visit two designated viewing sites: a sand spit at the mouth of the creek and a viewing tower located a mile upstream (the latter is accessed by a groomed trail through beautiful old-growth forest). You can fly, boat, or kayak to the refuge. Once on site, self-sufficiency is the byword. Even day-users need to be prepared for sudden storms that may cancel their flights. No facilities or lodging of any kind exist, and campers are restricted to a nearby island. You'll need a boat or kayak to get to the island's campsite.

The 10,778-acre **Seymour Canal Eagle Management Area** encompasses Tiedeman, Bug, Dorn, and Faust Islands, as well as several smaller islands, in the middle of Seymour Canal. Bald eagles tend to nest in old-growth spruce or hemlock trees within 200 yards of

Admiralty Island

salt water, so you'll see dozens of them here. Admiralty Island averages about one nest for every mile of shoreline, the highest density anywhere in the world.

Paddlers from Juneau can reach the head of the Seymour Canal (which is really a long inlet) courtesy of the tram located at the head of Oliver Inlet, 14 to 18 water miles from town. Load your kayak or small boat on the tram for the 1-mile overland jaunt. That way, you'll save yourself a long paddle down blustery Stephens Passage to the mouth of the canal.

Don't expect a fancy conveyance, however; in fact, don't expect the tram even to have an engine. The Oliver Inlet tram is a do-it-yourself operation: A small cart, big enough to hold a couple of kayaks and gear, is pushed by hand on narrow-gauge rails laid over a boardwalk. Sometimes the hand cart will be at the other end of the route, forcing you to retrieve it first. Still, a 2-mile walk beats 40 miles of paddling through choppy seas.

Admiralty Island waterfall

Mitchell Bay

Many canoers and kayakers head for Mitchell Bay on the "dry" (western) side of the island, which receives a mere 40 to 60 inches of precipitation a year.

The Tlingit community of **Angoon** is the main access point here. Located at the mouth of Kootznahoo Inlet, the bay offers a network of shoals, channels, and small wooded islands for you to explore. *(Caution: Strong tides near Angoon can be hazardous to small craft.)*

Deer and bears wander the beaches and forests. Harbor seals periscope up above the waves to check out paddlers. The 9-inch-long, black-and-white waterbirds you'll see in the bay are marbled murrelets. Sometimes these little birds flee at the first sign of an approaching boat; at other times they wait until the last second before diving to safety.

There are no developed hiking trails in Mitchell Bay, but its beaches are great for open-ended rambles. You'll find abundant secluded camping spots along the way. Beachcombing at low tide reveals barnacles, limpets, mussels, chitons, anemones, sea stars, sea slugs—and sometimes bears scavenging along the shoreline. Expect to meet local people engaged in fishing and hunting.

With a population of only about 600, Angoon is not set up for tourism. You'll find one or two bed-and-breakfasts, a general store, and a small motel (which is nearly always fully booked in summer). There is no public campground. You can rent canoes and kayaks at the general store. A few charter boats are available for fishing; some also cater to whale-watchers. For information on accommodations and charters, call the Angoon city offices *(907-788-3653).*

Scheduled seaplane service to Angoon from Juneau is relatively inexpensive, but the Alaska State Ferry is the cheapest access if you're toting your own boat and gear. Both the ferry and the seaplanes drop passengers off at a pier about 3 miles from Angoon. You can walk to town, call a taxi, or begin your trip right there at the dock.

Cross Admiralty Canoe Route

This 32-mile-long route links Mitchell Bay on the west coast of Admiralty Island with Mole Harbor on the east coast. *(Be careful crossing Mitchell Bay; tides particularly strong.)* Along the way, the route passes through as many as eight lakes, all of them connected by Forest Service portage trails. Relatively easy portages make this a fun and enjoyable trip. A few of the lakes have public-use cabins; others offer only rudimentary campsites.

Along the route, you'll see smatterings of red and Alaska cedar, black cottonwood, subalpine fir, lodgepole pine, and Pacific silver fir, as well as plants such as sedge, prickly devil's club, and skunk cabbage. Watch for deer, bears, beavers, common loons, goldeneyes, and the exquisite harlequin duck.

Don't be surprised to see hummingbirds. Weighing a minuscule one-tenth of an ounce and with a wingspan of less than 4 inches, the rufous hummingbird is Alaska's smallest migrating bird. Named for its reddish brown feathers, the rufous winters in Mexico and travels almost 4,000 miles to get here, arriving in early April, just when the columbines, tiger lilies, and paintbrushes come into bloom. The hummingbirds' tiny size does not mean they stick close to the ground; in fact, they appear to use the same flight lanes, and the same altitudes, as Canada geese.

Fishing for cutthroat trout and Dolly Varden can be excellent here in late spring, during the initial insect hatch; however, you must be extra cautious when fishing or when cleaning or cooking fish. All three activities can attract bears.

■ 937,000 acres ■ 15 miles west of Juneau ■ Best months May–Oct.
■ Camping, boating, fishing, whale-watching, wildlife viewing ■ Access by ferry, small boat, canoe, kayak, or aircraft ■ Contact the monument, 8461 Old Dairy Rd., Juneau, AK 99801, 907-586-8790; or Forest Service Information Center, 101 Egan Dr., Juneau, AK 99801; 907-586-8751. www.fs.fed.us/r10/tongass/districts/admiralty

Bear in Mind

Home to as many as 40,000 black bears and brown bears (also known as grizzlies), Alaska truly is bear country. Physical characteristics distinguish the two species, but color alone is not a reliable indicator. Some brown bears are very dark, in fact almost black. Black bears, meanwhile, can vary from jet black to white. Some brown-colored black bears, called cinnamon bears, are often misidentified as grizzlies.

Although black bears usually are smaller than brown bears, size alone is not an ironclad identifier either. By distinguishing the following physical features, you should be able to tell the two apart: Black bears have a long, skinny snout, big ears, no shoulder hump, and short claws; grizzly bears have a dish-shaped face, short ears, a prominent hump, and long, straight claws.

No matter what their claw shape or snout size, all bears are potentially dangerous. Be alert when you're around them, and strictly observe the following safety procedures:

Never surprise a bear. Make a lot of noise, sing, or talk loudly. Never hike alone. And detour around thick brush.

Never approach a bear. Some bears seem unafraid of people, whereas others feel threatened if approached. Females with cubs should be given an especially wide berth; not for nothing did the she-bear earn her reputation for defensiveness.

Never feed a bear. Bears that associate people with food can be very dangerous. Therefore, keep a clean camp; never cook in or near your tent, and always take pains to store all food and garbage a good distance from your campsite, either high in a tree or in bearproof containers. Anglers should clean their catch well away from camp, then dispose of the remains in water.

If you do encounter a bear at close range, remain calm. Talk in a normal voice, raise your arms, and back away slowly. If the bear follows, stop and hold your ground. Whatever you do, don't run; bears can cover the distance between the two of you at 35 miles an hour and, like dogs, will chase a fleeing creature.

What if a bear charges you? Bears often "bluff charge," pulling up within just feet of their adversary. If a grizzly bear grabs you, experts warn that you should not fight back. Instead, fall to the ground, curl up in a ball with your hands behind your neck, and play dead. A mauling from a grizzly usually lasts a matter of seconds.

Brown bear

If you are attacked by a black bear, however, fight back with everything you've got: Sometimes a stout tree limb will see them off. If you fall to the ground and play dead, a black bear might attempt to eat you.

The best defense, of course, is to avoid situations that put you at risk in the first place. State law allows you to shoot a bear in self-defense (and as a last resort). If this happens, you will be required to file a report. You'll also have to relinquish the animal's hide and skull. In addition, you may face a charge of a different kind if it is suspected that you provoked the confrontation with the bear.

For self-protection, some people carry aerosol "bear sprays" containing the pepper extract capsicum. Although these sprays can deter attacks, they have an effective range of less than 10 yards and are useless in strong winds or heavy rain. Don't spray your gear and your tent with the stuff in hopes of keeping bears away; the odor may actually attract them.

Thankfully, bear attacks are rare. Of the hundreds of encounters that occur each summer, very few result in contact and injury.

Tracy Arm–Fords Terror Wilderness

160 miles southeast of Glacier Bay

To sail into **Tracy Arm,** you have to cross a bar left by the glacier that once filled this valley. Known as a terminal moraine, the underwater ridge of rocky debris marks the glacier's farthest advance down the fjord.

Beyond the bar, your tour boat eases its way among the flotilla of icebergs that seem to dance in the turquoise waters. This is one of the most magnificent fjords in southeastern Alaska, with towering walls of granite reminiscent of a cathedral.

Departing from Juneau, tour boats make daily trips to Tracy Arm. As your captain navigates the 22-mile-long fjord toward two beautiful, and very active, tidewater glaciers—**Sawyer** and **South Sawyer**—you'll want to be on deck to soak up the sights and sounds. (If you listen carefully, you will hear the distinctive "popping" of the ice.) Keep watch for harbor seals and their pups riding on the drifting icebergs, and sure-footed mountain goats traversing the cliffs. If you're lucky, you may see a black bear scavenging for mussels at low tide.

These are fairly good waters for kayaking. Watch the tides, however, and keep a safe distance from potentially rolling icebergs and calving glaciers.

Neighboring **Endicott Arm** offers more camping spots as well as a more peaceful wilderness experience because the cruise ships don't go there—yet. Adventure Bound Alaska *(907-463-2509 or 800-228-3875)* runs a small cruise boat out of Juneau that will deliver you and your kayak to the entrance to Endicott Arm.

At the inland end of Endicott Arm, you'll find **Fords Terror.** This narrow, T-shaped fjord was named more than a century ago for an unfortunate sailor named Harry L. Ford. A master-of-arms in the U. S. Navy, Ford, who was rowing a small skiff, entered the fjord at slack water to make a survey of the coast here. On his way out, he was forced to paddle against the outgoing tide and battle the unpredictable currents and churning whirlpools at the entrance to the fjord. If you plan to come here to kayak, take all precautions seriously.

■ **653,179 acres** ■ **50 miles south of Juneau** ■ **Best months May–Sept.**
■ **Camping, kayaking, wildlife viewing, boat tours** ■ **Contact Forest Service Information Center, 101 Egan Dr., Juneau, AK 99801; 907-586-8751. www.fs.fed.us/r10/tongass**

Mendenhall Glacier

50 miles east of Glacier Bay If you fly into Juneau for the first time on a clear day, you may see a startling sight: a massive ribbon of blue-and-white ice winding down the steep surrounding mountains to the edge of Alaska's capital city. This is Mendenhall Glacier.

Located just a dozen or so miles from downtown Juneau, the glacier plunges from its immense reservoir of ice in the **Juneau Icefield** (in the upper reaches of the Coast Mountains) to near sea level. At its terminus, the face of the glacier is 1.5 miles wide.

The best way to experience the glacier and the field of ice at its source is to fly over them. A helicopter can whisk you up above Juneau and deposit you on the ice in a matter of minutes.

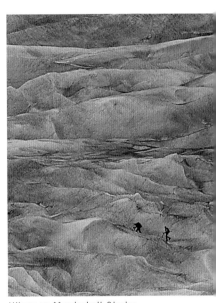

Hikers on Mendenhall Glacier

Atop the glacier, you can take a short walk with a guide. More energetic, and experienced, trekkers may opt for a guided glacier hike and ice-climbing package.

Outfitted with an ice ax and crampons (climbing cleats that attach to your boots), you can explore more intimately this frozen world: jump deep, blue crevasses; drink from tumbling meltwater streams; climb small ice towers; and marvel at the glacier's stark beauty.

If you prefer to keep your feet planted on terra firma, you will find information about walking and hiking trails at the visitor center at the bottom of the glacier. The **nature trail** is a gentle half-mile outing, while the 3-mile round-trip **East Glacier Loop** leads to a scenic overlook of the glacier.

■ **12 miles long** ■ **Northwest of Juneau** ■ **Best months May–Aug.**
■ **Hiking, ice climbing, flight-seeing, guided glacier hikes** ■ **Contact Mendenhall Glacier Visitor Center, Mendenhall Loop Rd., Juneau, AK 99802; 907-789-0097. www.fs.fed.us/r10/tongass**

Mount Roberts

50 miles east of Glacier Bay

You have a choice to make on Mount Roberts: Take it easy and rest your legs or give your heart a workout? Or maybe a bit of both?

If the first option appeals, the tram is for you. On a clear day, go down to the cruise-ship dock and board the **Mount Roberts Tramway** (the cars are painted with traditional Tlingit eagle and raven motifs). You'll be whisked halfway up the mountain, where you can visit a **nature center.** For information, call 907-463-3412 or 888-461-8726.

For a more energetic outing, take the 4.5-mile **Mount Roberts Trail,** which starts at the top of Sixth Street near downtown Juneau. After 2.5 miles of forest, the trail emerges above tree line (about 2,500 feet) at a large wooden cross. From here, you can hike over steep, rocky ridges, through flower-filled meadows, to **Gastineau Peak** and then on to the top of Mount Roberts. Enjoy fabulous views of **Gastineau Channel,** and, if your timing is good, parasailers leaping from the summit to glide on the thermals.

Sea kayaks, Point Adolphus

To take advantage of the third option, you can ride the tram to the halfway point, then hike the rest of the way an additional 2 or so miles, to the top of the mountain.

■ **3,819 feet high** ■ **Southwest of downtown Juneau** ■ **Best months May–Sept.** ■ **Hiking, parasailing, tram rides** ■ **Contact Forest Service Information Center, 101 Egan Dr., Juneau, AK 99801; 907-586-8751**

Point Adolphus

10 miles south of Glacier Bay

At the height of the Alaska summer, the waters off Point Adolphus in **Icy Strait** are the place to see humpback whales. They come here for good reason: The ebb and flow of the tides, together with the confluence of waters from Icy Strait, **Glacier Bay** and **Mud Bay,** churn up rich nutrients that provide a lavish feast for whales and other marine creatures. Bald eagles and gulls eagerly skim off whatever is left over.

To sight a whale, scan the surface of the water for a vapor plume about 15 feet high. Also watch for tail flukes; the humpback almost always shows its flukes before diving. Turbulence in the water and screeching gulls overhead are good signs that whales are feeding. You may even see a flipper waving and slapping the surface.

One of the humpback's most unusual feeding techniques is to catch prey in a net of bubbles. The whale dives below a school of fish, then slowly spirals up around it, releasing air bubbles from its blowhole as it goes. The bubbles act as a seine net, corralling the fish and forcing them into a tight circle. The whale then dives back under to rocket up through the middle of the bubbles, its mouth wide open to swallow its prey.

The most thrilling sight of all, however, is that of a 35-ton humpback whale breaching—that is, hurtling itself out of the water in a graceful backward, even balletic, arch. Daily boat tours or guided kayaking trips can be arranged from Gustavus or Juneau through Sea Otter Kayak *(907-697-3007).*

■ **Northern tip of Chichagof Island, across Icy Strait from Glacier Bay** ■ **Best months late June–mid-August** ■ **Whale-watching, guided kayaking trips, sailboat and passenger cruises** ■ **Contact Glacier Bay National Park and Preserve, P.O. Box 140, Gustavus, AK 99826; 907-697-2230. www.nps.gov/glba**

Alaska Chilkat Bald Eagle Preserve

70 miles north of Glacier Bay Founding father Benjamin Franklin did not approve of the creature that the young American republic had chosen to represent it as its national symbol. The bald eagle, he declared, was "a bird of bad moral character." He preferred the turkey.

Franklin's judgment seems more than a trifle harsh. With its regal white head, enormous wingspan (about 8 feet), and sharp eyes that can sight a target a quarter of a mile away, the bald eagle is in fact a magnificent creature worthy of its moniker, the king of birds.

In the early 20th century, the United States declared its national symbol of freedom to be a virtual outlaw. Claiming that the birds preyed on salmon and therefore competed with fishermen, the federal government offered a bounty of 50 cents (later increased to $2) for every eagle killed. Between 1917 and 1952, more than 100,000 Alaska bald eagles suffered that fate.

Scientists, however, have learned since then that bald eagles actually posed no threat to the salmon industry. Scavengers, they feed primarily on dying or dead salmon. Thanks in part to that discovery, the bird's rehabilitation in Alaska is now complete. Although the bald eagle remains on the threatened species list in the rest of North America, it is thriving in Alaska and in Canada.

A visit to the Alaska Chilkat Bald Eagle Preserve proves just how well the species is doing. Like solemn, hook-nosed judges bewigged

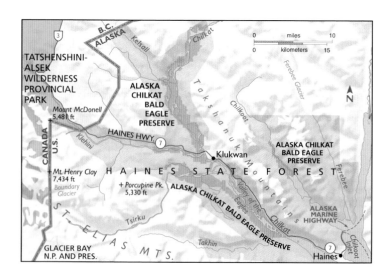

in white and robed in black, the birds fly in every fall from hundreds of miles away to gather along the banks of the **Chilkat River.** Ask at the ranger station in Haines *(907-766-2292)* for the location of viewing sites that do not disturb the birds.

Bald eagle

From October to December, the largest concentration of bald eagles in the world gathers in and around Chilkat. In addition to the 200 to 400 eagles that reside in the preserve year-round, the new arrivals swell the birds' ranks to more than 3,000.

You'll see them lining the snowy branches of cottonwoods, where they perch for hours, conserving their energy. At their feet is a veritable banquet: Warm water, welling up from the bottom of the Chilkat River in winter, keeps the river flats free of ice, allowing the birds to gorge on spawned-out, dying, and rotting salmon.

The **Valley of the Eagles** is located between Miles 10 and 26 on the **Haines Highway.** The first 26-mile stretch of the highway, which is open year-round, runs between Haines and Klukwan. Along a 5-mile stretch beside the Chilkat River *(between Miles 18 and 24),* you'll find the **Eagle Council Grounds.** Here, the birds congregate in large numbers along the river flats, making this area the premier spot for viewing them.

Every year, the town of Haines marks the return of the bald eagles with the **Alaska Bald Eagle Festival.** Usually held during the second weekend of November, the festival features performances by musicians and local artists. Photography workshops and guided eagle-viewing excursions may be offered as well. For information about the festival, contact the Haines Chamber of Commerce *(P.O. Box 518, Haines, AK 99827. 907-766-2202).*

■ **48,000 acres** ■ **10 miles northwest of Haines** ■ **Best months Oct.–Dec.; eagles begin gathering in early Oct. and taper off by Feb.** ■ **Bird-watching, wildlife viewing** ■ **Contact Alaska State Parks, Southeast Area Office, 400 Willoughby Ave., Juneau, AK 99801; 907-465-4563. www.dnr.state.ak.us/ parks/units/eagleprv.htm**

Chilkat State Park

70 miles north of Glacier Bay

A delightful smorgasbord for the short-term traveler, seaside Chilkat State Park offers you a chance to scale **Mount Riley**—at 1,760 feet, the highest peak on the Chilkat Peninsula. You'll be rewarded with fine views of nearby summits, glaciers, and the Lynn Canal. The climb is not nearly so rigorous as the steep trail up **Mount Ripinski,** the mountain that rises directly behind Haines. Stop at the Haines Visitor Information **Center** for maps and directions.

Three routes will get you to the top. The easiest to find is the trail off **Mud Bay Road** *(2.8 miles to summit)*. Allow about 4 to 5 hours round-trip.

For a pleasurable forest and beach walk, head to the park campground *(about 7 miles from town at end of Mud Bay Rd.)*.

There you'll find the beginning of **Seduction Point Trail** (6.8 miles one way). Across the water, **Davidson** and **Rainbow Glaciers** cascade down the mountains. From the trail, you'll have opportunities to see bears, moose, whales, seals, sea lions, and blue herons. Seduction Point separates the **Chilkat** and **Chilkoot Inlets**.

Fit hikers should be able to complete the hike in about 9 hours round-trip. The best time to tackle it is in midsummer, when you can take advantage of the longer hours of sunlight. Be sure to check tides before setting out and carry extra water.

■ **6,000 acres** ■ **South of Haines on the Chilkat Peninsula** ■ **Best months May–Sept.** ■ **Camping, hiking, boating** ■ **Contact the park, P.O. Box 430, Haines, AK 99827; 907-766-2292; or Haines Visitor Information Center, 2nd Ave., Haines, AK 99827; 907-766-2234 (summer). www.haines.ak.us**

Klondike Gold Rush National Historical Park

70 miles north of Glacier Bay

"Gold! Gold! Gold!" trumpeted the *Seattle Post-Intelligencer* of July 17, 1897. "Sixty-Eight Rich Men on the Steamer Portland—Stacks of Yellow Metal!" Thousands cheered from the Seattle docks as the prospectors carted their gold (wrapped in caribou hides or stuffed in socks, leather satchels, and old jam jars) off the ship. Many of them had spent years panning the creeks of the Klondike River deep in the Yukon Territory. They, like everyone else, were unprepared for the size of their windfall. News of their good fortune spread throughout the lower 48, triggering a stampede to the north the likes of which had never before been seen—and would never again be seen.

Skagway marked the beginning, and the end, of the Klondike gold trail. Accessible by sea, the town provided the quickest and easiest routes over the mountains and into the goldfields. The whole story unfolds as you stroll through history at the unique Klondike Gold Rush National Historical Park. Along with Skagway's well-preserved downtown, complete with wooden sidewalks, cabins, and renovated saloons, the park contains the trail and mountain pass used by thousands of gold seekers traveling to and from the Klondike.

"Skagway was little better than a hell on earth," recalled the incorruptible Samuel Steele, superintendent of the North West Mounted Police, after he visited the town. Gunfire rang out through the night, he recalled in his memoirs, and bullets crashed through the walls of the boardinghouse where he slept. Cries of "Help!" and "Murder!" punctuated the rollicking music blaring from dance halls.

A two-bit con artist named Jefferson Randolph "Soapy" Smith and his gang of hoodlums ruled the town. Soapy came by the nickname while selling bars of soap earlier in his career, but he just couldn't keep his hands clean: In Skagway, Soapy and his cronies set up bogus businesses practically overnight—barbershops, telegram offices, church fundraising operations—and invented ingenious ways of fleecing hapless newcomers or returning prospectors.

Soapy's days were numbered, though. On the evening of July 8, 1898, he got wind of a meeting of town fathers, who well understood that every dollar he skimmed off the citizenry was a dollar destined never to line their own pockets. The meeting had but one item on the agenda: how to deal with Soapy.

Armed and angry, Soapy stormed into the meeting, where he was confronted by Frank Reid. Nominally the town's engineer and surveyor, Reid was determined to protect his own shady money-making enterprises and to eliminate his rival in the bargain. When he accosted Soapy that July night, Soapy responded by pulling a gun. Reid did the same, and both men died as a result of the ensuing gun battle. History has been kind to Reid, however. He and Soapy are buried—one as hero, the other as villain— in the **Goldrush Cemetery** on the outskirts of town.

What to See and Do Around Skagway

The Park Service **visitor center** (*daily in summer, reduced hours in winter*) in the old railroad depot on Second Avenue and Broadway offers films, exhibits, ranger talks, and information on conditions along the **Chilkoot Trail** (*opposite*). Excellent ranger-led walking tours of historic Skagway depart several times daily. For a self-guided tour, go to the Skagway Visitor Center (*5th Ave. and Broadway. 907-983-2854*) and pick up the "Skagway Walking Tour" brochure. Other fun tour options include a horse and buggy, and even a vintage car with a costumed driver.

Ride the Train

From Skagway, Klondike-bound prospectors had two possible ways in. The old **White Pass Trail** is the route used today by the

White Pass & Yukon Route railroads

White Pass & Yukon Route Railroad (*800-343-7373. www.whitepass railroad.com*) for the 3-hour trip from Skagway to White Pass Summit. In the early days of the gold rush, this was known as the Dead Horse Trail because thousands of horses fell to their deaths while hauling miners' supplies.

The train ride makes for an interesting half-day excursion. After the first 4 miles, the gradient grows unusually steep (some of the grades reach 3.9 percent). The track is the handiwork of a brilliant engineer named Michael J. Heney. In 1898, he constructed a railroad over the Coast Mountains, deemed by most folks as too steep even for a billy goat. Heney's motto: "Give me enough dynamite and snoose [snuff] and I'll build a road to hell."

Hike the Chilkoot

The other route into the Klondike was the 33-mile **Chilkoot Trail,** which you can still walk today. The only footpath in Klondike Gold Rush park, the trail is managed through an agreement between the national park services of the United States and Canada.

Historic Skagway

If you have only a few hours, try some of the shorter hikes near downtown Skagway. **Lower Dewey Lake Trail,** which begins on Spring Street between Third and Fourth Streets on the east side of town, is a lovely 0.7-mile walk with an elevation gain of 600 feet. You can go on, if time permits, to **Upper Dewey Lake** for a round-trip of 7 miles.

■ **13,191 acres** ■ **Skagway Historic District in downtown Skagway; 33-mile Chilkoot Trail begins in Dyea, 9 miles from downtown Skagway** ■ **Best months late May–mid-Sept.** ■ **Hiking, backpacking, guided walks, tram rides** ■ **Contact the park, P.O. Box 517, Skagway, AK 99840; 907-983-2921. www.nps.gov/klgo**

Lituya Bay

Western shore of Glacier Bay National Park

Enchantress. Siren. Death trap. Beautiful Lituya Bay has been called many names, all of them well chosen. For Lituya Bay—the only shelter on a 150-mile-long stretch of the Gulf of Alaska's wild northwestern coast—is a microcosm of the geologic hazards of the North Pacific. The little bay is dominated by the backdrop of the majestic, ice-capped **Fairweather Range.** The entrance to the bay (about 350 yards across) is almost sealed shut by a terminal moraine that was deposited by the glacier that carved out the bay.

Twice a day the waters of the Pacific Ocean rush in and out of this bottleneck, setting up a chain of "haystacks" (sailorspeak for standing waves) and pounding turbulence that easily can overwhelm any ship.

When French explorer Jean-François de La Pérouse sailed in here in 1786, he sent three longboats to take depth soundings near the mouth of the bay. With little warning, two of the boats were swept out to sea and crushed. None of the sailors survived. As a memorial, La Pérouse buried a bottle on Cenotaph Island in the middle of the bay. It contained this poignant message: "Twenty-one brave mariners perished here, Reader. Mingle your tears with ours."

Lituya Bay lies directly across an active seismic fracture zone, called the Fairweather Fault. On the night of July 9, 1958, three fishing boats were anchored in the bay when an earthquake rumbled beneath the water. The boats were tossed about like bath toys by a great wave that rolled across the bay and surged onto the land, ripping out trees and advancing 1,720 feet up the mountain.

The wave then roared out of the bay and into the gulf, carrying two of the boats with it. One craft sank, but its crew was rescued. The second boat sank with all hands. And the third somehow managed to stay afloat inside the bay.

The captain of the third boat described what he had witnessed: "These great snow-capped giants [the Fairweather Range] shook and twisted and heaved. They seemed to be suffering unbearable internal tortures...At last, as though attempting to rid themselves of their torment, the mountains spewed heavy clouds of snow and rocks into the air and threw huge avalanches down their groaning sides. During all this, I was terrified, rooted to the deck...then I saw a wave come out of this churning turmoil...As we were swept along by the wave over what had recently been dry land and a timber-covered shore, I was sure that the end of the world had come for Sonny and me and our boat."

Miraculously, their boat not only rode out the monster wave, but the entire crew survived the ordeal.

■ 16 square miles ■ Gulf of Alaska, western shore of Glacier Bay National Park and Preserve ■ Backcountry hiking, kayaking, fishing ■ Best months late May–mid-September ■ Contact Glacier Bay National Park and Preserve, P.O. Box 140, Gustavus, AK 99826; 907-697-2624. www.nps.gov/glba

Katmai

Volcanoes and bears—powerful, unpredictable, and awe inspiring—embody the wild heart of Katmai National Park and Preserve. Lying along the Pacific Ring of Fire, Katmai has within its borders 15 volcanoes, some of them still steaming. It also boasts North America's largest population of protected brown bears (about 1,500 of them). You can hike, kayak, and canoe here. You can fish waist deep in rivers as clear as glass. And you can watch the best fish catcher of all, the great Alaskan brown bear, sometimes dive under the water for its prey, sometimes catch fish in midair. At day's end you can relax in a rustic lodge on the shore of a sapphire lake and recount the day's adventures.

In 1912 a volcano erupted here with a force ten times that of Mount St. Helens in 1980. The cataclysmic eruption of Mount Katmai's Novarupta vent began on June 6 and lasted 60 hours. Suddenly Katmai, a place hardly anyone had heard of, was making headlines around the world. People heard the blast in Juneau, 750 miles away. Ash filled the air, global temperatures cooled, acid rain burned clothing off lines in Vancouver, British Columbia; and on Kodiak Island, just across Shelikof Strait from Katmai, day became night.

Botanist Robert Griggs, leading a 1916 expedition sponsored by the National Geographic Society, ascended Katmai Pass from Shelikof Strait. "The whole valley as far as the eye could reach was full of hundreds, no thousands—literally, tens of thousands—of smokes curling up from its fissured floor," he wrote. The smokes were fumaroles steaming 500 to 1,000 feet into the air. Griggs, who named it the Valley of Ten Thousand Smokes, spearheaded the campaign to include Katmai in the National Park System.

The smokes are gone from the valley. But steam vents still appear elsewhere in the park. And it's only a matter of time before other fumaroles appear in the wake of another eruption.

- Southwest Alaska, 290 miles southwest of Anchorage
- 4.1 million acres
- Established 1980
- Best months June–early Sept.
- Camping, hiking, boating, fishing, wildlife viewing
- Information: 907-246-3305 www.nps.gov/katm

Brown bears at Brooks Falls, Katmai National Park and Preserve

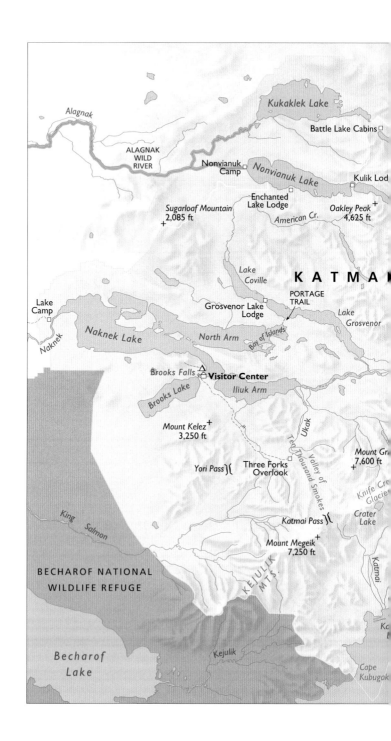

Alagnak

Kukaklek Lake

Battle Lake Cabins

ALAGNAK
WILD
RIVER

Nonvianuk
Camp

Nonvianuk Lake

Kulik Lod

Enchanted
Lake Lodge

Sugarloaf Mountain
2,085 ft

American Cr.

Oakley Peak
4,625 ft

Lake
Coville

K A T M A

PORTAGE
TRAIL

Lake
Camp

Grosvenor Lake
Lodge

Lake
Grosvenor

Naknek Lake

North Arm

Bay of Islands

Naknek

Brooks Falls

Visitor Center

Iliuk Arm

Brooks Lake

Mount Kelez
3,250 ft

Ukak

Mount Gr
7,600 ft

Yori Pass

Three Forks
Overlook

Valley of Ten Thousand Smokes

Knife Cre
Glacie

Crater
Lake

King

Salmon

Katmai Pass

Mount Megeik
7,250 ft

Ka

BECHAROF NATIONAL
WILDLIFE REFUGE

K E J U L I K   M T S.

Katmai

Becharof
Lake

Kejulik

Cape
Kubugak

COOK INLET

N

McNeil Cove

MCNEIL RIVER
STATE GAME
SANCTUARY

Kamishak

Douglas

Mt. Douglas +
7,063 ft

Cape
Douglas

NATIONAL PARK

Fourpeaked
Glacier

vonoski

Kaguyak
Crater

Swikshak
Bay

Wolverine Falls

inbow

Hook
Glacier

Ninagiak

Mount Denison
7,606 ft +

Hallo
Bay

Hallo Glacier

Serpent Tongue
Glacier

Kaflia
Bay

SHELIKOF STRAIT

Kinak Bay

Takli

KODIAK
ISLAND

Dakavak
Bay

| 0 | miles | 20 |
| 0 | kilometers | 30 |

How to Get There

From Anchorage, scheduled jets fly the 290 miles to park headquarters at King Salmon; from there *(June–mid-Sept.),* daily floatplanes fly the last 33 miles to Brooks Camp, site of a summer visitor center and center of activity. Air charters can be arranged to access other areas. You can drive the 9 miles from King Salmon to Lake Camp, at the western end of the park on the Naknek River, then go by boat to Brooks Camp, the Bay of Islands, and other areas of Naknek Lake.

When to Go

June to early September. Only then, with transportation available between Brooks Camp and the Valley of Ten Thousand Smokes, are the lodges, cabins, and Brooks Camp Campground open.

Bear-watching, an increasingly popular pastime, is best in July when the sockeye salmon spawn (bear-watching suffers a brief lull in June and again in August). Fishing and hiking are good throughout summer, but come prepared for rain. Heavy snowpack may remain in the upper elevations into July. Summer daytime temperatures range from the mid-50s to mid-60s; the average low is 44° F.

What Not to Miss

- Guided bus tour to Valley of Ten Thousand Smokes
- Bear-watching at Brooks Falls
- Picnicking or camping at Three Forks Overlook
- Hiking Dumpling Mountain and Ukak Falls Trails
- Paddling with sea lions in the Bay of Islands
- Aerial grand tour over the park and volcanoes
- White-water rafting on the Alagnak River

How to Visit

If time is short, get to **Brooks Camp.** This is the park's main destination; compared to the rest of the park, it's crowded. But the lodge and campground are comfortable *(reservations required),* the hiking and fishing are good, and the bear viewing is unforgettable. Plan to attend the program on bear safety.

If possible, sign up for the 23-mile guided tour by bus or van from Brooks Lodge to the **Valley of Ten Thousand Smokes.** Return the same day or hike into the valley and camp.

Extend your stay by boating or flying to the many other lakes, streams, rivers, and lodges in the park. Pick your area, make a safe plan, and go.

EXPLORING THE PARK

Brooks Camp & Valley of Ten Thousand Smokes

Some very pleasant hikes begin near Brooks Camp. The first trail you'll want to take leads to the bear-viewing platform. The half-mile boardwalk trail begins between Brooks Camp and **Brooks Lake** and winds gently through the forest to **Brooks Falls,** ending at the viewing platform. Climb the wooden steps to the balcony, where you can look down on a lively scene of jumping fish and feeding bears.Weighing on average a thousand pounds and measuring up to 10 feet in length, these Alaskan brown bears are the largest land carnivores in North America.

The trail up **Dumpling Mountain** makes a good day hike. Starting at the campground, you'll climb 1.5 miles to an overlook. From there you can continue another 2 miles through dense forest and alpine meadows to the 2,440-foot-high summit. Both the overlook and summit have sweeping views of Brooks Camp, Naknek Lake, and the distant volcanoes.

The park's most and spectacular, and popular, hiking is in the Valley of Ten Thousand Smokes. There's no other landscape like it, anywhere. Daily tours connect Brooks Camp with the **Three Forks Overlook** and a cabin at the north end of the valley, where you can camp or picnic. From the Three Forks Visitor Contact Station, the 1.5-mile **Ukak Falls Trail** drops 700 feet to the edge of the valley, with

Visitors photograph brown bears feeding on salmon

Hungry as a Bear

Often called the largest land carnivores, brown bears (known as grizzlies when more than 100 miles from the coast) are in fact omnivores: They range from tidal flats to mountaintops in search of anything edible, be it clams or berries. In spring they graze for hours on tidal sedges and grasses. When the salmon begin to run in summer, grizzlies gorge themselves, gaining 20 percent of their body weight. (A small bear weighed by biologists on the Alaska Peninsula actually doubled its body weight.) Late season berry binges add extra pounds; by hibernation time in late October, healthy brown bears are waddling fat. Some large males approach three-quarters of a ton. Upon emerging from hibernation in late March or early April, they quickly shake off their lethargy and resume their search for food.

Brown bear

its ash-and pumice-covered floor. From here you can walk over the volcanic tuff to **Ukak Falls,** where the **Ukak River** roars through a bedrock canyon, or to the **Three Forks Convergence,** where the river and its tributaries have cut deep gashes in the ash.

The most popular hike into the valley is via the (unnamed) **trail** that begins a half mile back from the end of the road; plan to camp overnight. The trail crosses Windy Creek, passes the north end of the Buttress Range, crosses the River Lethe, and finally climbs a thousand feet to the Baked Mountain Cabin, a shelter available for overnights. The challenging 12-mile trip takes a full day; drinking water is scarce. The river crossing can be extremely dangerous; be sure to be briefed at the visitor center before you hike.

Due south 5.5 miles from the cabin is **Katmai Pass,** where Robert Griggs first beheld the valley in 1916. Strong winds often funnel through here. A fascinating side trip between Katmai Pass and Baked Mountain is to **Novarupta,** a 200-foot-high dome of volcanic rock that was the extrusion plug of the 1912 eruption. Scientists believe that most of the ash and lava spewed out through a fissure here, drawing magma from nearby Mount Katmai and causing its summit to collapse into a caldera.

To reach the caldera (a strenuous 1- to 2-day trip), head east from Novarupta or Baked Mountain to the stagnant, ash-covered **Knife Creek Glaciers;** then climb 3,800 feet up ash and ice to the caldera rim, where, if you peer over the edge, you'll see what Robert Griggs saw: "a wonderful lake, of a weird vitriolic robin's-egg blue."

Water & Air Trips

Boaters, kayakers, and canoeists find no shortage of places to explore in Katmai. Guides and equipment are available for hire through Brooks Lodge or one of the other, smaller lodges catering mostly to fishermen. An especially popular and picturesque spot is the **Bay of Islands** in the **North Arm** of **Naknek Lake,** 22 miles from Brooks Camp.

For serious paddlers looking for the truly wild side of Katmai, the **Savonoski Loop** is an 85-mile round-trip from Brooks Camp that takes 4 to 8 days, depending on the weather. You paddle through the Bay of Islands, portage to **Lake Grosvenor,** and float the **Grosvenor** and **Savonoski Rivers** into the **Iliuk Arm** of Naknek Lake for the return to Brooks Camp. Follow the shorelines; the wind can suddenly transform lakes from tranquil to tempestuous.

If you'd like to take a river trip, inquire about the **Alagnak River,** a designated Wild and Scenic River, and the **Ukak River,** which, with its Class V rapids, is only for experienced river runners.

Like Alaska's other national parks, Katmai is spectacular from the air. Flight-seeing trips can be arranged in King Salmon or Brooks Camp. The grand tour might swing over the Valley of Ten Thousand Smokes, through Katmai Pass, up the coast from Katmai Bay to Swikshak Bay, over Kaguyak Crater, and down the Savonoski River back to Brooks Camp. Take plenty of film and a calm stomach.

INFORMATION & ACTIVITIES

Headquarters
P.O. Box 7, King Salmon,
AK 99613. 907-246-3305
www.nps.gov/katm

Seasons & Accessibility
Park open year-round, but
regular scheduled flights from
Anchorage to King Salmon
(with connecting seaplane flights
into the park) are available June
to mid-September only. Reserve
well in advance. Accessible by
private or charter plane all year.
Contact the park for a list of
licensed air charter companies.

Visitor & Information Centers
Brooks Camp Visitor Center
and the concessions are open
from June to mid-September.
All visitors to Brooks Camp
are required to attend the 15-
minute orientation on bear
etiquette. For visitor information, contact the park or
Katmailand, Inc., the park's
main concessionaire *(4125 Aircraft Dr., Anchorage, AK 99502.
907-243-5448 or 800-544-0551.
www.katmailand.com)*. King
Salmon Visitor Center
is open year-round.

Entrance Fee
None, but $10 per person fee
for day users of Brooks Camp.
Call National Parks Reservation
Service *(800-365-2267)* for
advanced permits. Limited
day-use permits and advanced
reservations are required.

Facilities for Disabled
Brooks Lodge is accessible, but
with assistance.

Things to Do
Free ranger-led activities
include daily interpretive
programs, evening programs,
nature walks. Also, bus trips
to the Valley of Ten Thousand
Smokes, bear-watching, hiking,
kayaking, canoeing, float trips,
mountain climbing, flight-
seeing, and fishing *(license
required)*. Katmailand, Inc.,
has guides, boating, and fishing
equipment available at Brooks
Lodge; reserve ahead. Ask the
park for a list of other outfitters and guides authorized to
operate within its borders.

Special Advisories
■ Alaskan brown bears are
unpredictable and dangerous;
stay far away from them
unless you're at one of the
bear-viewing platforms.
■ Exercise caution when crossing glacial streams.

Overnight Backpacking
Camping allowed anywhere in
the park without reservations,
except at Brooks Camp. Back-

Canoeing on Naknek Lake at Brooks Camp

country permits required, but are free and unlimited. Information pamphlet available. Bear-resistant food canisters, required for overnight stays, are available free at visitor center.

Campgrounds

Park's one backcountry campground, Brooks Camp, open June to mid-September. $8 for up to six people, reservations required. 7-day limit in July and September. Showers available at Brooks Lodge, tent sites only, three-sided shelters for cooking; limited food services in park. Call National Parks Reservation Service *(800-365-2267)*.

Hotels, Motels, & Inns

(Unless otherwise noted, rates are for two persons in a double room, high season.)

INSIDE THE PARK:
Katmailand, Inc., offers a variety of package tours from Anchorage that include airfare; lodging at **Brooks Lodge, Grosvenor Lake Lodge,** or **Kulik Lodge;** meals; guides; fishing tackle; rafts; licenses; and/or transportation by boat or plane to fishing spots. For information, call 907-243-5448 or 800-544-0551.

■ **Brooks Lodge** 16 cabins. Packages starting from $302 per person. Open June to mid-September.

■ **Grosvenor Lake Lodge** 3 cabins. Packages starting from $2,200 per person. Open June to late September.

■ **Kulik Lodge** 12 cabins. Packages starting from $2,275 per person. Open mid-June to late September.

Excursions from Katmai

McNeil River State Game Sanctuary

Adjoins Katmai to the north

Just west of Augustine Island (an active volcano), the **McNeil River** drains into the mudflats of Kamishak Bay. About a mile upstream from its mouth, boulders and fast water form frothing waterfalls that pose a challenge to migrating salmon. The fish leap and fight against the current and cataracts in their attempts to navigate the falls, and dodge hungry, pawing bears. At times, hundreds of salmon clog the pools below the falls.

With no comparable fishing sites in the area, the **McNeil River falls** attract the world's greatest concentration of brown bears. Nowhere else can you expect to see a similar gathering. Using threats, growls, bare-fanged assaults, thousand-pound males defend their fishing grounds against other bears. Smaller bears position themselves on exposed rocks in midstream. Juveniles and females with cubs patrol back and forth. You'll typically see 20 to 30 bears here, and as many as 60.

Uncontrolled public use in the early 1970s (when people sometimes outnumbered the bears at the falls) endangered this area, and the bears abandoned the river or fished at night. Preservation of this unique ursine feeding ground is the sanctuary's main goal; managers instituted a permit system limiting the number of daily visitors to ten people. Permits are awarded by a lottery; deadline is March 1. (*Apply by mail to Alaska Department of Fish and Game, Division of Wildlife Conservation, P.O. Box 228080, Anchorage, AK 99522. Attn: McNeil River Application. Or at: www.admin.adfg .state.ak.us/license.*)

In June, red (sockeye) salmon migrate into **Mikfik Creek,** which drains into **McNeil Cove.** From several locations along the creek you can watch bears fishing or grazing on the sedge flats, usually eight or nine at a time. When the abundant 7- to 18-pound chum salmon enter McNeil River in July, bears begin to congregate at the falls, along with bald eagles and magpies, not to mention the occasional wolf, red fox, or wolverine.

Other than a communal cook shack and pit toilets, the only campground is undeveloped; there are no concessions of any kind. You must be entirely self-sufficient and prepared for cold, wind-driven rain. Storms delay or cancel flights, so bring at least two days' additional food. From the campground, you hike 2 miles one way to the McNeil River falls, at times wading through knee-deep water and slogging through boot-sucking mud (backpack and hip boots are necessities). Expect mosquitoes on calm days.

Regulations prohibit solo inland jaunts; visitors travel in groups led by a sanctuary employee. These stringent rules work: By always returning to the same locations, humans are seen by the 140 bears as nonthreatening, thus allowing visitors a closer, more intimate look at the animals as they go about their daily activities.

■ 114,100 acres ■ 250 miles southwest of Anchorage, 100 miles west of Homer ■ Access by air June–Aug. ■ Camping, wildlife viewing ■ Lottery permit system and user fees ■ Contact the sanctuary, Alaska Department of Fish and Game, Division of Wildlife Conservation, 333 Raspberry Rd., Anchorage, AK 99518; 907-267-2182. www.state.ak.us/adfg

Kodiak Island Archipelago

125 miles southeast of Katmai

This string of islands parallels the Alaska Peninsula about 30 blustery miles across the **Shelikof Strait.** Geologically speaking, the archipelago (about 180 miles long and 67 miles across) is a continuation of the Kenai Mountains. The main islands—Shuyak, Afognak, Raspberry, Uganik, Kodiak, Sitkalidak, and the Trinity group—together approximate the size of Connecticut. Kodiak, at 3,588 square miles, is the nation's second largest island, surpassed only by the island of Hawaii. Still, no point of land in the archipelago is farther than 15 miles from tidewater because of all the bays and inlets.

Thousands of years ago, glaciers carved the archipelago's mountainous landscape into pinnacles, fjords, and wide valleys. Volcanic and seismic forces have also contorted the landscape, while ferocious winter storms and surf rolling in off the North Pacific continue to shape the islands.

Vegetation here ranges from dense Sitka spruce forest in the north to rolling, hummocky tundra in the south. Willows, alders, and flowering plants, nurtured by the rich soils and 67 inches of average annual precipitation, stand 5 feet tall or higher, choking many low-lying inland areas.

All five types of Pacific salmon spawn here. Fourteen marine mammals—including sea otters and sea lions; and humpback, gray, orca, and finback whales—feed offshore or migrate through.

Biologists list 140 seabird colonies and estimate that 1.5 million seabirds and more than 150,000 waterfowl winter along the bays and shores. Despite its size, Kodiak Island originally supported only six native land mammals. Some now well-established species arrived here as transplants: Sitka black-tailed deer in 1924, mountain goat in 1952, and beaver, snowshoe hare, reindeer, and Roosevelt elk on Afognak in 1929.

Several agencies manage parts of the islands. The Fish and Wildlife Service administers Kodiak National Wildlife Refuge, created by President Franklin D. Roosevelt in 1941, largely to protect the Kodiak brown bears. The Alaska State Parks system manages several smaller sites.

The city of Kodiak (population about 8,000) serves as the islands' main supply and transportation hub, with an airport and access from the mainland via Homer, Seward, and Anchorage. For information, call 907-235-8449 or 800-382-9229 (www.akmhs.com).

What to See and Do
Kodiak National Wildlife Refuge is a nearly two-million-acre preserve, with no roads, that includes the southwestern two-thirds of Kodiak Island, all of Uganik Island, and parts of Afognak. The refuge encompasses 800 miles of coastline, 11 large lakes, and 7 major watersheds. But its greatest claim to fame is its wildlife.

Biologists estimate that 2,500 to 3,000 Alaska brown bears—the world's greatest known concentration of these creatures—live in Kodiak NWR. Your best chance to see them is in July and August, when the animals congregate along salmon streams. In other seasons, the bears often move about in dense alders where they are harder to see—and easier to encounter unexpectedly.

Many guides and air taxi operators specialize in bear-viewing trips within the refuge, and some will even guarantee sightings. For a list of guide services, contact the Kodiak Convention and Visitors Bureau (907-486-4782). The refuge visitor center will also provide recommendations for bear-sighting locations as well as advice about safe viewing and camping techniques.

In general, you're likely to see bears at **Frazer Lake, Uganik Lake, Little River,** and **Blue Fox Bay.** While other drainages have equally impressive congregations of bears, they are harder to access. Although bears are not usually seen near the roadside, they can be encountered almost anywhere else within the refuge.

Kodiak National Wildlife Refuge mainly attracts hunters and fishers, but others increasingly are finding their way here. Rafters come to paddle the **Ayakulik** and **Karluk Rivers.** And kayakers are discovering the beauty and tranquillity of the refuge's large lakes. *(You may need permission to access private lands within the refuge.)*

Fishing lesson, Kodiak Island

Although summers here tend to be wet, cool, and cloudy, the refuge offers an endless array of subjects for nature photographers—from exquisite wildflowers to dramatic landscapes and seascapes, entertaining seabirds and marine mammals to bald eagles, land otters, deer, and foxes.

There are no developed hiking trails within the refuge, but don't let that stop you: Visitors are welcome to wander almost anywhere; brush and terrain make hiking difficult, however, except on high alpine ridges.

You are also free to camp wherever you want, provided that you employ bear-safety precautions. The refuge maintains seven public-use cabins, available by lottery *(apply in April; 907-487-2600)*. Several lodges and private cabins are scattered around Kodiak Island.

Access to the refuge is by air or sea from the city of Kodiak, or from one of four native villages adjacent to the refuge: Karluk, Larsen Bay, Akhiok, or Old Harbor. Be prepared for delays due to weather, especially on flights through the mountains. Overcast skies might prevail at your departure location, but Kodiak National Wildlife Refuge could be completely fogged in.

If you can wait out the weather and tides, you might charter a boat and explore the coast of the refuge. You'll see bears and deer, seals and sea lions, eagles and oystercatchers, murres and horned puffins. In spring, look for Pacific (black) brant, among Alaska's most impressive migratory visitors, as they make their way slowly northward. The birds' return trip to Mexico in the fall is apparently nonstop; they complete the 3,500-mile-long journey in just 60 to 120 hours.

En route, the four-pound birds lose a third of their body weight. In fall, most of the 150,000 brant migrate through **Izembek Lagoon** near Cold Bay, drafting low-pressure systems that propel them to speeds of 50 miles per hour and as far south as Vancouver Island.

Alaska State Parks

Inspiring wilderness experiences await outside the refuge, too. Alaska State Parks *(1400 Abercrombie Dr., Kodiak, AK 99615; 907-486-6339)* administers two remote parks: 47,000-acre **Shuyak Island State Park** and 48,742-acre **Afognak State Park.**

Shuyak Island, which is located 50 air miles north of Kodiak city, has four public-use cabins, which are most in demand in August *(reservations required; applications accepted in Feb.)*. This is a popular spot for fishing and wildlife-watching. Sea kayakers also come

here to explore the numerous sheltered bays and channels around the island.

Afognak offers a public-use cabin at **Pillar Lake** *(7-day limit)*. Hikers and climbers can explore the surrounding mountain slopes with the chance to see roaming bear, elk, or deer.

Afognak Wilderness Lodge *(907-486-6442)*, the only lodging within the state park, is one of the best places in Alaska to see marine mammals.

Exploring by Road

Access to Kodiak NWR and the state parks can be expensive. You can get a good sense of the place, however, simply by driving the 100 miles of mostly gravel roads that radiate from Kodiak city and lead you from seashore to mountaintop. You'll see a variety of habitats and wildlife. The downtown visitor center

Orthodox church, Kodiak

(100 Marine Way. 907-486-4782) provides a detailed road log and up-to-date reports on road conditions. Rent a car at the airport or bring your own vehicle over on the state ferry, M/V *Tustumena,* from Homer.

Kodiak Audubon Society puts out a guide to trails and hikes that are accessible from Kodiak's road system. The guide includes details about each walk, such as the length, difficulty, and points of interest. In addition, the local Audubon chapter offers weekend hikes. Pick up a map and information at the visitor center downtown or from the refuge.

Watch for wildlife as you drive. It's unlikely that you'll see bears, but you will see various other creatures depending on the season and the time of day (dawn and dusk are best for sighting wildlife). Migrating gray whales pass fairly close to the island from March through early May, while deer fawns appear in June. Salmon begin running in late May and peak in July. Bald eagles congregate near town and on **Pasagshak River** in December. Also, wildflowers bloom most profusely in July, while berries follow later in the month.

Other Attractions

In addition to its beautiful forested setting on Monashka Bay, **Fort Abercrombie State Historical Park** *(1400 Abercrombie Dr., 907-486-6339)* showcases the concrete bunkers of a World War II defensive position. Trails, beach walks, and tide pools provide plenty of invitations for exploration. Also accessible from the 11-mile-long Monashka Bay Road are **Mill Bay Beach Park**, **Monashka Bay viewpoint,** and **Pillar Creek Beach,** a favorite spot for picnics, pink salmon fishing, and beach walks. At the end of the road, the **Point Otmeloi Trailhead** leads into the forest and uplands.

Pasagshak River State Recreation Area, located at the mouth of the Pasagshak River, is a great destination for experienced sea kayakers. At certain times, this area also offers good fishing, especially at the **"fishing bridge"** *(Mile 8.5 on Pasagshak Rd.).* Try your luck surf casting at about Mile 10.

The park's campground, 2.5 miles farther up the road, offers beach access. You'll find nice **walking trails** here, as well as beautiful views of the sea and Ugak Island.

Woody Island, a short skiff ride from the Kodiak harbor, is a great place to see sea lions and harbor seals. A good trail crosses the island.

Before leaving town, visit the **Alutiiq Museum and Archaeological**

Gravesite, St. Paul Island, Pribilofs

Repository *(215 Mission Rd. 907-486-7004)* and the Russian-built **Baranof Museum** *(101 Marine Way. 907-486-5920)*. Both are downtown near the ferry dock. The Baranof, listed as a National Historic Landmark under the name Erskine House, was built in 1792, making it the oldest wooden building on America's West Coast.

When Russian fur hunters seeking the archipelago's abundant sea otters arrived in the late 1700s, they encountered the Alutiiq, who had occupied the islands for 7,500 years. The ensuing disease and armed conflict took a terrible toll on these native people. You may leave with new respect for those who continue to eke out a living here on these beautiful but harsh islands.

■ 5,000 square miles ■ 250 miles southwest of Anchorage ■ Access by air, ferry, and charter boat ■ Best months May–Oct. ■ Camping, kayaking, fishing, wildlife viewing ■ Contact Kodiak National Wildlife Refuge, 1390 Buskin River Rd., Kodiak, AK 99615; 907-487-2600. http://kodiak .fws.gov/index.htm

Alaska Maritime National Wildlife Refuge

220 miles southwest of Katmai
Ocean waves crash against lonely pinnacles of rock. Tiny bare islands, sheer cliffs, misty headlands, reefs, islets, and volcanic spires punctuate Alaska's coastline from the southern rain forest to the northern, ice-choked waters of the Chukchi Sea. More than 2,400 of these outposts make up the Alaska Maritime National Wildlife Refuge. Most of them lie in the Gulf of Alaska, along the Aleutian chain, and up into the Bering Sea.

To the human eye they seem uninhabitable, but their cliffs, crevices, and surf-washed ledges teem with wildlife. In spring, as many as 30 million seabirds (55 species) return to nest. They swarm around the islands and settle in gregarious colonies up and down the cliff faces, beneath which swim the whales—blue and gray, sei and sperm, orca and minke, bowhead and humpback, fin and northern right, Baird's beaked and Cuvier's beaked.

The refuge is also host to thousands of marine mammals. There are the seals, those curious and ghostly spirits from the deep. You'll see them surface just enough to take some air, survey the scene with their large and luminescent dark eyes, and then with a periscopic turn slip silently beneath the waves.

Sea lions, hauled out in their rookeries, bellow and roar defending their harems. Like their terrestrial namesake, the lions of Africa, sea lion bulls have a large neck and shoulders and a distinctive mane. Males weigh on average about 1,250 pounds.

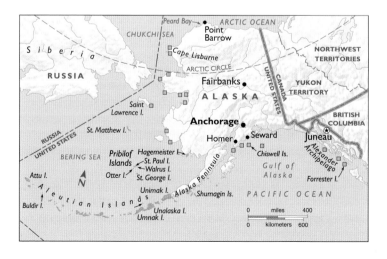

In contrast, little sea otters frolic in the waves and float on their back snacking on crabs and sea urchins. Its whiskers earned the sea otter the moniker, "the old man of the sea."

The portly, tusked walruses are perhaps the most comical of the bunch. On the other hand, the male walrus will serenade his mate for hours with a love song that biologists say sounds like a chorus of church bells. These nearly two-ton creatures generally follow the drifting ice pack, except in summer when they gather in noisy bachelor parties on Round Island.

Remote and pristine as these western Alaskan waters appear, they have seen a precipitous drop in once abundant populations of marine mammals, including Steller sea lions, harbor seals, Alaska king crabs, and sea otters in the Aleutians. This has alarmed scientists. Far from being protected by their remoteness, these waters contain an intricate and vulnerable web of life. Although the exact causes of the declines remain biological mysteries, current theories suggest a combination of stresses:

A Seal's Life

Majestic if a trifle fat (up to 600 pounds), the northern fur seal strikes a singular pose at the ocean edge on tiny St. Paul Island, where he reigns over a noisy stretch of beach for two months in summer. Refraining from eating—and leaving his rocky perch only to deal with cocky contenders for his throne —the male fur seal spends his days defending his territory and mating with the 20 to 100 females in his harem.

On warm days, you may see a northern fur seal of either sex waving its long rear flippers in the air. Hairless and webbed with blood vessels, these flippers serve to cool off the fur seal (which is otherwise bundled up in dense fur and blubber) while it is on land.

Except when they haul out to mate, northern fur seals spend the bulk of their time at sea. Their shore leave begins in the middle of May, when the bulls stake out beaches for their breeding territories.

Females impregnated the summer before arrive about four weeks later, at the end of their 11- to 12-month gestation period. A few days later, they give birth to a single pup, then mate again within a week. Most of the fur seals return to sea in November.

warmer water temperatures, heavy commercial fishing, predators forced to seek new prey, and industrial pollution from distant lands swept up by currents and delivered to these shores.

By contrast, the return of the diminutive Aleutian Canada goose from the brink of extinction is one of Alaska's great conservation success stories. Even though these geese nested in the Aleutians, which are among the most isolated islands in the world, they were nearly wiped out in the early 1900s when fox farmers introduced hundreds of foxes there, which killed the geese and other birds.

At one point the Aleutian Canada goose was deemed extinct— and probably would be today were it not for the dedication and courage of one man, Robert D. "Sea Otter" Jones. Known for his love of the animals, the biologist first visited the islands with the U.S. Navy during World War II. In 1947, Jones became the first resident manager of the 1,100-mile-long Aleutian Islands National Wildlife Refuge, which has since been incorporated into the Alaska Maritime National Wildlife Refuge.

Jones and his staff scoured the islands for the elusive Aleutian Canada geese, navigating dories and inflatable watercraft through unimaginably heavy and treacherous weather. During spring forays into the refuge, they occasionally would spot a few migrating geese.

One joyful day in 1962, however, they discovered a nesting population of about 200 to 300 geese on Buldir Island, the most remote outpost in the archipelago. From captive flocks, Aleutian geese were reintroduced to their former, now fox-free habitats.

Jones died in 1998, just a few months before the Fish and Wildlife Service proposed removing the Aleutian Canada goose from the threatened species list. Whereas the world population of these small but spectacular birds was fewer than 500 in 1967, the global population of Aleutian Canada geese is now estimated to be more than 30,000.

What to See and Do

Inaccessible as the refuge is, birding expeditions nevertheless find their way to the island of **Attu** (it's so far out in the Aleutian chain that the International Date Line has to jog around it) to watch for "accidental" birds—that is, Asian birds on the eastern edge of their customary spring migrations north.

Closer to civilization, there are popular day cruises offered out of Seward into **Resurrection Bay** *(907-224-8068 or 800-468-8068)*. **Beehive Island,** part of the **Chiswell Islands,** is a good place to view horned and tufted puffins, common and thick-billed murres, kittiwakes, and even oystercatchers, which are distinguished by their long, orange bills. You may also see sea lions, porpoises, and whales here.

Pribilof Islands

Floating far out in the Bering Sea, about 300 miles off the coast of western Alaska, the Pribilofs—nicknamed Islands of the Seals—are a popular summer destination for birders, botanists, and flower lovers. They are most famous, however, as seasonal territory for the world's largest population (about 800,000) of breeding northern fur seals. From observation blinds around the island, you can watch beefy "beachmasters" defending their harems from the challenges of cocky young bachelors. Equally intriguing is to see the females slithering over the rocks from one harem to another. Pups are born on the beaches, where mating occurs about a week later.

Between the cacophony of the seals and thousands of nesting seabirds, the Pribilofs are quite lively. But they are also some of the most enchantingly peaceful islands in the world. It only takes a few days here amid all the beauty, serenity, and wild things to restore balance to your spirit.

Four tiny volcanic islands—**St. Paul, St. George, Walrus,** and **Otter**—make up the Pribilofs. Of these, St. Paul is the largest and most visited. Blue arctic foxes bound over the island and reindeer, descendants of a Siberian herd imported in the 1890s, roam the interior. Clinging to the cliffs are colonies of nesting seabirds, among them parakeets and least auklets, red-faced cormorants, rare red-legged kittiwakes, horned and tufted puffins, and thick-billed murres.

Perhaps most amazing of all is that in July you can sit for hours in the tundra enjoying a rainbow of beautiful flowers—purple monkshood, chocolate lilies, pink Unalaska saxifrage, white rock jasmine, fields of blue lupine—and no mosquitoes! (If you've experienced the onslaught of whining, biting insects for which Alaska is famous, you will believe that you have arrived in heaven.) The reason? The wind blows here.

Parrot of the Sea

In gift shops throughout Alaska, puffin images adorn everything from T-shirts to antismoking signs ("No Puffin' Here!"). Most of this kitsch honors the horned puffin, but the tufted puffin also lives in Alaska. Distinguished by their large, colorful beaks, penguinlike coloring, and webbed orange feet, puffins of either type are nicknamed "parrots of the sea."

Wintering far out to sea, puffins are uniquely adapted for life on the ocean. In fact, they can "fly" quite well underwater. They flap half-folded wings for propulsion and use their feet as a rudder to change direction.

A puffin may emerge from the sea with as many as 15 fish in its mouth. Stiff spines inside its upper beak help hold the individual fish draped in place across the lower beak, their heads and tails poking out on either side. Not the most gifted aviators, puffins often run along the surface of the water for some distance on takeoff, giving the impression they'll never get airborne.

Puffin

You can travel on your own to St. Paul or St. George, but it's more fun on your first visit to be guided by the Aleut people who live here. They offer great tour packages *(877-424-5637)* with local guides and knowledgeable naturalists.

■ **4.5 million acres** ■ **From Forrester Island near tip of southeast Alaska, down Aleutian Island Chain, up into Bering and Chukchi Seas to Cape Lisburne** ■ **Be prepared for weather delays: Bring rain gear and warm clothing (wool or fleece) to layer. Temperatures in summer rarely rise above 60° F** ■ **Best months mid-May–mid-Aug.** ■ **Bird-watching, wildlife viewing** ■ **Contact the refuge, 2355 Kachemak Bay Dr., Suite 101, Homer, AK 99603; 907-235-6546. http://alaskamaritime.fws.gov/index.htm**

Getting Around

Terrifying encounters with Alaska bears make headlines, but those creatures may be the least of your outdoor concerns when traveling in the state. Due to the lack of roads, getting around Alaska involves boats and planes, both of which are subject to weather whims. Remember: It's better to pass up a flight-seeing trip or a boat ride than to come back a day or two late—or not at all. To ensure flexibility and safety, plan extra time at both ends of your trip.

Dozens of commercial flying services, called air taxis, haul passengers and freight statewide. Some offer scheduled flights; others specialize in charters. Flight-seeing trips cater to thousands of travelers, although weather-related delays and cancellations are common. Maybe you'll reach your destination but you get weathered in. If so, do you have extra food?

Most flights go flawlessly, but each summer a few pilots chance the weather and planes go down. Use your common sense. If the weather looks dicey, don't go. Also, look out for "outlaw" bush pilots who sell their services but fly without the proper training, licensing, or insurance. Ask for proper documentation.

Sudden storms, underwater hazards, and extreme tides— tidal rips, bore tides, and fluctuations to 38 feet—can make any ocean boat trip problematic. Many charter boat operators who hold "six-pack" licenses (which limit them to six passengers or fewer) take part in a voluntary U.S. Coast Guard inspection program; visit www.uscg.mil/d17 to find out a boat's safety rating.

Large tour boats face more stringent licensing and inspections. Many unlicensed charter boats ply offshore waters, so ask for credentials before paying for any trip.

Properly licensed boats occasionally experience bad weather or mechanical trouble (even giant cruise ships go aground), and the law requires them to carry survival gear. If you are inexperienced with Alaska tides and waters, hire a guide. Even if you're going out only for a day, follow the Coast Guard's advice: "Always file a float plan before you go boating."

Never board a boat, canoe, raft, or kayak for even a short jaunt without a flotation device and rain gear. Once the lake gets choppy or seas start coming over the bow, it's too late to remember life jackets (nearly 40 people drown yearly in Alaska).

Pilot on Bagley Icefield

Think of the small things; guides can do only so much. If you wear eyeglasses, for example, always secure them with a sports strap or a neck cord.

Midsummer water temperatures are cold enough to quickly immobilize even powerful swimmers. Hypothermia develops when the body can no longer maintain its normal temperature, a potentially lethal situation. Shivering is an early danger sign. Untreated hypothermia results in impaired judgment and coordination, eventually leading to stupor, collapse, and death.

You don't have to fall in the water or be in a snowstorm to develop hypothermia. Common summer conditions—wind, rain, temperatures in the low 50s—can trigger its onset. Experienced Alaskans carry packs stuffed with rain gear,

food, and extra clothes, even on day hikes.

Take extra care when walking on tidal flats. Wet mud loses its cohesiveness, so you could sink and be trapped. Also, be wary wading streams and rivers: It's easy to underestimate the depth and current, or stumble over a slippery rock. A glacial or mountain stream that's easy to ford in the morning may become uncrossable in the afternoon from increased runoff.

Keep in mind that off-trail hiking can be extremely taxing, especially under a heavy backpack. Brush, boulders, bogs, and bugs are normal parts of almost any hike. Most treks take longer than planned; 2 miles per hour is a respectable pace in Alaska. No matter what you do or where you go, always tell someone your plans. Otherwise, help can be a very long time in coming.

Kenai Fjords

D istill the essence of coastal Alaska into one place and you have Kenai Fjords, the smallest national park in Alaska. Here the land pushes into the sea with talonlike peninsulas and rocky headlands. Here, too, the sea reaches inland with long fjords and hundreds of quiet bays and coves.

Only a geologic heartbeat removed from the last ice age (it is a vestige of the massive ice sheet that covered much of Alaska during the Pleistocene era), the immense Harding Icefield dominates the park. Pierced only by peaks of granite called *nunataks* (Eskimo for "lonely peaks"), the ice field covers 700 square miles and is nearly a mile high and hundreds, perhaps thousands, of feet deep.

Draping the Kenai Mountains in snow and ice, it is the reservoir for the spectacular glaciers that rumble toward the sea. Nearly three dozen named glaciers (and many others unnamed) dangle in high mountain valleys, spill down rock faces, and plunge into the headwaters of fjords. Six of them flow to tidewater.

Kenai's fjords formed as the earth warmed after the last ice age, causing the world's glaciers to begin melting back. Saltwater rushed in to fill U-shaped valleys left by the retreating ice, creating habitats for throngs of sea animals.

Seabirds congregate here by the tens of thousands; about 20 species nest along the rocky coastline. Bald eagles soar off the towering cliffs, while peregrine falcons frequent the outer islands.

A narrow fringe of spruce and hemlock forest, sprinkled with fireweed, lupine, and dwarf dogwood, limns the coast on land reclaimed from the ice. Interspersed among the living trees, "ghost forests" preserve the legacy of the great earthquake of 1964: The land dropped 7 feet, swamping the coast-line and killing huge stands of spruce with intruding saltwater.

Bleached and scoured by sun and weather, preserved in salt, the dead trees

- South-central Alaska, 13 miles from Seward

- 607,000 acres

- Established 1980

- Best months May– August

- Camping, hiking, boating, kayaking, fishing, cross-country skiing, wildlife viewing, boat tours

- Information: 907-224-7500 www.nps.gov/kefj

Harris Bay, Kenai Fjords National Park

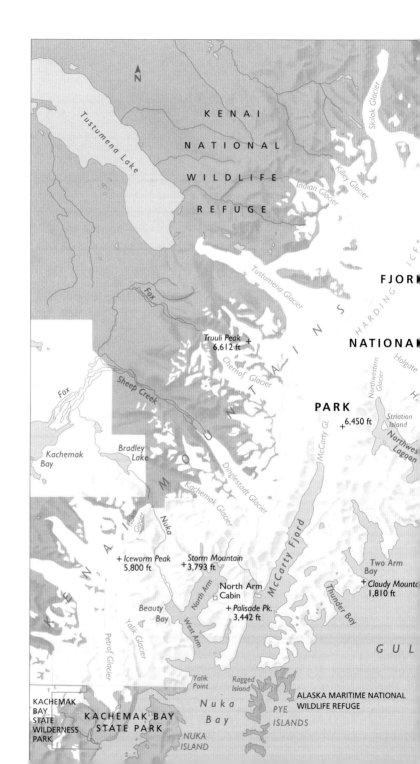

RESURRECTION
RIVER TRAIL
LOST LAKE
TRAIL
□ U.S.F.S. Cabin
CHUGACH
NATIONAL
FOREST
9
ger Station
EXIT
GLACIER
DING   Exit Gl.   Willow   ROAD
FIELD   Cabin
TRAIL
Lowell Gl.
Phoenix Peak   Seward
5,155 ft +
Park Headquarters and
ENAI   Visitor Center
COASTAL
TRAIL
CAINES
HEAD
S.R.A.
Bear Glacier
Resurrection Bay
Fox
Island
Bulldog   Callisto
Cove   Head
Aialik
Cabin
Rugged
Island
Holgate
□ Cabin
Glacier
AIALIK PENINSULA
Harding
Gateway
Aialik Bay
Cheval Island
Aialik Cape
ALASKA
MARITIME NATIONAL
WILDLIFE REFUGE
Aligo
Point   CHISWELL
Granite
Cape   ISLANDS
F   ALASKA
0   miles   10
0   kilometers   15

rise like eerie sentinels, endur-
ing symbols of nature's power.

Life abounds elsewhere,
though. In Resurrection Bay
and the fjords, jellyfish—
gossamer-white moon and
giant lion's mane jellies and
others—float near the surface.

Fish, both freshwater and
saltwater, proliferate, including
all five species of Pacific
salmon, Dolly Varden trout,
halibut, lingcod, and rockfish.

Some 23 species of mam-
mals, including harbor seals,
northern sea lions, and sea
otters, live here.

Throughout the summer
months, whales, including
fins, minkes, grays, orcas, and
humpbacks, inhabit the park's
cold waters.

Of these, the most readily
spotted are the humpbacks,
which return each year from
their breeding grounds in
Hawaii and Mexico.

The smaller, 8-ton orcas,
distinguished by their black-
and-white markings and triangular dorsal fins that slice the
water, are also easy to spot.

Moose, black bears, lynx,
wolverines, and marten roam
the narrow bands of forest
between the park's coastline
and the ice field, while at
higher elevations, sure-footed
mountain goats graze on the
treeless slopes.

How to Get There

Seward is the gateway to Kenai Fjords. Take the Seward Highway (Alas. 9) south from Anchorage for 130 miles. Buses and small commuter planes connect Anchorage and Seward, and the Alaska Marine Highway (ferry) links Seward with Homer, Seldovia, Kodiak, Valdez, and Cordova.

You also can charter a flight from Seward or Homer to the park. In summer, the Alaska Railroad serves Seward from Anchorage, with connections to Fairbanks and Whittier.

When to Go

Summer. The road to Exit Glacier generally opens in May and closes with the first snowfall, usually in October. In winter, many visitors ski or snowmobile on the road into Exit Glacier.

How to Visit

The most popular and accessible area in the park is **Exit Glacier**, 13 miles northwest of Seward. You can drive to it or take a tour bus. Trails offer half-hour hikes to the glacier and a half-day hike to the **Harding Icefield.**

Otherwise, hiking is a matter of exploring wilderness shores and ridges accessible only by boat and plane.

What Not to Miss

- Drive or bus tour to Exit Glacier
- Hiking to Harding Icefield
- Hiking the Main Trail to overlook and glacier terminus
- Charter-boat tours of Resurrection Bay, Chiswell Islands, fjords, and glaciers
- Kayaking in Aialik Bay
- Wildlife viewing at Nuka Bay
- Guided kayak tour around Northwestern Lagoon

From mid-May to late September, daily tour boats depart from Seward for half-day and full-day round-trip excursions to the park's fjords and outlying islands.

Charter boats take kayakers and campers to any fjord they wish (most commonly to **Aialik Bay)**; you can be picked up the same day or later as prearranged. Kayaking, fishing, and backpacking guides are available; ask park staff for a list of authorized operators.

From Seward or Homer, you can book a breathtaking, hour-long flight over the ice field and Kenai coast. Ski planes also drop off and pick up skiers on the ice field; floatplanes do the same for kayakers in the fjords, weather permitting.

EXPLORING THE PARK

Exit Glacier & Harding Icefield

Exit Glacier is one of many rivers of ice that flow off the Harding Icefield. It is the only glacier in the park to which you can drive.

From Seward, follow the highway north to Mile 3.7, where a paved road leads 9 miles to the Exit Glacier parking lot *(open early May, weather permitting; winter access to glacier by cross-country skis, snowmobile, or dogsled)*. You'll find a ranger station here where you can get information about the area.

From here you can access three trails: The **Main Trail** is paved for a quarter of a mile to a viewing area. It then separates into two loops. The **lower loop** continues another quarter-mile to the out-wash plain for a close view of the glacier terminus. Don't get too

Hikers at Exit Glacier

close, however; a tourist was killed here in 1987 when she posed for a photo beneath overhanging ice. Remember, glaciers are constantly moving.

The **upper loop** climbs steeply for a quarter of a mile, rewarding with views of deep crevasses and towering seracs along the glacier's flank. A half-mile **nature trail** begins at the glacier and winds over old moraines and through cottonwood, alder, and willow before following **Exit Creek** to connect with the Main Trail leading back to the ranger station. Interpretive signs provide information on glaciers, moraines, and plant and animal succession.

For hardier hikers, the well-marked **Harding Icefield Trail** branches off the Main Trail and climbs 3,000 feet through alpine terrain in 3.5 miles, ending on the ice field. On the slopes you may see mountain goats and black bears.

The upper section of the trail is usually snow covered; the lower portion is slippery and muddy after rain. Ask a ranger about current conditions and sign in at the trail register. Expect the round trip to take you 6 or 7 hours; wear warm clothing and good hiking boots, and carry plenty of food and water.

For those wishing to camp, a public-use cabin is available for rent at Exit Glacier.

The Fjords

The waterfront in Seward is the embarkation point for all-day boat tours into **Resurrection Bay.** Tour boats travel daily down the bay, past picturesque **Caines Head** and **Callisto Head,** then around rugged **Aialik Cape** and into **Aialik Bay,** the most visited fjord in the park.

The **Holgate** and **Aialik Glaciers** flow into this fjord. Tour boats usually visit the Holgate, then return to Seward via the **Chiswell Islands,** part of the **Alaska Maritime National Wildlife Refuge** (see pp. 131–135) and an excellent place to observe nesting seabirds and sea lions hauled out on rocks. You're most likely to see humpback whales from June to mid-August.

Endless exploring awaits boaters and hikers on the shores of Kenai Fjords. If you are without a guide, be sure to inquire at the visitor center about weather, landing sites, tides, and hazards. The farther you go down the coast to the southwest, the fewer the people.

Narrow **Granite Passage** is an exciting entrance into **Harris Bay.** From 1910 to 1960, **Northwestern Glacier** retreated 9.5 miles and

Infallible Fireweed

Though Alaska's official flower is the tiny blue forget-me-not, many people think it should be the fireweed. Brilliantly highlighted against green coastal forests and blue glaciers, the crimson flower brightens meadows, woods, and roadsides. Yet its first blooming brings a kind of wistfulness: The opening of its last flowers in August signals the end of summer. The cold autumn days that follow turn the leaves of the fireweed a flaming orange-red.

Fireweed

Fireweed is a tenacious, quick-growing herb. When fire ravages the Alaskan wilderness, fireweed is one of the first plants to recolonize the devastated area. As a result of its deep roots, which usually escape damage, it is quick to grow, bringing life back to the land.

opened up **Northwestern Lagoon** at the head of Harris Bay. The lagoon should be entered on calm water (preferably in a kayak) and at high tide only. Once you are inside and on the shore, you will find excellent hiking, especially to **Northeastern, Southwestern,** and **Sunlight Glaciers.**

Down the coast, **Thunder Bay** is a welcome anchorage during inclement weather. A narrow waterway cuts between the mainland and the **Pye Islands.** From here, **McCarty Fjord** slices 23 miles into the coast, its steep walls rising more than 4,000 feet overhead on either side of **McCarty Glacier.**

The **West** and **North Arms** of **Nuka Bay** offer a variety of terrain and wildlife. Watch for the craggy profile of **Palisade Peak** (a 900-foot waterfall) and historic gold mine sites. Also look for black bears, moose, and river otters near the **Nuka River;** shorebirds along the mud flats at **Shelter Cove;** and black-sand beaches around **Yalik Point** at the park's southern end. Few people come here; travel to Nuka Bay and you might have it all to yourself.

INFORMATION & ACTIVITIES

Headquarters
P.O. Box 1727, Seward,
AK 99664; 907-224-7500.
www.nps.gov/kefj

Seasons & Accessibility
Park open year-round, but
from roughly mid-October to
May, snow may close the road
to Exit Glacier. Access then is
by skis, snowmobile, dog team,
or snowshoes only. Call headquarters for information about
weather and road conditions.

Visitor & Information Centers
Visitor center in Seward, on
Alas. 9 just outside the eastern
border of the park, open daily
from Memorial Day to Labor
Day; weekdays only rest of
the year. Ranger station at
Exit Glacier open intermit-
tently in summer only. Contact
park headquarters for visitor
information.

Entrance Fees
Daily fee of $5 per vehicle;
$15 annual fee.

Pets
Permitted leashed on the Exit
Glacier Road and in parking
areas. Prohibited on all trails.

Facilities for Disabled
Exit Glacier is the most accessible area. From the Ranger
Station, wheelchairs can negoti-
ate the glacier trail (for the first
third of a mile) to an interpretive shelter with exhibits and
views of the glacier. Visitor center is also wheelchair accessible.

Things to Do
In summer, free ranger-led
activities (from the Ranger
station at Exit Glacier) include
walks to the base of the glacier
and all-day hikes to the ice
field. Also available are
advanced mountain climbing,
sailing, fishing (license
required), wildlife-watching,
cross-country skiing, dogsledding, and snowshoeing.

Authorized commercial
guides offer camping, fishing,
kayaking, flight-seeing, and
boat trips for viewing the
fjords and observing seabirds,
whales, porpoises, and other
wildlife. Contact park headquarters for a list of companies authorized to do business
in the park.

Special Advisories
■ If planning a backcountry
trip without a guide, first check
conditions with park staff.
■ Hypothermia is a danger on
the ice field, even in summer.
■ Do not venture out in a boat
unless you have experience
with rough water.

Near Harding Icefield

Overnight Backpacking

Permits, free at the visitor center, are required; registration requested for Harding Icefield.

Campgrounds

One walk-in campground at Exit Glacier. Four cabins in the fjords available May through September for overnight use, with permit. Access by boat or plane only. In winter, a public-use cabin is available at Exit Glacier. Contact the visitor center for information.

Hotels, Motels, & Inns

(Unless otherwise noted, rates for two persons in a double room, high season.)

In Seward, AK 99664:

■ **Breeze Inn** 1306 Seward Hwy., P.O. Box 2147. 907-224-5237. 86 units, 1 with a kitchenette. $130-$218. Restaurant.

■ **Hotel Seward** (on 5th Ave.) P.O. Box 670. 907-224-2378. 38 units. $125-$224. AC.

■ **Marina Motel** (on Alas. 9) P.O. Box 1134. 907-224-5518. 26 units, 1 with a kitchenette. $110-$125.

■ **Murphy's Motel** 911 4th Ave., P.O. Box 736. 907-224-8090. 24 units. $99-$149.

■ **Van Gilder Hotel** 308 Adams St., P.O. Box 609. 907-224-3525, 907-224-3079, or 800-204-6835. 24 units, 20 with private baths. $149; suites $219.

Excursions from Kenai Fjords

Chugach National Forest

north and
northeast of
Kenai Fjords

President Theodore Roosevelt created Chugach National Forest *(see map p. 154)* in 1907, when the national forest system was still in its infancy. Encompassing fjords, lakes, islands, glaciers, mountains, and vast stretches of trees, the national forest sweeps across the coasts and islands of Prince William Sound, covering 3,500 miles of coastline from the Bering Glacier on the northeastern edge of the Gulf of Alaska to the salmon-choked waters of the Russian River on the western half of the Kenai Peninsula.

Like Tongass National Forest near Juneau, the Chugach is a temperate rain forest. Translation: Cherish sunny days! Rainfall and snowfall are abundant. MacLeod Harbor on Montague Island, at the entrance to the sound, holds the Alaska record for the most rainfall in a year: nearly 28 feet in 1976. It also holds the record for a single month: November 1976 swam in 6 feet of rain. The alpine tundra (as low as 2,000 feet in elevation in Chugach National Forest) is snow free only a few months out of the year. As you can see, it won't do to trip lightly into this country. Come prepared for wet and cold, even in summer. Clouds and fog are dramatic, and storms even more so.

Chugach's heights are raw and rugged, with sculpted rock, glaciers, and imposing peaks. At lower elevations, deep coastal forests of spongy moss and spruce and western hemlock are interspersed with aspen and birch that turn beautiful shades of yellow in the fall. Buttercups, columbine, and Indian paintbrush thrive in the short growing season here.

Bears and moose abound here. With the exception of Montague and Hinchinbrook Islands in Prince William Sound, black bears can be found everywhere in Chugach National Forest. You can see them foraging for berries and carrion on the open slopes or digging grasses and catching fish in the intertidal zones. Brown bears, which can outweigh black bears by 800 pounds, prowl the eastern shore of Prince William Sound on the Copper River Delta and the Kenai Peninsula, where moose and small herds of caribou roam as well.

In winter, shy and lovely Sitka black-tailed deer wander onto island shores in the sound to feed on beach grasses. As the snows disappear, the deer follow the vegetation up the mountainsides, feeding on skunk cabbage and blueberry bushes. Much higher up

Horseback riding by Kenai Lake

on rocky outcroppings, you may spot clusters of white dots, identifiable through binoculars as Dall's sheep. Look for them particularly around **Kenai Lake** on the rocks of **Langille Mountain.** Mountain goats live on steep cliffs, closer to salt water. Try spotting them high up on the mountainsides of Prince William Sound and the Copper River Delta. Many smaller mammals wander the forest as well, including coyotes, lynx, red fox, wolverines, porcupines, red squirrels, and beavers.

An impressive array of marine mammals swims through Prince William Sound and the Gulf of Alaska, such as fin, gray, humpback, and killer whales, as well as Dall's porpoises and sea otters.

And birds? Come at the right time in spring and you'll hit the jackpot: Within the space of only a few hours, thousands fly overhead. The **Copper River Delta** is a resting and staging area for millions of birds migrating north in late April and May. More than 200 species of resident and migratory birds find their way here to these bountiful, intertidal waters.

What to See and Do

Because there's so much to see in Chugach National Forest, you might want to spend several days exploring. Scattered throughout Prince William Sound and Chugach National Forest are dozens of public-use recreational cabins available for rent. For information contact the Forest Service and ask for the 30-page pamphlet, "Public Recreation Cabins: Chugach National Forest, Alaska," which describes each cabin and how to reach it. Call the National Recreation Reservation Service *(877-444-6777)* for reservations or visit www.reserveusa.com

Hiking

From the Sterling and Seward Highways, you can access more than 200 miles of trails on the **Kenai Peninsula,** many of which are also used by travelers on horseback. The book, *55 Ways to the Wilderness,* by Helen Nienhauser contains descriptions of walks in the national forest. It is available for purchase through the Alaska Natural History Association *(907-274-8440).*

Flattop Mountain viewed from Chugach National Forest

Boating

Chugach National Forest offers a wealth of rushing rivers, quiet alpine lakes, hidden coves, and spectacular fjords for canoeists and kayakers, white-water rafters, sailors, and anglers.

Kayakers can take day or multiday trips to explore the waterfalls of **Shoup Bay** or paddle around **Sawmill Bay** with its dramatic backdrop of mountains. Guided trips hosted by Anadyr Sea Kayaking *(907-835-2814)* and Pangea Adventures *(907-835-8442)* depart from Valdez and Whittier. If you prefer to explore on your own, both outfits rent equipment.

Keep in mind when planning your trip that the waters here are exceedingly cold. (Water draws the heat out of your body 20 times faster than air; after just 10 minutes in these ocean waters, a person begins to lose mobility.) If you are a beginner, go with a guide. And if you are experienced, don't be overly cocky; Alaska has the highest number of drownings per capita of any state in the entire country.

Fishing

There are plenty of secret (and not-so-secret) places to fish, both saltwater and freshwater, in the Chugach. With 3,500 miles of coastline, you can wet a line on an empty beach with only seals and sea otters for company.

Some of the more popular destinations, however, include **Billy's Hole** in **Long Bay,** where you may spot brown bears in mid-July; **Eickelberg Bay,** which is known for its stunning granite peaks; and **Finski Bay,** where you can explore sea caves and hike to alpine lakes or **Glacier Island.**

You might also charter a motorboat out of Whittier or Valdez *(contact Valdez Convention & Visitors Bureau 907-835-4636 or 800-770-5954)* and head into deeper water, where it's not unheard of to reel in a 200-pound halibut.

In June and July when the red salmon arrive en masse, you can expect to stand shoulder to shoulder with other anglers on the **Russian River.**

If you're a freshwater angler, you might consider escaping by floatplane *(Ketchum Air Service. 907-243-5525 or 800-433-9114. www.ketchmair.com)* to a remote lakeshore cabin, where you can paddle out in a canoe and toss out a line.

Or you can hike to great fishing on lakes and streams all the way from the Kenai to the Copper River. Many of the Kenai rivers and streams are migration routes for Dolly Varden trout, rainbow trout, and silver, king, and red salmon. Other freshwater fish found in these waters include arctic grayling, burbot, lake trout, and cutthroat trout.

Glacier Viewing

Located just 55 miles south of Anchorage, **Portage Glacier** is the national forest's most popular attraction. The **Begich, Boggs Visitor Center** on Portage Glacier Road offers interpretive displays on area glaciers and natural history *(907-783-2326. Daily in summer, weekends in winter)*.

Columbia Glacier, out of Valdez on the eastern side of Prince William Sound, is one of the largest tidewater glaciers in North America. Several years ago it began a dramatic retreat, opening up the fjord in front of it. You can sail or paddle to the glacier and nose among small icebergs. Just remember to stay a respectful distance (at least a quarter of a mile) from the face of any glacier or large iceberg. Because the ice is constantly melting, it is unstable and can roll at any time.

Bird-watching

The Copper River Delta outside Cordova in eastern Prince William Sound is an extraordinarily lush and diverse ecosystem fed by several glacial rivers. In late April and early May, hundreds of bird-watchers descend with their rubber boots and binoculars for the annual **Copper River Delta Shorebird Festival** to watch millions of migrating birds.

Nearly the entire world population of western sandpipers cruises through here in the company of thousands of other shorebirds, swans, sandhill cranes, raptors, and geese. The local Audubon Society chapter *(907-424-7260)* often sponsors a naturalist-led cruise from Valdez to Cordova during the festival.

■ **5.6 million acres** ■ **Coast and islands of Prince William Sound and parts of Kenai Peninsula** ■ **Best months March–Sept.** ■ **Hiking, white-water rafting and kayaking, fishing, horseback riding, skiing,bird-watching, whale-watching** ■ **Contact: the national forest, 3301 C St., Suite 300, Anchorage, AK 99503; 907-271-2500. Glacier Ranger District, 907-783-3242; Cordova Ranger District, 907-424-7761; or Seward Ranger District, 907-224-3374. www.fs.fed.us/r10/chugach**

Seward Highway

Anchorage to Kenai Fjords

127 miles, a half to full day Only one road, the Seward Highway, leads south from Anchorage, but it's a doozy: It snakes along exquisite Turnagain Arm, past the prolific bird population of **Potter Marsh,** through Chugach State Park and into **Chugach National Forest** (*see pp. 148–152),* past the ski slopes of Alyeska and the Portage Glacier, into the **Kenai Mountains,** over Turnagain Pass, along the edge of **Kenai Lake,** and past Exit Glacier.

After all that (a drive of about three hours if you don't stop), the Seward Highway winds up at Resurrection Bay, the jumping-off point for **Kenai Fjords National Park.**

As you drive along the edge of **Turnagain Arm,** you'll marvel at the backdrop of mountains and valleys. The body of water came by its unusual name in 1778, when British explorer Capt. James Cook sailed up in search of the elusive Northwest Passage,

Potter Marsh

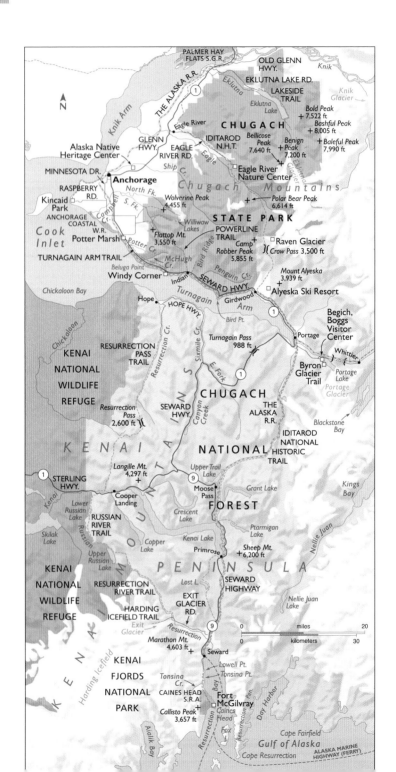

Tidal Bore

With one of the largest tides in the world, Cook Inlet fluctuates more than 35 feet between low and high tide. The ebbing tide runs so strongly against the rising tide that it temporarily dams up the water until the incoming tide literally bursts into the narrow inlet. The tide then advances as a wave or wall of water known as a tidal bore.

Such waves form in shallow, tapering inlets where the water levels fluctuate greatly between low and high tides. In North America, tidal bores occur in only two places: the Bay of Fundy in Nova Scotia, and the upper Cook Inlet near Anchorage in the narrow Knik and Turnagain Arms. In Turnagain, the most dramatic of the two arms, the bore can travel 10 to 15 miles per hour and reach a height of 6 feet.

The bore begins forming at the mouth of Turnagain Arm about one hour after each low tide for Anchorage. Its journey to the end of the arm takes a little more than five hours. One of the best places to view these bore tides is along the Seward Highway, about 30 miles south of Anchorage. You'll find pull-offs here. The best time to be at this viewpoint is about two hours after Anchorage's predicted low tide.

commonly believed to be the direct link between Europe and the riches of the Orient.

On Cook's third and final voyage, he had to turn his ship around here yet again. Clearly an expression of his disappointment, he called the waterway Turnagain River. Later, it was renamed Turnagain Arm.

On the north side of Turnagain Arm, the Seward Highway forms a boundary of **Chugach State Park** *(see pp. 160-66).* Check out the scene at **Beluga Point** at Mile 110. If you're there a couple of hours or so after Anchorage's low tide, watch for the waves of salt water, called tidal bores, that rush down the arm *(see above).* In summer, you may see the colorful sails of windsurfers skimming the water or pods of surfacing white beluga whales.

You'll likely see Dall's sheep picking their way along the cliffs near **Windy Corner,** which is known for its exposure to strong breezes. From here, as well as from many other turnouts (watch for the Alaska hiker signs), you'll find some great hiking trails along the

Turnagain Arm Trail *(see p. 164)* with its bird's-eye views of the water.

A new interpretive overlook at **Bird Point** *(Mile 96)* juts out into the ocean. From here you can hike or bike the new, 6-mile paved **interpretive trail** to Girdwood; it's part of the old Seward Highway that was bypassed with the building of a new highway in 1998. The trail also makes an easy bike ride, with pretty views of the arm. Bike rentals are available at either end of the trail. For information, call Chugach State Park *(907-345-5014)*.

Like so many towns in Alaska, **Girdwood** *(Mile 90)* owes its existence to gold fever. Skiers turn off here for **Alyeska Ski Resort** *(907-754-1111)*, which is known for its challenging downhill runs. It's the only ski resort in the country where you can schuss down powdery slopes with views of an ocean (albeit a frozen one) directly below.

At Mile 79 is the turnoff to **Portage Glacier** and iceberg-filled **Portage Lake.** Thanks to its easy access, this glacier draws more tourists than any other attraction in the state. Your best view (depending on weather and ice conditions, of course) may be from the deck of one of the daily Portage Glacier Cruises *(907-783-2983)*.

At one time, Portage Glacier extended all the way to where the Chugach National Forest's **Begich, Boggs Visitor Center** *(End of Portage Glacier Rd. Open daily in summer, weekends in winter. 907-783-2326)* now stands, and the entire lake was filled with ice. The glacier has since retreated more than 4.5 miles. The visitor center offers films and exhibits on the forest and glacier, as well as information about local hikes.

The short (less than 1 mile) **Byron Glacier Trail** near the visitor center is a level and easy walk. Here you get a close view of the hanging valley glacier, the snowfields left by winter avalanches, and the silty glacial creek formed from the glacier's meltwater. Black and brown bears, moose, marmots, and bald eagles all inhabit Portage Valley.

Back on the highway from Portage, the road winds into the mountains and crosses 988-foot-high **Turnagain Pass,** a popular cross-country skiing and snowmobiling area in winter. For a list of licensed snowmachine outfitters, contact the Glacier Ranger District *(907-783-3242)*.

Beyond Turnagain Pass, an interesting side trip is the 34-mile round-trip cutoff road at Mile 57 to **Hope,** an old gold-mining

Dall's Sheep

Named for pioneering naturalist William H. Dall, these sheep are one of Alaska's most common species of large mammals.

Numbering perhaps 70,000 statewide, the animals prosper in dry inland mountain ranges. You seldom find them in the wetter and snowier coastal ranges. Their preferred habitat is grazing meadows and slopes adjacent to cliffs.

While the sheep's distinctive white coloration serves as winter camouflage, biologists theorize that the color also mitigates the heat from the unrelenting summer sun in the animal's tree-less alpine habitat.

The sheep's normal life span is 10 to 12 years. Adults weigh between 150 and 250 pounds. Both sexes grow horns, the ram's being large and curling, and the ewe's short, slender, and slightly curved. During breeding season, which runs from November into December, males sometimes break their horns as they battle each other head-on for the right to mate.

Look for Dall's sheep along the Seward Highway (*20 miles S of Anchorage*), on Sheep Mountain, between Mileposts 110 and 120 on the Glenn Highway, and near Cooper Landing (Mile 45) on the Sterling Highway.

Dall's sheep

town on the southern edge of Turnagain Arm. This is a favorite route among cyclists because of the fabulous scenery and the minimal road traffic.

Before the turnoff to Kenai and Homer on the Sterling Highway, you'll pass a sprinkling of alpine lakes. Continue to **Moose Pass,** which was named for a well-known local incident in which a particularly cantankerous moose refused to budge, forcing a musher to detour his dog team.

Shortly before you reach Seward, turn off at Mile 3.7 for **Exit Glacier** *(see pp. 143–44).* Nine miles of driving and half a mile of walking will take you to the foot of this river of ice that flows down from the **Harding Icefield** in Kenai Fjords National Park.

At the end of your journey lies Seward on Resurrection Bay, an important ice-free port and sea link from the coast into the interior

Turnagain Arm near Portage Glacier

of Alaska. It is Mile 0 on the historic gold rush and mail route, known by early mail carriers as the Seward-to-Nome Trail. Today it's referred to as the **Iditarod National Historic Trail.**

You should take precautions while driving the Seward Highway. Keep your headlights on at all times. Take special care on the twisty section of road between Potter Marsh and Portage, which is often buffeted by high winds and subject to avalanches and mud slides. Be prepared to slow for animals; moose often bolt across the highway and Dall's sheep sometimes come down near Windy Corner and Beluga Point.

■ **127 miles long** ■ **Anchorage to Seward** ■ **Year-round** ■ **Hiking, biking, skiing, wildlife viewing** ■ **Contact Chugach National Forest, 3301 C St., Suite 300, Anchorage, AK 99503; 907-271-2500. www.fs.fed.us/r10/chugach**

Chugach State Park

100 miles
northeast of
Kenai Fjords

Bounded on the north by the **Knik Arm** and on the west by the city of **Anchorage** on the edge of Cook Inlet, Chugach State Park's southern boundary is scenic **Turnagain Arm** *(see pp. 153–56),* where pods of white beluga whales congregate throughout the summer. **Knik Glacier** and **Chugach National Forest** *(see pp. 148–152),* the second largest national forest in the United States, together constitute the park's eastern limit.

What makes this park so extraordinary? It's wild, pure, and simple. The amazing thing is, all of this wildness (nearly half a million acres) sits in the backyard of metropolitan Anchorage, where a quarter of a million people reside. In the park's 30 years, it has not been explored in its entirety. A few peaks have never been climbed and many summits go nameless. Most valleys and headwaters within the park's interior see only a few hardy visitors each year.

Of course, residents near the park border live with certain challenges that come with proximity to a wild place. It's not unusual to see moose chomping away in summer vegetable gardens or nibbling at trees in winter.

More than the moose, though, it's the bears that concern residents. Every year black and brown bears come sauntering around hillside homes, wreaking havoc with property not to mention frightening folks in the vicinity. Despite the scares, though, most residents claim they would live nowhere else. The joy of seeing an animal in the wild, even if it's peering in your window, is a gift.

Most of the park *(see map p. 154)* is comprised of mountains, their peaks rising dramatically from sea level to more than 8,000 feet. If you're hiking, it won't take you long to get above tree line. In the high alpine meadows, you'll find at your feet a myriad miniature flowers: moss campion, dwarf fireweed, mountain harebells, shooting stars, buttercups, and dwarf dogwood. Late summer brings blueberries, raspberries, crowberries, and cranberries.

Humans aren't the only fruit lovers up here. If you are picking berries, be sure to glance up occasionally to make sure you haven't been joined by a bear. On a summer's evening, if you hear a piercing whistle, it may be a hoary marmot on a rocky perch warning colleagues of an approaching brown or black bear.

Other mammals in the park include wolves, lynx, foxes, ermines, coyotes, mountain goats, river otters, flying squirrels, muskrat,

Chugach Mountains off Glenn Highway

mink, and beavers. In addition, some 2,000 Dall's sheep scramble around the rocky summits of the park.

In the lowlands, you wander through forest of birch, spruce, aspen, poplar, and willow. Up near tree line, you begin to see stunted and gnarled, bonsai-like forests of mountain hemlock, a sight reminding that this terrain is not always hospitable. Winds may blow as hard as 130 miles per hour during winter storms.

Eagle River Nature Center

Located in Chugach State Park near the rushing waters of Eagle River, this former log-cabin lodge has been renovated and is now a nature center. The **Eagle River Nature Center** *(907-694-2108. Parking fee)* has an active, year-round naturalist program. Programs range from wildflower and mushroom walks in summer to animal tracking and northern-lights viewing in winter. Also here are animal exhibits and displays on the natural history of Chugach State Park, as well as self-guided nature walks, trail maps for independent hikers, and telescopes for observing Dall's sheep on the mountain crags.

For good views of Hurdy Gurdy, Cumulus, and Polar Bear Peaks, walk down the 3-mile **Albert Loop Trail** that takes you alongside the river and offers beautiful views of the valley. The **Rodak Nature Trail** is less than a mile long and has interpretive signs about the natural history of the valley. On the trail, you'll find a viewing platform that overlooks a beaver pond. In late August, you can watch spawning red and silver salmon.

A hundred years ago, gold miners and trappers bound for the interior would cross from Girdwood on Turnagain Arm, over **Crow Pass Trail** past Raven Glacier, and down into Eagle River Valley. This was a dangerous route in winter, with "avalanches up the yinyang," as one former park ranger described it. It's still perilous today in winter.

If you're going for the full experience, the 26-mile **Iditarod-Crow Pass Trail** from the Girdwood side of the mountains into Eagle River Valley, do it in summer. From Girdwood, take Crow Creek Road to its end to reach the trailhead. Lots of bears live here, both black and brown, and midway through the trail you'll come across an exciting fording of Eagle River.

For visitors who wish to spend a few days in the area, the center rents a cabin and yurt, which are located 1 to 2 miles along the Iditarod trail near **Eklutna Lake.** You will have to carry in any supplies that you need because the cabins are accessible only on foot.

To reach the nature center from downtown Anchorage, take the Glenn Highway to Eagle River Road at Mile 19. The center is 12 miles down the road—about a 45-minute drive.

On a long and mild summer evening, however, when the sun sets close to midnight, the views from the park's ridges and peaks are stunning. And on a clear day, you'll see Mount McKinley 130 miles to the north, the volcanoes of the Alaska Range 100 miles to the west, and the Kenai Peninsula across Turnagain Arm to the south.

Although the mountains in the front range of the park are small (about 3,500 to 5,000 feet) compared with those in the park's interior, they assume their own majesty with the first dusting of snow in autumn and the mantle of whiteness in winter. As summer approaches, a lovely blanket of green makes its way up the slopes. Statistically, June is the driest summer month; however, "termination dust"—an Alaskan euphemism for the first snow—can fall as early as mid-July.

To get deep into Chugach State Park, you'll have to work a little bit. Most importantly, you must have solid backcountry camping skills to fend for yourself. There are innumerable ways you can get lost or into trouble due to crevasses, avalanches, river crossings, bear encounters, hypothermia, and frostbite.

Check with park rangers for the latest weather advisories. No matter how mild or sunny the weather might be when you start out, it can change quickly and dramatically. Always carry a day pack with plenty of water, some high-energy food, an extra fleece, a wind/rain jacket and pants, a hat and gloves, a map, a lighter, basic first-aid supplies, a knife, mosquito repellent, sunglasses, and a flashlight.

What to See and Do
Chugach State Park has dozens of access points. The old federal building in downtown Anchorage houses the **Alaska Public Lands Information Center** (*605 W. 4th Ave. 907-271-2737*). Here you can obtain maps and books about the park, as well as information about trails and cabins. The center also has exhibits on other Alaska parks, refuges, and forests.

Hiking
To make the two-hour climb to the most popular peak on the Anchorage horizon, 3,550-foot-tall **Flattop Mountain,** head for the Glen Alps parking lot: From the Seward Highway, go east on O'Malley Road, then continue east via Hillside, Upper Huffman, and Toilsome Roads. Though polka bands, dancers, wedding

celebrants, winter campers, and solstice revelers all have gained Flat-top's summit, getting there is no stroll. Climbers train every winter and spring on the mountain's flanks to get in shape for Mount McKinley. Watch out for some steep pitches below the summit.

Be careful as you scramble up these slopes. Climbers jokingly call the region's volcanic rock "metamorpha-grunge-it" or "Chugach crud." You will discover the aptness of those monikers the moment you reach for a solid handhold—and get a fistful of rotten rock instead.

If you prefer flatter walking, try the 12-mile-long **Powerline Pass Trail,** which also begins at the Glen Alps parking lot. The trail dips below **False Peak** and follows the **South Fork Campbell Creek.** If you are so inclined, head across the valley and up **Little O'Malley Peak** (3,257 feet). Should the next valley, the **Middle Fork Campbell Creek,** beckon as well, cross the wide stretch of open land known as the "football field" and descend to **Williwaw Lakes,** a pretty place for overnight camping or a picnic.

On the southern boundary of the park, where the Seward High-way winds beside **Turnagain Arm,** the beautiful **Turnagain Arm Trail** runs 9 miles along the side of the mountains, paralleling the high-way and providing mostly flat walking. Originally the railroad route in the days before roads connected Anchorage and Seward, this trail brims with raspberries, highbush cranberries, and water-melon berries. It also offers spectacular glimpses of Turnagain Arm and the Kenai Mountains.

You can access the Turnagain Arm Trail at numerous trailheads along the highway between Miles 115 and 106. The 3.3-mile section from **Potter Creek** to **McHugh Creek** is the easiest walking. The 6.1 miles from McHugh Creek to **Rainbow Valley** and beyond to **Windy Corner** are more difficult, but they offer excellent views. A map of this interpretive trail is available at the Potter Creek trailhead at Mile 115.

For a steep, vigorous hike embellished by spectacular wild-flowers such as lupine and chocolate lilies, trek about 1.5 miles up **Bird Ridge** along Turnagain Arm to the lookout point; the trailhead is at Mile 100.5 of the Seward Highway. If your knees are in less than mint condition, take along a pair of ski poles to steady yourself on the descent.

If you walk part of the historic **Iditarod trail** over Crow Pass to Eagle River, you'll cross over **Yakedeyak Creek.** The creek got its name in the mid-1970s. A troop of Girl Scouts was restoring the old trail, which involved building a bridge over an unnamed creek. After the girls had spent much time discussing what they should name it, Doug Fesler, the young park's very first ranger, suggested, "You've been yakking so much about it, why don't you name it Yakedeyak." And so they did.

To the north, the 13-mile-long **Lakeside Trail** at Eklutna Lake *(accessed via Glenn Hwy.)* meanders along the gently rolling eastern shore from one end of the lake to the other. It is good for hiking as well as for mountain biking and cross-country skiing.

Climbing

Humor. Respect. Honor. Terror. The spectrum of human experience in these mountains is recorded in their names. Trappers and miners traveling the Iditarod trail from Girdwood to Eagle River named a string of peaks in the Chugach range after birds that frequent the region, such as Magpie, Camp Robber, Gray Jay, Raven, Crow, Finch, Bunting, Roost, and Golden Crown. (Several

Hiking the Turnagain Arm Trail, Chugach State Park

features in the park are named Penguin, though you won't find the bird in the Northern Hemisphere.)

Aspiring mountaineers gave an alliterative string of "B" names to some of the highest peaks in the park's interior: Baleful, Bold, Bashful, Benevolent, Boisterous, Bellicose, Baneful, Bounty, and Benign. At 8,005 feet, Bashful ironically is the park's tallest mountain. "Bold, Bashful, and Baleful Peaks," says former park ranger Fesler, "are rights of passage for young climbers. There's lots of rotten rock, definite exposure, and you need ropes. They're very rugged and not easy to get into."

The technical route up **Eklutna Glacier** ascends over Inferno Pass by Mount Soggy, Devil's Mistress, and Mount Beelzebub. A second technical climb ascends **Bird Ridge** to **The Beak** at 4,730 feet, then climbs 240 feet higher to its true summit at **Bird's Eye Peak** before descending a mere 10 feet to **Tail Feather Peak.** Contact the park for specific route information; keep in mind that the duration of any climb varies depending on its difficulty and the climber's experience level.

Boating

Glacier-carved, 7-mile-long **Eklutna Lake** is the park's largest. Tucked between jagged, 7,000-foot mountains, it offers lots of recreational opportunities, such as kayaking or rowing. *(Beware of wind; get off lake as soon as it rises.)* You can rent a kayak in Anchorage or from the park's concessionaire, Lifetime Adventures *(907-746-4644. www.lifetimeadventures.com).* There's no boat ramp so you'll have to carry your craft at least 100 yards to the water.

Eagle River is the only river here suitable for canoeists, kayakers, and rafters. From the put-in at Mile 7.5 on the Eagle River Road downstream to the first bridge, the water is Class I and II, which requires basic navigating skills. The trip takes about 3 hours.

Pull out at the left bank before the bridge. Unless you are a veteran paddler and have scouted the rapids, do not venture below the first bridge. Experienced boaters have died in the Class II and III white water that runs between the first and second bridges.

■ 495,000 acres ■ 12 miles south of Anchorage ■ Year-round ■ Hiking, kayaking, paragliding, fishing, cross-country skiing, snowshoeing
■ Contact the park, HC 52, Box 8999, Indian, AK 99540; 907-345-5014. www.dnr.state.ak.us/parks/units/chugach

Mount Marathon

5 miles east of Kenai Fjords

Blood, guts, and glory are what Marathon Mountain means to many people. A bar bet in 1915 sent the first runners racing up its slopes to "the rock," the mountain's lower summit (3,022 feet).

Nowadays, specifically every Fourth of July, Seward hosts the **Mount Marathon Race.** Some 30,000 revelers—that's ten times the town's winter population—descend here to watch the scramble for the lower summit and back across rock, shale, and snow. One contestant described it as "a controlled free-fall." The record from the center of town to the rock and back is 43 minutes and 23 seconds, set in 1981 by former Olympic skier Bill Spencer.

You don't have to be a racer to venture up the mountain. By following the trail that begins near the center of town, you can enjoy a 4-hour round-trip hike to the rock. Pick up a map at the visitor information center at the north end of town *(Mile 2 on Seward Hwy.)* before you set out.

Although the terrain is steep, and at times you may have to resort to all fours and pull yourself up by tree roots, the hike is a rewarding one. On a clear day in summer, you will enjoy sweeping views over a panorama of mountain peaks, glaciers, and the breathtaking fjord of **Resurrection Bay.**

Marmot

Be advised that the mountain always has some snow on its higher reaches; snow arrives on the lower slopes in October and remains until May. This makes the steep slope quite slippery; take ski poles to stabilize yourself. In addition, check in town for avalanche warnings, or call the Alaska Mountain Safety Center *(907-345-3566).*

■ **4,603 feet high** ■ **Seward** ■ **Best months June–Sept.** ■ **Hiking, mountain race** ■ **Contact Seward Chamber of Commerce, P.O. Box 749, Seward, AK 99664; 907-224-8051. www.sewardak.org**

Hiking with the Gods

I n ancient Greek and Roman mythology, immortals entered Mount Olympus, the home of gods and goddesses, through the Great Gate of Clouds. Hiking in Alaska, upward into the clouds that crown her peaks, discovering an enchanting alpine lake or the breathtaking sweep from a summit—you may feel that you, too, have crossed into the realm of the gods.

In all of Alaska's vastness, you'll find few official trails. **Chugach State Park** *(see pp. 160–166)* and the **Kenai Peninsula** probably have the best developed trails because of their accessibility.

In Chugach State Park, **Wolverine Peak** is a popular day hike (10.5 miles round-trip). Named for the wolverine tracks visible in the snow at the summit, the mountain affords great views of Mount McKinley and the Alaska Range, Cook Inlet, and the rugged peaks of the Chugach. Dall's sheep often wander over the summit into the next valley. Pick up the trail from the **Prospect Heights Trailhead** above Anchorage.

South of Anchorage, 26.5 miles along the Seward Highway and Turnagain Arm, is the start of the trail up **Bird Ridge.** With southern exposure, this trail is one of the first to be free of snow in spring, around April.

You soon emerge from the trees to find fabulous views over Turnagain Arm. Continue on up to the top of the ridge or walk about 20 minutes to an alpine meadow, where you can have a picnic, relax, and just enjoy soaking up the scenery.

At the end of Turnagain Arm is the turnoff for Girdwood and Alyeska Ski Resort. **Mount Alyeska** is fun to hike in summer: The route goes up a toll road, along a tumbling river and past some prolific blueberry bushes, and ends up in alpine meadowland.

The 38-mile (one way) **Resurrection Pass Trail,** an old gold-miners' route on the Kenai Peninsula, crosses the mountains from the little town of Hope to just south of Kenai Lake. The trailhead is just southeast of Hope on the airport road. This route takes about 3 to 5 days of hiking. Reservations are required through National Recreational Reservation Service if you want to overnight in the public-use cabins along the trail *(877-444-6777; www.reserveusa. com).*

Near the end of this trail on the Kenai River side is the trail to **Lower** and **Upper Russian Lakes,** extremely popular fishing spots for sockeye salmon in June and July. You'll find trails for both hikers and anglers.

Scaling Flattop Mountain

Hikers use the **Lower Russian Lake Trail** (6 miles round-trip), which connects to the **Upper Russian Lake Trail** (24 miles round-trip). Anglers access the river via a separate trail. Both lakes have public-use cabins.

En route to Seward are two absolute beauties: **Ptarmigan** and **Lost Lakes.** You can pick up the trail to **Ptarmigan Lake** (6 miles round-trip), a turquoise jewel twinkling in a mountain setting, at Mile 23 on the Seward Highway.

To access the trail to Lost Lake (it sits prettily amid high-alpine meadows of forget-me-nots and wild geraniums and a sprinkling of other small lakes and mountain tarns), drive to **Primrose** at the eastern end of Kenai Lake or to the other **Lost Lake Trailhead** (*in Lost Lake*

subdivision off Seward Hwy.).

Or, you can start at one end and trek across to the other. The round-trip to Lost Lake is about 14 miles; the traverse is 16 miles. Even in early July there may be still a fair amount of snow so be prepared.

For more information on trails and trailheads, the **Alaska Public Lands Information Center** (*605 W. 4th Ave. 907-271-2737*) in Anchorage has an array of useful maps and books.

Remember, this is wilderness; you must be prepared to be self-sufficient. Collapsible ski poles ease wear and tear on the knees for ascents and descents. Even if you are going just for the day, pack extra water and food, warm clothing, rain gear, a map, a lighter, and basic first aid supplies.

Alaska SeaLife Center

In 1998, the Alaska SeaLife Center opened at the edge of Resurrection Bay. It was the devastating oil spill from the *Exxon Valdez* nearly a decade before that fueled the movement to establish a world-class, state-of-the-art facility for marine research, rehabilitation, and public education here where the land meets the sea.

10 miles east of Kenai Fjords

The largest oil spill in U.S. history, it was responsible for the deaths of thousands of creatures. (At the entrance to the center, notice the mural depicting many of the marine species affected by the catastrophe.) The scientific jury on the long-term consequences of the spill is still out. Scientists at the SeaLife Center continue to investigate the big picture.

Designed to function more as a research facility than a tourist

Steller sea lion, Alaska SeaLife Center

attraction, the SeaLife Center offers a naturalistic setting where visitors can observe marine mammals, fish, seabirds, and other denizens of the northern waters.

The center's aquariums provide a fascinating window on underwater marine life. Young visitors particularly enjoy the panoramic view of sea lions diving and gliding around the huge aquarium.

At the habitat pools, visitors have the opportunity to observe marine species that inhabit environments above the ocean's surface and along the coast. Here you can watch biologists feed an array of diving seabirds, known collectively as alcids. Among the birds you'll see here are murres (which resemble penguins but are unrelated, and unlike their Southern Hemisphere look-alikes they can fly) as well as orange-beaked puffins and pigeon guillemots.

The newest additions to the seabird habitat are red-legged kittiwakes, which are rarely seen outside of the remote Aleutian or the Pribilof Islands. Not divers but excellent fliers, they are distinctive with their brilliant white feathers and dark wings, and striking scarlet-colored feet—and a treat to watch as they flit above the habitat pool.

■ **Downtown Seward on Resurrection Bay** ■ **Year-round** ■ **Wildlife viewing, exhibits, films** ■ **Adm. fee** ■ **Contact the center, Mile 0, Seward Hwy., P.O. Box 1329, Seward, AK 99664; 907-224-6300 or 800-224-2525. www.alaskasealife.org**

Caines Head State Recreation Area

20 miles southeast of Kenai Fjords

The old adage that time and the tide wait for no one is borne out by the 4.5-mile-long **coastal trail** from Seward to Caines Head in the Caines Head State Recreation Area. Three miles of the trail along the beach can be accessed only at low tide. If you're caught there during high tide, you may find yourself doing some swimming in the icy waters, a dangerous prospect that is best avoided.

Before you venture out on the trail, pick up a tide table from a local sporting goods store or newsstand. Rangers advise you to start your journey at least 2 hours before low tide to be on the safe side.

The trailhead begins at **Lowell Point,** which lies just south of Seward. The first 1.5 miles of the trail take you along clifftops and through forests of spruce, alder, and western hemlock. During the summer, the footpath is lined with a wild garden of lupine, dwarf fireweed, beach peas, dogwood, and cow parsnip. The trail drops steeply, through patches of berry bushes and devil's club, to the bridge over **Tonsina Creek.**

Keep your eyes open; this is prime black bear country. Among the many other creatures you may see here are sea otters, harbor seals, salmon, whales (humpbacks and orcas), puffins, oyster-catchers, and, at a distance, mountain goats. Be sure to bring along binoculars for this hike.

A quick jaunt through open woods takes you across another bridge and to the beach. Don't expect a strand of powdery white sand; like many beaches in Alaska, this coastal stretch is lined with shale, gravel, and rocks. On a sunny day, the view across the bay is absolutely stunning—a panorama of glaciers and mountain peaks on the **Resurrection Peninsula.**

Hike the next 3 miles of beach from **Tonsina Point** to **North Beach** only at extreme low tide—and plan to return at the next low tide. As an alternative, you might consider staying overnight before journeying back to Lowell Point. There are campsites and cabins available at Derby Cove, Porcupine Glacier, or Spruce Glacier; reservations are required for cabins.

An interesting place to explore is the abandoned **Fort McGilvray,** which crowns the 650-foot-high promontory of **Caines Head** at the entrance to Resurrection Bay. The fort was built to defend the Port of Seward against enemy attack. This was no abstract threat, considering that by 1942, Japanese ground forces had captured two tiny Aleutian islands.

Although Resurrection Bay never saw combat, there were a few unconfirmed reports of enemy submarines sighted in the Gulf of Alaska. You can access the fort on your own, but take a flashlight with you, and use caution when navigating the tunnels and underground passages.

■ 6,000 acres ■ 4.5 miles from Seward on western side of Resurrection Bay ■ Best months June–Sept. ■ Camping, hiking, boating, fishing, wildlife viewing ■ Fishing license required ■ Contact Alaska Department of Natural Resources, Division of Parks and Outdoor Recreation, Kenai/Prince William Sound Area Office, P.O. Box 1247, Soldotna, AK 99669; 907-262-5581. www.dnr.state.ak.us/parks/units/caineshd.htm

Fox Island

20 miles southeast of Kenai Fjords On the old topo maps of 1951, Fox Island is identified by its French appellation, Renard Island. However you say it, there are no foxes left on Fox Island. And no bears either—which makes the idea of gathering the island's sweet, plump blueberries in late August that much more appealing.

During the height of summer tourist season, boat tours from Seward make daily stops at Fox Island, usually for about an hour—long enough for you to enjoy a salmon bake lunch.

Unfortunately, that precludes a hike to the top of **Fox Island Peak** (its unofficial name), which takes about an hour one way, including a bit of a scramble at the end. The spectacular views of Resurrection Bay, however, make the climb worthwhile.

For those who would like to stay and explore the island, you can reserve one of the eight guest cabins here through Kenai Fjords Wilderness Lodge (*Alaska Tour & Travel 800-208-0200*).

For another perspective on Fox Island, see it from the water. You can take a guided kayaking trip to the north or the south of the island (*contact Sunny Cove Sea Kayaking 907-224-8810*).

If you prefer a more adventurous excursion, the island's 12-mile-long coastline can be circumnavigated in about 4 hours on a calm day.

You'll paddle past natural rock arches and sea caves, as well as eerie "ghost forests" left by the devastating earthquake of 1964.

Watch for puffins, cormorants, bald eagles, sea otters,

Red fox

jellyfish, and orca and humpback whales.

Interestingly, Fox Island is composed of sedimentary rock, while neighboring Hive and Rugged Islands are granite, and Cape Resurrection (to the east) is pillow basalt.

On rare occasions, you'll see orcas (also known as killer whales) swimming around Fox Island's sculpted, flat stone. The whales occasionally approach to massage themselves on the rocks in the shallow coastal waters. (Human beachcombers find that the flat rocks make ideal skipping stones.)

In 1918, American artist Rockwell Kent spent a winter on Fox Island accompanied by his young son and an old Swedish trapper and fox farmer. Kent recorded the experience in words and drawings in *Wilderness: A Journal of Quiet Adventure in Alaska*. His fascination with the world of Fox Island aptly evokes the inexorable pull of the Alaskan wilderness.

He wrote: "I crave snow-topped mountains, dreary wastes, and the cruel Northern sea with its hard horizons at the edge of the world where infinite space begins. Here skies are clearer and deeper, and for the greater wonders they reveal, a thousand times more eloquent of the eternal mystery than those of softer lands."

■ **Approximately 3 square miles** ■ **Resurrection Bay** ■ **Best months May–mid-Sept.** ■ **Hiking, kayaking, bird-watching, whale-watching, berry picking, boat tours** ■ **Contact Kenai Fjord Tours, CIRI Alaska Tourism, 2525 C St., Suite 405, Anchorage, AK 99503; 907-276-6249 or 800-478-8068. www.kenaifjords.com**

Kenai National Wildlife Refuge

100 miles northwest of Kenai Fjords

Created in 1941 to protect the area's moose population and the wildlands over which they ranged, this refuge was originally called the Kenai National Moose Range. In 1980, it was renamed the Kenai National Wildlife Refuge and expanded to embrace new lands and a new mission: to protect habitat for all wild creatures within its boundaries. The refuge now covers half of the Kenai Peninsula. Most of that acreage has a special wilderness area designation, which means that refuge managers use "least intrusive methods" to administer the area.

Moose, the largest members of the deer family, still have star status here. No surprise, considering their size: Alaska moose are

View of Redoubt Volcano from Ninilchik

the largest in the world. Bulls can weigh up to 1,500 pounds. Their racks, or antlers, may extend 6 feet across and weigh 70 pounds when dry (125 pounds when wet).

During the fall mating season, they use these to impress females and to fend off challengers simply by displaying the size of their weaponry. Such an exhibit, biologists say, is intended to win the war without fighting a battle. Come December, male moose shed their antlers. Other mammals found on the refuge include caribou, bears, otters, wolverines, porcupines, wolves, snowshoe hare, beavers, and lynx.

Sixty-seven bird species make their home here. Among them are trumpeter swans, whose white feathers were once so prized that the birds became endangered by the early 1900s. Their population rebounded in the 20th century and they are now off the endangered list. More than 80 percent of the world's population of trumpeter swans live in Alaska today.

The Kenai National Wildlife Refuge encompasses **Skilak Lake** and **Tustumena Lake.** The latter, covering 117 square miles, is one of

Alaska's largest lakes. The refuge contains some 4,000 lakes, many of which harbor rainbow trout, grayling, and arctic char.

What to See and Do
To reach the refuge's **visitor center and headquarters** in Soldotna, turn left off the Sterling Highway onto Funny River Road, then turn right on Ski Hill Road and follow it to the end. You'll find lots of useful material, including maps, dioramas, books, videos, and information on canoeing, hiking, and camping.

Hiking
The refuge contains more than 50 miles of established trails. The **Keen Eye Trail,** a mile-long interpretive nature walk, begins at the visitor center and leads through a boreal forest of spruce and birch to a small lake.

Most hiking trails in the refuge are in the **Skilak Wildlife Recreation Area** around Skilak Lake and are accessible by road. Many lead to good fishing lakes; follow the trail to **Lower Fuller Lake** to fish from the banks for grayling.

Additional trails are listed in *Kenai Pathways,* published by the Alaska Natural History Association and available at the visitor center.

Country store, Seldovia

Canoeing & Kayaking
The **Kenai Canoe Trails** are nationally recognized wilderness routes noted for their exceptional wildlife viewing and recreation. Choose between two canoe systems in the northern wetlands area: The 60-mile-long **Swan Lake Canoe Route** links 30 lakes and is the more popular day-use route. The 80-mile-long **Swanson River Canoe Route** connects 40 lakes and 50 miles of river.

The trails start at Mile 84

on the Sterling Highway. Pick up a guide, or buy Daniel Quick's *The Kenai Canoe Trails,* at refuge headquarters. Guided tours are available around Skilak Lake *(Alaska Wildland Adventures. 800-334-8730. www.alaskawildland.com).*

The larger lakes here offer lovely views of the snow-crested Kenai Mountains rising in the distance. Blueberries and lowbush cranberries brighten the landscape in summer. As you paddle by lakeshore and riverbank, look for the refuge's famous moose, as well as coyote, wolves, and bears. Resident birds include loons, green-winged teal, mallard, mergansers, and eagles.

Afternoon breezes can whip up a frenzy of whitecaps, particularly on Skilak and Tustumena Lakes; get off the water if the wind comes up.

Rafting

A great day outing is a guided rafting trip down the Kenai River from **Cooper Landing** to Skilak Lake *(contact refuge for outfitter information).* As you float down the peaceful upper river, your guides will inform you about the region's natural history and point out sockeye salmon, moose, Dall's sheep, and bald eagles. You also get to ride the rapids through the canyon, then float into Skilak Lake for the grand finale. If you are lucky, you may see moose, coyote, wolves, or bears en route.

Bird-watching

Birders will be interested to know that the refuge provides habitat for more than 67 species of birds, including three-toed woodpeckers, sharp-shinned hawks, and great horned owls. You may also see sandhill cranes, which count among the world's tallest and leggiest birds. Males are known for their courtship rituals, when they flourish their wings, dance about, toss sticks in the air, and bob their heads.

In wetlands and marshes, and on ponds and lakes, listen for the call of the trumpeter swan, which sounds like a loud French horn.

■ **1.96 million acres, including 1.35 million acres designated as wilderness** ■ **Kenai Peninsula** ■ **Best months May–Sept.** ■ **Hiking, boating, cross-country skiing, fishing, bird-watching, wildlife viewing** ■ **Contact the refuge, P.O. Box 2139, Soldotna, AK 99669; 907-262-7021. www.r7.fws.gov**

Kachemak Bay S.P. and State Wilderness Park

west of Kenai Fjords, near Homer

Sweeping in from the Gulf of Alaska, the sea ebbs and flows into the magnificent fjord known as **Kachemak Bay,** on the southern end of the Kenai Peninsula. A waterway with many faces, Kachemak rushes into smaller bays, coves, and lagoons. It laps onto rocky beaches and into tide pools, and caresses the edges of a coastal rain forest.

Kachemak Bay State Park and Kachemak Bay State Wilderness Park together encompass ocean and alpine lakes, forests and meadows filled with wildflowers. Their mountain peaks are capped with ancient ice fields and draped with glaciers.

Kachemak Bay State Park was established in 1970 to protect the area from logging. Within its boundaries, it contains a more bio-diverse ecosystem than almost any park in the world. It serves as the flagship for a remarkable group of state parks that rival the best parks anywhere on the planet.

On the southeast side of Kachemak Bay, the boundaries of the two parks stretch from **Tutka Bay, China Poot Bay, Sadie Cove, Halibut Cove Lagoon,** all the way to the edge of **Aurora Lagoon.** This thin strip of coastline sees most of the parks' visitors. Here you will find a few trails, campsites, and public-use cabins. Beyond is wilderness, where it's possible to hike without seeing another person for weeks.

Although both parks are treated as one, the wilderness park was established later in 1972. It encompasses mountain peaks, glaciers, and large bodies of water, including **Port Dick, Tonsina Bay, One-Haul Bay,** and **Bootlegger Cove.** All of these face the Gulf of Alaska and are exposed to stormy weather. The park takes its wilderness designation seriously: There are no trails within its boundaries.

A variety of individuals—from commercial fishermen to home-steaders to artists—call this bay home. The sea influences all aspects of life, including much of the art that is made here.

"The ocean is so powerful and unyielding," says artist Diana Tillion, who maintains a studio in Halibut Cove on Ismailof Island. "I use octopus ink to paint things of great intensity. To me, it's a living color."

What to See and Do

You'll find water taxis, ferries, and floatplanes available in Homer. Contact the parks for a list of operators, or visit the website.

Homer charter-boat crew and their record-setting halibut

Boat Tours

The *Danny J,* known locally as the Kachemak Bay Ferry *(Central Charter 800-478-7847),* is a colorful former fishing boat that makes two daily trips to **Halibut Cove,** located on the south side of Kachemak Bay, just outside the state park's boundary.

The first trip of the day usually passes near **Gull Island** (not officially within park boundaries). The island is home to a large colony of kittiwakes, as well as tufted puffins, cormorants, and murres.

A larger tour boat, the *Rainbow Connection (907-235-7272),* carries tourists down Kachemak Bay to the fishing village of **Seldovia** via Gull Island. For information about fishing, marine wildlife tours, or ferry service to Kachemak Bay State Park, call Inlet Charters *(907-235-6126).*

Hiking

Kachemak Bay State Park has several developed trails. For an easy walk through a mature spruce and cottonwood forest, take the 3.5-mile **Grewingk Glacier Trail** from your water-taxi drop-off at Rusty Lagoon *(outside Halibut Cove)* to Grewingk Lake at the foot of the glacier.

Hikers seeking a tougher challenge might head for **Poot Peak** (also called Chocolate Drop for its distinctive shape), which you can see from Homer. From a water-taxi drop-off at the head of

Halibut Cove Lagoon, you can climb to the lower summit and back in 4 hours *(upper summit climb recommended only for those with rock-climbing training).*

If you prefer a more leisurely pace, this is a fun place to camp. For a good campsite, walk to **China Poot Lake,** located 2.6 miles from the trailhead at Halibut Cove Lagoon. Leave your backpack in camp the next day and climb the Chocolate Drop unfettered.

Natural History Tours

At Peterson Bay, the **Center for Alaskan Coastal Studies** *(907-235-6667. www.akcoastalstudies.org)* is a nonprofit organization dedicated to the study of marine and coastal ecosystems of

Gull Island

Kachemak Bay through educational outreach.

The center's naturalists lead beach walks and conduct informative public programs on tide pools, rain forest flora and fauna, geology, and marine land. On the way to the center, you will pass Gull Island.

■ **380,000 acres** ■ **Southern tip of Kenai Peninsula; access by small plane or boat only** ■ **Best months May–Sept.** ■ **Camping, hiking, kayaking, fishing, wildlife viewing, boat tours** ■ **Contact Alaska State Parks, Kachemak District, Mile 168.5 Sterling Hwy., Homer, AK; 907-235-7024. Or Division of Parks, Kenai Area Office, P.O. Box 1247, Soldotna, AK 99669; 907-262-5581. www.dnr.state.ak.us/parks/parks.htm**

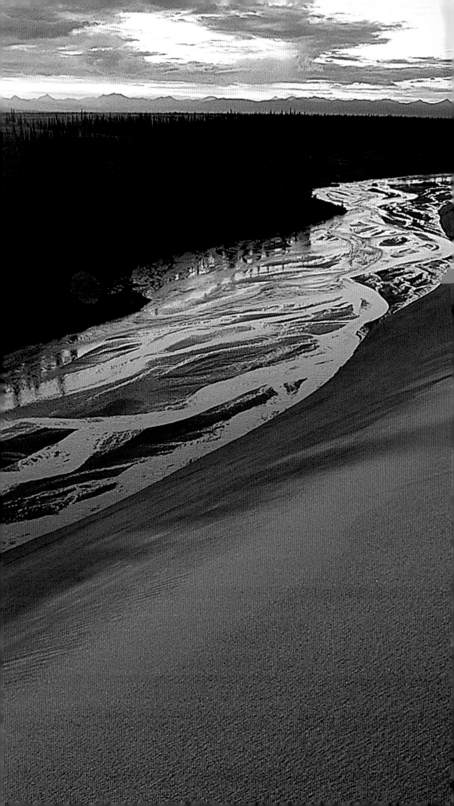

Kobuk Valley

"Now we were alone between fringes of spruce by a clear stream where tundra went up the sides of mountains," wrote John McPhee in *Coming into the Country*. The Kobuk Valley, said McPhee, "was, in all likelihood, the most isolated wilderness I would ever see."

Located entirely above the Arctic Circle, and cordoned off by the Baird and Waring Mountains, Kobuk Valley protects the midsection of the Kobuk River, the drainage of the wild and scenic Salmon River, the Great Kobuk Sand Dunes, and an array of wildlife. This undeveloped national park sees fewer tourists than any other. Float a river here in late August and the only other humans you're likely to encounter are Inupiat hunters who, like their ancestors, ambush the caribou that migrate through each year.

Twelve thousand years ago, when continental glaciers covered much of North America and a land bridge connected Alaska and Asia, Kobuk Valley was an ice-free refuge with grassy tundra similar to that found in Siberia today. Bison, mastodons, and mammoths roamed the valley, along with the humans who hunted them.

Since then, the climate has shifted, and sea level has risen to flood the land bridge; many of the early mammals have disappeared. But today's shrubby flora harbors relicts of the preglacial steppe, and in the cold, hard ground lie the legacies of ancient animals and peoples.

Here in Kobuk Valley the boreal forest reaches its northern limit, and the North American and Asiatic flyways cross. Pockets of tundra blend into birch and spruce, dwarfed by blasts of freezing air. And along the Kobuk River stretch 25 square miles of active sand dunes, where summer temperatures can climb to 100° F.

Kobuk Valley National Park's management plan encourages traditional native subsistence practices over tourism, so no facilities or trails lie within the park.

- Alaskan Arctic, 75 miles east of Kotzebue
- 1.8 million acres
- Established 1980
- Best months June–mid-Sept.
- Hiking, rafting, kayaking, fishing
- Information: 907-442-3890 www.nps.gov/kova

Great Kobuk Sand Dunes, Kobuk Valley National Park

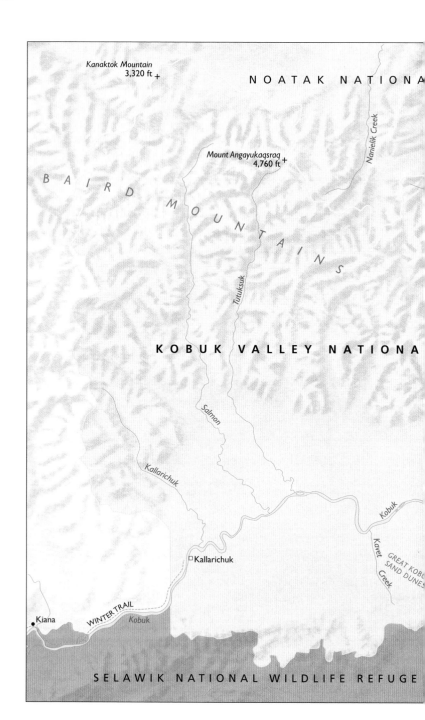

Kanaktok Mountain
3,320 ft +

N O A T A K   N A T I O N A

Nanielik Creek

Mount Angayukaqsraq
4,760 ft +

B A I R D

M O U N T A I N S

Tutuksuk

K O B U K   V A L L E Y   N A T I O N A

Salmon

Kallarichuk

Kobuk

Kavet Creek

GREAT KOBU
SAND DUNE

☐ Kallarichuk

WINTER TRAIL

Kiana

Kobuk

S E L A W I K   N A T I O N A L   W I L D L I F E   R E F U G E

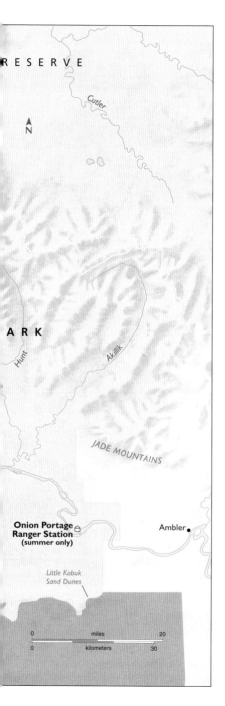

RESERVE

Cutler

N

ARK

Hunt

Akillik

JADE MOUNTAINS

Onion Portage
Ranger Station
(summer only)

Ambler

Little Kobuk
Sand Dunes

0   miles   20
0   kilometers   30

How to Get There

Commercial planes fly daily from Anchorage to Kotzebue, where the park's information center is located. Connecting flights serve the native villages of Kiana and Ambler, both of which lie along the Kobuk River, on the park's western and eastern sides respectively. From either location, you can charter a boat or plane into the park. Alternatively, a boat or plane can be chartered from the village of Kotzebue.

When to Go

Summer. Days are long (from about June 6 to July 3 the sun doesn't set at all), and temperatures in many places can reach into the 80s or higher.

Ice breaks up on the Kobuk River in May and begins to form again by mid-October. The ranger station at Onion Portage is staffed periodically from June to September.

The latter half of June is best for wildflower viewing. August can bring rain, and September snow. In late August, the aspens start to turn yellow and the tundra red, and the caribou begin their annual migration.

How to Visit

Consider a combination **river-hiking trip** so as to have some

Inflatable boats for river running

What Not to Miss

- **Paddling or motorboating down the Kobuk River from Ambler to Kiana**

- **Viewing caribou migration at Onion Portage in August or September**

- **Paddling and hiking to the Great Kobuk Sand Dunes**

- **Cultural tours of Inuit communities with native guides**

- **Flight-seeing over Cape Krusenstern National Monument from Kotzebue**

The wide and placid **Kobuk River** makes for an ideal trip, whether by canoe, kayak, or motorboat. Most people put in at Ambler and take out at Kiana, both of which are located outside the park boundaries. You can charter a boat in Kiana.

You can also float or paddle the **Salmon,** a designated Wild and Scenic River; however, it is rougher than the Kobuk and also more difficult to reach.

Hiking in most areas of Kobuk National Park is excellent; however, the park has no maintained trails or river crossings, so be sure to plan your trip carefully.

While you are in the park, be respectful of Inuit lands, most of which are located along the Kobuk River.

time on the water as well as a chance to explore the land. You can paddle to different landing points, leave your gear in the canoe, and then hike unencumbered. Bring everything you need; there are no visitor facilities within the park.

EXPLORING THE PARK

Kobuk River: **347 miles one way**

Many visitors travel through the park on the Kobuk River. Flowing from the Endicott Mountains in the Brooks Range into **Hotham Inlet,** the river has served as a highway between Alaska's interior and the sea for thousands of years. It remains a key artery today.

Many boaters put in near the Kobuk's headwaters at **Walker Lake** in **Gates of the Arctic National Park** *(see pp. 57–81)* and then float through Kobuk Valley National Park. Guided floats are led by Arctic Treks *(907-455-6502),* Alaska Wildtrek *(907-235-6463),* and Equinox Expeditions *(907-222-1219).*

You can design your own trip and put in or take out at any of the five riverside Inupiat villages: **Kobuk, Shungnak, Ambler, Kiana,** or **Noorvik.** The flexibility allows you to determine the length of your trip, from one to four weeks. However long your trip, go in late August or early September, when you can sit on a bluff and, if you're lucky, watch migrating caribou swim across the river.

Near **Onion Portage,** a historic caribou crossing where the river enters the park (and named for the local wild chives), archaeologist J. Louis Giddings in 1961 unearthed a major find here dating back at least 10,000 years. His 2-acre plot yielded 30 artifact-bearing layers reflecting several different cultures, each of which depended on caribou for survival. The site is now inactive, but there's great hiking nearby.

Three spots in the river's first 30 miles demand extreme caution: About two-thirds of a mile downstream from the lake is a stretch of dangerous Class IV to V rapids. Do *not* attempt to run it; follow the portage route on the left bank. The second stretch of rapids lies 10 miles below the lake at **Upper Kobuk Canyon;** it should be lined on the right, as should the third stretch, which follows about 20 miles down where the river plunges through **Lower Kobuk Canyon.** Below this canyon the river quiets to Class I. If you prefer to skip the white water, have a plane drop you off west of the park at **Ambler.**

Powerboats ply the river below the canyons, serving native fish camps along the shore. The slow water and many oxbows downstream from Shungnak prompt many paddlers to take out there.

Fishing can be incredible on the Kobuk. The catch includes grayling, arctic char, and giant sheefish. Boaters have the best luck, but you can reach choice spots by hiring a floatplane from Ambler Air *(907-445-2157)* or Bettles Air *(907-692-5655).*

Great Kobuk Sand Dunes

About 40 miles downstream from Ambler is a curious sight on the river's south side: the Great Kobuk Sand Dunes, a 25-square-mile mini-Sahara sitting 30 miles above the Arctic Circle. Come by river and leave your boat on shore, then hike 1.5 miles to reach the dunes, some of which soar 100 feet high.

During the Pleistocene, glaciers ground away at the Brooks Range, filling the rivers with outwash. Strong winds swept away this alluvial detritus, forming the 33,000-year-old dune fields you see today. A special combination of topography and eastern and northern winds keeps the dunes moving and inhospitable to vegetation.

At their western edge, the Great Kobuk Sand Dunes overrun sections of boreal forest. Here you'll see the tops of 150-year-old black spruce jutting above the sand, which is often crisscrossed by caribou and bear tracks.

Kavet Creek offers the best access to the dunes. Do *not* try to wade upstream or follow the creek margin. Instead, head a few hundred yards to the west, then hike south on the open, easy ridge.

There are native allotments within the park. The Park Service asks visitors not to disturb these cabins or camps, or to interfere in any way with subsistence activities.

Great Kobuk Sand Dunes

Alaska Natives

Although the term "Alaska natives" (or simply "natives") often is used to describe the state's indigenous peoples, that designation actually encompasses several cultures, each with its own customs and traits and history.

Fourth of July, Pribilof Islands

Three distinct groups—the Athapaskans, the Inupiat (including the Nunamiut), and the Yup'ik—make their home in the Arctic.

The Inupiat, who reside along the shores of Arctic rivers and the Arctic Ocean, and the Yup'ik, who live at the edge of the Bering Sea, also are called Eskimos, or Inuit.

Athapaskans, who are frequently referred to as Indians, inhabit the interior of Alaska north to the Brooks Range.

Variations in customs and dialects exist within each large cultural community. Unlike the majority of Inupiat, the Nunamiut are not maritime hunters. Rather, they live in the mountains, relying on caribou for subsistence, as do the Gwich'in Athapaskans.

Over the centuries, cultural interactions among Alaska natives have ranged from friendly trading to veiled distrust and open warfare. As a way to guarantee the safe conduct of commerce, certain areas apparently were designated as neutral trading sites.

Many contemporary natives continue lifestyles similar to those of their ancestors; however, change is taking its toll on many villages. To better understand contemporary native life, consider taking a cultural tour.

If you would like information about Nunamiut and Inupiat tours, contact Alaskan Arctic Adventures (*907-852-3300*), Arctic Tour Company (*907-852-4512*), Northern Alaska Tour Company (*907-474-8600*), or Tour Arctic (*907-442-3301*). For information about Athapaskan village tours, contact Athabascan Cultural Journeys (*907-829-2261*), or Yukon River Tours (*907-452-7162*).

If you go on a tour, remember that you are a guest: Be polite, respect the privacy of others, and always ask for permission before taking photos.

INFORMATION & ACTIVITIES

Headquarters
P.O. Box 1029, Kotzebue,
AK 99752; 907-442-3890.
www.nps.gov/kova

Seasons & Accessibility
Open year-round; access by
boat or charter aircraft from
Kotzebue generally available
June through September.
*(Kobuk River usually thaws by
early June freezes by mid-Oct.)*

There are no roads into or
inside the park. Be prepared
for severe arctic weather at
any time. Contact park headquarters before visiting; if
you wish to charter in by
air, request a list of licensed
companies.

Information Centers
Located 80 miles from the
park, the Kotzebue Headquarters and Information Center
is open daily in summer and
Monday through Friday the
rest of the year.

Entrance Fee
None.

Pets
Strongly discouraged.

Facilities for Disabled
Kotzebue information center
accessible to wheelchairs;
otherwise none.

Things to Do
Kotzebue information
center shows films; check
schedule. The park does not
offer organized activities;
however, rafting, kayaking,
canoeing, hiking, sportfishing
(license required), and flight-
seeing are all available.

Commercial outfitters offer
a variety of private guide
services for floating, fishing,
and trekking trips. Contact
park headquarters for a list
of outfitters and guides authorized to work in the park.

Special Advisories
■ Travel with a guide unless
you have substantial wilderness
experience and skills.
■ Mosquitoes and gnats can
be brutal; bring plenty of
repellent, a head net, and
an insect-proof tent.
■ Inuit own much of the land
along the river and practice
subsistence hunting and fishing. Be respectful of the people
and their property.

Overnight Backpacking
No permit is required, but
contact park headquarters
for current information
regarding weather, river
conditions, bears, and any
native subsistence activities
before venturing out.

Brown bear cubs

Campgrounds

None; backcountry camping only.

Hotel

■ **Nullagvik Hotel**
P.O. Box 336, Kotzebue, AK

99752. 907-442-3331. 74 units.
$143 for double. Restaurant.

Excursions from Kobuk Valley

Cape Krusenstern National Monument

10 air miles northwest of Kotzebue For more than 6,000 years, Eskimos have forged a living on this treeless stretch of gravelly coastal plain projecting into the Chukchi Sea. The cape—named by, or for, Capt. Johann Von Krusenstern, an Estonian-born German who led Russia's first round-the-world voyage in 1803—is the site of 114 remarkable beach ridges.

Rich in ancient artifacts, this cluster of ridges is an archaeological gold mine. Each ridge once served as an oceanfront campsite for early hunters. Formed over thousands of years by winds, waves, and currents that deposited sand and gravel on the shore, the ridges chronicle 9,000 years of human use. Today, the cape's large land and sea mammals are still crucial to local subsistence.

Eschewing trails, campgrounds, or any other "improvements," Cape Krusenstern National Monument protects Inupiat cultural heritage past and present. Removal of artifacts is prohibited as is

Cape Krusenstern

interfering with Inupiat hunters and fishers whose tents dot the outer beach.

This is a harsh land. Coastal temperatures in summer seldom exceed 60° F; the chill wind reminds that snow is always possible. Still, every summer a few hardy birders come in hopes of sighting migrant and vagrant species that share their habitat with musk-oxen, arctic hare, and other mammals. In spring and fall, you can see walrus and beluga and bowhead whales pass by on their annual journey to ice-free waters. If you choose to visit in winter, you can get here by plane, boat, dogsled, or snowmobile.

A charter flight over the monument from nearby Kotzebue *(contact Northwestern Aviation 907-442-3525)* is the best way to appreciate the changes wrought by sea ice over the millennia. You'll have the best view of the sand ridges, which lie along the cape's southern coast, if you go early in the morning or late in the day. For a good introduction to coastal Inupiat culture, visit the **NANA Museum of the Arctic** *(907-265-4157)* in Kotzebue.

If you visit the monument *(primitive camping only)*, you will be walking where ancient Inupiat cultures first emerged 5,000 years ago. Contemporary Inupiat still practice many of their ancestors' ways, hunting and fishing on this precarious threshold of the planet's habitable terrain.

■ **444,673 acres** ■ **10 air miles northwest of Kotzebue** ■ **Access by air or boat** ■ **Best months June–Aug.** ■ **Camping, hiking, kayaking, fishing, wildlife viewing** ■ **Contact the monument, P.O. Box 1029, Kotzebue, AK 99572; 907-442-3890. www.nps.gov/cakr**

Noatak National Preserve

north of Kobuk Valley, access from Kotzebue

There's no doubt that Noatak National Preserve is one of the finest wilderness areas left in North America. UNESCO conferred International Biosphere Reserve status on the site when it was established in 1980. One of the continent's largest undeveloped river basins, dramatically encircled by mountains, Noatak's sweeping views are awesome in the true sense of the word. Indeed, the preserve comprises a world unto itself by virtue of sheer size—more than 12,000 square miles.

Noatak encompasses deep canyons, crystal rivers, undulating tundra, and coastal wetlands. The Noatak River rises from residual glaciers clinging to the flanks of 8,510-foot-tall **Mount Igikpak,** the highest peak in the western Brooks Range. The Noatak flows west 350 miles from **Gates of the Arctic National Park** *(see pp. 57–81)* through the national preserve into the Chukchi Sea.

The remote Noatak preserve is one of Alaska's least traveled areas. There are no lodges, campgrounds, or trails here; however, visitors with well-honed backcountry skills will find countless opportunities for backpacking and exploring. You can float the Noatak River or one of its ten tributaries, including the **Cutler, Kelly,** or **Nimiuktuk Rivers.** Whether you hike, float, or fly in and camp, take time to savor the silence and solitude that are this preserve's unique gift to the visitor.

What to See and Do

The **Noatak National Wild and Scenic River** offers superlative wilderness trips from the Brooks Range to the Chukchi Sea. Most visitors fly in from area villages such as Kotzebue and Bettles *(allow extra time for delays due to fog).*

The upper access lakes at the head of the river between **Portage** and **Douglas Creeks** get heavy use, so try not to camp near your put-in. Alternatively, you can arrange to be dropped off and picked

Noatak River

up by floatplane (*contact preserve for list of approved operators*), or you can float all the way downstream to Noatak village.

If you raft the Noatak River on your own, allow 10 days to float from the access lakes to the Cutler River (a common take-out point) or 21 days to Noatak. If you wish to hire a guide, try to find an outfitter who will combine backpacking and river running.

To enhance your enjoyment of this long trip, be sure to take sunscreen, insect repellent, and a head net or bug jacket. In summer, expect swarms of mosquitoes; in autumn, whitesox—tiny, biting flies that leave nasty welts.

Limited access and shallow water above the put-in lakes put the Noatak's upper 25 miles largely off the radar of boaters and hikers. For the first 50 miles, the river flows through a deep, U-shaped valley in the Gates of the Arctic park, hemmed to the south by the **Schwatka Mountains.** Here the river is mostly placid (Class I and II), although some sections can be tricky. The whirlpool below Douglas Creek, called the Jaws, should be lined.

Arcing westward, the river enters its great basin—3,000 square miles of wildlife habitat ringed by the **Baird Mountains** to the south and the **De Long Mountains** to the north. Aside from a few balsam poplars and willows edging the river, the surrounding countryside

is open; be aware, however, that grizzlies can hide in even small pockets of brush.

These spare slopes and vast stretches of tundra offer excellent chances to view wildlife. You may see caribou, gyrfalcons, whistling swans, pacific loons, and perhaps even a wolf or wolverine. Songbirds include Asian strays such as bluethroats, as well as migrants from South America.

In April and August, you may observe a primal spectacle from the Ice Age: the Western Arctic caribou herd migrating south through the preserve. Over the millennia, when land bridges periodically linked Siberia to North America, mammals such as lions, short-faced bears, horses, hare, caribou, musk-oxen, and saber-toothed cats crossed into the New World. As you watch the thundering caribou pass, try to picture the same scene with the additional presence of camels and woolly mammoths.

Halfway to the sea, the Noatak enters 70-mile-long **Grand Canyon,** a beautiful, carved valley with minimal white water. There's some great hiking around the **Nimiuktuk River,** which joins the Noatak here. (Don't be surprised to see Inupiat hunters motoring by in powerboats.) Below the Kelly River, the Noatak dissolves into braids and loses its Wild and Scenic designation.

About 70 or 80 river miles from the ocean, the Noatak River reaches **Noatak,** the only village along its entire length. You'll know you're approaching this Inupiat town by the unmistakable sounds of "civilization"; be sure to take the right channel or you will miss the place. Most boaters take out here and catch a scheduled flight to Kotzebue.

■ **6.3 million acres** ■ **Northwest Alaska; access by aircraft from Bettles, Fairbanks, or Kotzebue** ■ **Best months June–Sept.** ■ **Camping, hiking, bird-watching, wildlife viewing, float trips** ■ **Contact the preserve, P.O. Box 1029, Kotzebue, AK 99572; 907-442-3890. www.nps.gov/noat**

Bering Land Bridge National Preserve

125 miles southwest of Kobuk Valley

The mandate of Bering Land Bridge National Preserve is to commemorate the peopling of the Western Hemisphere and to provide information about complex natural processes, particularly the effects of climate change, including greenhouse gases, global warming, and ozone depletion.

Bridging the Gaps

Did human beings migrate to the New World over the Bering Land Bridge 10,000 to 13,000 years ago? Many scientists think so. For evidence, they point to sites at Cape Krusenstern and on the Bering Land Bridge that have yielded artifacts dating back 9,000 to 10,000 years.

In the 1990s, investigations of the Mesa and Putu sites in the Brooks Range uncovered stone spearpoints 9,700 to 11,000 years old. Particularly intriguing to archaeologists is the close resemblance between these weapons and the stone tools found thousands of miles to the south.

Combined with research from other Alaska sites such as Onion Portage on the Kobuk River, the evidence now suggests that several human migrations—both by land and by sea—to the New World may have taken place. As each new clue is unearthed, the puzzle of who peopled the Americas, as well as when and how, moves closer to completion.

Several times during the Pleistocene Ice Ages, the now submerged continental shelf linking Alaska and Siberia dried up. The bridge of land, called Beringia, was a thousand miles wide and covered with grasslands across which people, wildlife, and plants moved.

Before you make your way to the preserve, stop by the **visitor center** in **Nome.** Here you can pick up information about the site. You can also view the 7-foot-long tusk and bones of a 20,160-year-old woolly mammoth.

Access to Bering Land Bridge is a challenge. There are no roads leading directly into the preserve, and the six public-use cabins are intended mainly for emergency use in winter. Inland from the coast and barrier islands that make up the preserve's frontier, you'll find extensive wet tundra. Trekking here is the stuff of hiking nightmares (think teeming tussocks and swarming mosquitoes).

Considerably more inviting are the rolling hills of the preserve's interior. Here, volcanic history is preserved in lava flows near **Imuruk Lake** and in five large maar (crater) lakes in the area of **Devil Mountains–Cape Espenberg.**

Serpentine Hot Springs, a geothermal feature, is a popular fly-in spot. There's a rustic bunkhouse here that sleeps up to 20 people,

Serpentine Hot Springs

and a wooden tub in a bathhouse fed by a spring with waters of 140°
to 170° F. Between soaks, you can hike among the granite tors on
surrounding ridges and look for alpine birds and large mammals.

■ **2.7 million acres** ■ **90 miles north of Nome** ■ **Access by boat or aircraft**
■ **Best months June–July** ■ **Camping, hiking, fishing, wildlife-viewing, hot**
springs ■ **Contact the preserve, P.O. Box 220, Nome, AK 99762; 907-443-**
2522. www.nps.gov/bela

Seward Peninsula

50 miles
southwest of
Kobuk Valley

The westernmost point of the continental U.S., the
little-traveled Seward Peninsula boasts a diversity of
botanic, zoologic, and geologic riches. Best of all, the
place is easily accessible because all roads lead from Nome.

The **Kougarok, Council,** and **Teller Roads** collectively offer some
300 miles of gravel byways to explore. They lead through the
wilderness to gold-rush ruins, Pleistocene fossils, and indigenous
cultural sites. A representative range of Alaskan wildlife, from the
grizzly bear to the mosquito, are here too. So are Siberian reindeer,
which were introduced at the turn of the 20th century. Today they
wander the hills and are the staple of a cash economy that supple-
ments the traditional native subsistence lifestyle.

The Inupiat and Yup'ik peoples who live here still hunt, fish,
and gather berries as their ancestors did. A source of food for the

communities, these activities play a central role in native culture.

Thirty miles north of Nome, the jagged spires of the **Kigluaik Mountains** beckon. To get to the mountains, take the Kougarok Road to the north or the Teller Road to the west. There's something for everyone here: Photographers find subjects in the sunsets, cirques, and **Crater Lake.** Hikers traverse **Mosquito Pass** with its spectacular canyons. Fishers gravitate to **Canyon Creek** and **Sinuk River.** Birders stalk wheatears, longspurs, and gyrfalcons. History buffs inspect the unfinished 1905 **Wild Goose Pipeline.**

On Kougarok Road, you can fish and camp at the **Salmon Lake campground** (red salmon gather at the lake's outlet from late July through August). Drive up **Anvil Mountain** for a great view of the Bering Strait.

Along Council Road, you can trace sections of the **Iditarod National Historic Trail.** Because this road crosses each of the nine habitats found on the peninsula, it's the best route for sighting some of the 215 species of birds that frequent this area.

This is truly a birder's paradise. The peninsula lies at the crossroads of the Asiatic-North American flyway, offering unique opportunities to see resident birds, migrants, and Asian strays. In spring, for example, rare bluethroats appear in thickets along Kougarok Road, while bristle-thighed curlews populate ridges. (You won't see this species along any other road in North America.)

The Fish and Wildlife Service, which administers segments of the Seward coast, teamed up with the state of Alaska in 1994 to build a parking lot and **nature trail** at the Safety Bridge on Council Road. From here birders can scan **Safety Sound** for seabirds, waterfowl, and shorebirds, including rare strays such as red-necked stints and Mongolian plover.

Even **Nome** is a birding hot spot; a **walking tour** here may reward with sightings of yellow wagtails or threatened spectacled eiders. The town's other attractions include small museums, visitor centers, historic buildings, and nature tours *(contact Nome Discovery Tours 907-443-2814; or Arctic Winter Expeditions 907-443-2680).*

■ **15 million acres** ■ **Western Alaska** ■ **Best months late May–early Sept.** ■ **Camping, hiking, fishing, bird-watching** ■ **Contact Nome Convention and Visitors Bureau, P.O. Box 240, Nome, AK 99762; 907-443-6624. www.nomealaska.org/vc; or BLM Nome Field Office, P.O. Box 925, Nome, AK 99762; 907-443-2177**

Lake Clark

"Think of all the splendors that bespeak Alaska," wrote conservationist John Kauffmann, "glaciers, volcanoes, alpine spires, wild rivers, lakes with grayling on the rise. Picture coasts feathered with countless seabirds. Imagine dense forests and far-sweeping tundra, herds of caribou, great roving bears. Now concentrate all these and more into less than one percent of the state—and behold the Lake Clark region, Alaska's epitome."

Diversity is the hallmark of Lake Clark National Park and Preserve: The Turquoise–Telaquana Plateau has tundra similar to Alaska's North Slope, while the coast has forests similar to the southeast panhandle. Black bears and Dall's sheep reach their southern limits here, and Sitka spruce, Alaska's state tree, reaches its northern limit. Three rivers—the Mulchatna, Chilikadrotna, and Tlikakila—have been officially designated Wild and Scenic.

The Chigmit Mountains, spine of the park, are as rugged as mountains get. They lie on the edge of the North American plate where the oceanic plate slides beneath it, and their jumbled contours reflect centuries of geological violence. Three volcanoes—Spurr (north of the park), Iliamna, and Redoubt, otherwise known as "the steaming sisters"—are still active and vent gases regularly. Redoubt erupted in 1966, spewing clouds of ash 40,000 feet into the air; it erupted dramatically again in late 1989 and early 1990. The area averages one to two earthquakes per year that register at least a 5.0 on the Richter scale.

Archaeological finds show that humans, most recently Dena'ina Athapaskan, have lived in the area for nearly a thousand years. The Kijik National Historic Landmark is Alaska's largest known Athapaskan archaeological site.

The closest national park to Alaska's largest city, Lake Clark remains one of the least visited because of the logistics and expense involved in reaching it.

- Southwest Alaska
- 4 million acres
- Established 1980
- Best months June–mid-Sept.
- Hiking, white-water rafting and kayaking, fishing, hunting, cross-country skiing
- Information: 907-271-3751 www.nps.gov/lacl

Dogsledding in Lake Clark National Park and Preserve

How to Get There

Take a plane into the heart of the park, or a boat or plane to the coast. Charter a plane in Anchorage to Port Alsworth; or to Iliamna, 30 miles outside the park, and take an air taxi from there. Air taxis also fly from Homer and Kenai. To travel by boat, you must travel down Cook Inlet from Anchorage or across the inlet from Kenai.

When to Go

Summer. Wildflowers peak in late June, and fall colors in early September (upper elevations) and mid-September (lower). Daytime temperatures in June through August range from the 50s to low 60s in the park's eastern section and a bit higher in the western and interior areas.

How to Visit

Most visitors fly into the interior lake region. Air taxis can drop and pick up at prearranged locations. Smaller lakes offer excellent **kayaking;** several rivers give kayakers and rafters great white-water rides. **Hiking** is good around the lakes and from lake to lake. **Fishing** is usually first class. Contact park headquarters in Anchorage for information about guide services and lodges. Reserve early and make all arrangements in advance, or plan to be completely self-sufficient.

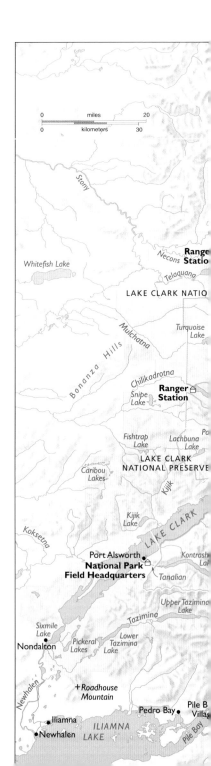

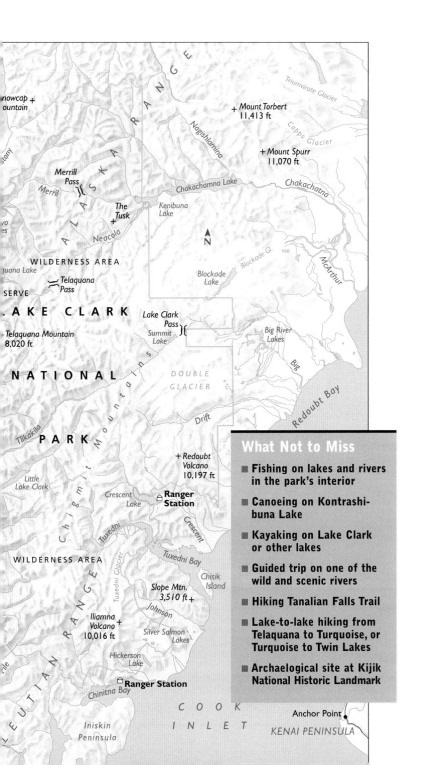

Snowcap
Mountain +

Stony

Merrill
Pass

Merrill

The
Tusk +

Neacola

WILDERNESS AREA

uana Lake

Telaquana
Pass

SERVE

LAKE CLARK

Telaquana Mountain
8,020 ft

NATIONAL

Tlikakila

PARK

Little
Lake Clark

WILDERNESS AREA

Iliamna +
Volcano
10,016 ft

Hickerson
Lake

Ranger Station

Iniskin
Peninsula

A L A S K A   R A N G E

Nagishlamina

+ Mount Torbert
11,413 ft

Triumvirate Glacier

Capps Glacier

+ Mount Spurr
11,070 ft

Chakachamna Lake

Chakachatna

Kenibuna
Lake

N

Blockade Gl.

McArthur

Blockade
Lake

Lake Clark
Pass

Summit
Lake

Big River
Lakes

Big

C h i g m i t   M o u n t a i n s

DOUBLE
GLACIER

Drift

Redoubt Bay

Redoubt
Volcano
10,197 ft

Crescent
Lake

Ranger
Station

Crescent

Tuxedni Glacier

Tuxedni

Tuxedni Bay

Chisik
Island

Slope Mtn.
3,510 ft +

Johnson

Silver Salmon
Lakes

A L E U T I A N   R A N G E

Chinitna Bay

COOK

INLET

Anchor Point

KENAI PENINSULA

What Not to Miss

- Fishing on lakes and rivers in the park's interior

- Canoeing on Kontrashi-buna Lake

- Kayaking on Lake Clark or other lakes

- Guided trip on one of the wild and scenic rivers

- Hiking Tanalian Falls Trail

- Lake-to-lake hiking from Telaquana to Turquoise, or Turquoise to Twin Lakes

- Archaeological site at Kijik National Historic Landmark

EXPLORING THE PARK

Lakes & Rivers

Most visitors head to the heart of Lake Clark National Park and Preserve, where pristine waterways and excellent hiking await. The flight in, through narrow, twisting mountain passes and heart-stoppingly beautiful country, is half the adventure.

Fishing is superb on the lakes and rivers of this mountain wilderness. Rainbow trout, arctic grayling, northern pike, and five kinds of salmon—king, chum, coho, humpback, and sockeye—lure anglers, many of whom take off from Port Alsworth, the site of the park's field headquarters.

As in many Alaska parks, a kayak in Lake Clark's wilderness is an invitation to freedom. You can explore large areas, carry a lot of gear, and take intermittent hikes as the mood strikes.

The park's large lakes, including **Telaquana, Turquoise,** and **Twin,** make for wonderful paddling trips. (They also offer access to good, though undeveloped, hiking.) To the southwest, **Upper** and **Lower Tazimina Lakes** are lovely, too, and closer to reach by floatplane. Of course, there's also stunning, 40-mile-long **Lake Clark** itself.

Soaking near Fishtrap Lake

Canoeists are partial to 13-mile-long **Kontrashibuna Lake.** *(Canoes must be flown in; ask your air taxi operator about boat-size restrictions.)* In the language of the Dena'ina Athapaskan people, Kontrashibuna means "lake in which water extends against the mountains." The narrow lake jogs between steep mountains and rushing creeks.

These lakes can be so still that they mirror the mountains without a ripple; that placidness, however, can change in a matter of minutes. Heed the advice about Lake Clark from Dena'ina elder Pete Trefon and apply it to any lake you paddle here: "If the wind starts to blow, get the hell off the lake!"

Another way to see the country is to let a river carry you through it. Only experienced river runners should attempt a trip (3 to 4 days on average) down one of the park's national wild and scenic rivers. If you have the chops, your options are the shallow and rocky Mulchatna, the swift and twisting Chilikadrotna, or the glacier-fed Tlikakila.

The **Mulchatna** flows from aptly named Turquoise Lake through the Bonanza Hills to the broader valley below. Access is by air taxi.

Known as "the Chilly," the **Chilikadrotna** experiences high water in June and August, when rafts and kayaks traverse Class II and III rapids through the wilderness. Begin your trip via air taxi to Twin Lakes, then fly out from any sandbar strip.

The small **Tlikakila** follows a major fault from Summit Lake to Lake Clark. The scenery en route—glaciers, sheer cliffs, waterfalls, craggy Chigmit peaks—is truly awesome. Be prepared to encounter Class IV rapids along this run. You can get here by floatplane to Summit Lake and depart by air taxi from Lake Clark or Port Alsworth, a 70-mile-long paddle.

Alternatively, you can opt for a kinder, gentler—and shorter (1 to 2 days)—run on the **Tanalian** or the Tazimina.

Hire a guide or check with rangers about water conditions, places to put in and take out, and landmarks and wildlife to watch for along the way.

Hiking

Lake Clark has no trail system and only one established hiking trail; therefore, you need to choose your route with care and be prepared with gear and supplies. Bring wind and rain gear for sudden changes in the weather, and repellent for mosquitoes.

Aerial view of Lake Clark

If you intend to hike without a guide, consult with a park ranger before starting out and take a good map with you.

Some general rules for hikers: Stay as long as possible on dry tundra where footing is good, avoid heavy brush, and choose your river crossings carefully. Hiking is generally best above 2,000 feet in the interior (where the dry tundra begins), or along the coast on any of the numerous gravel river bars. Below tree line, the vegetation can be thick and nearly impenetrable, especially the alder.

The park's only maintained route is the 2.5-mile-long **Tanalian Falls Trail.** Beginning in Port Alsworth *(trailhead just beyond the Homestead Cafe),* this easy hike takes you through a forest of black spruce and birch, past bogs and ponds, up along the tumbling Tanalian River, to Kontrashibuna Lake, and on to the falls, a half mile beyond. The country it leads through exemplifies all that is grand about this park. Watch for moose in the ponds, arctic grayling in the river, Dall's sheep on Tanalian Mountain, and bears everywhere.

Another hike from Port Alsworth is the strenuous 3,600-foot climb up **Tanalian Mountain.** You can begin the climb off the Tanalian Falls Trail, or by hiking the shore of Lake Clark and heading up a ridge where the walking is easier, a round-trip of about 7 miles.

North of Lake Clark, several lakes offer excellent hiking. You can take an air taxi to one and hike to another, or base yourself at one lake and day-hike along the shore and up the ridges.

If a lake-to-lake trek appeals to you, try the 16-mile hike from Telaquana Lake south to Turquoise Lake, or from Turquoise Lake 13 miles south to Twin Lakes. From Twin Lakes, you can hike 17 miles to **Portage Lake,** a beautiful tarn in an alpine valley, and from there another 11 miles to **Lachbuna Lake,** over a ridge and down the **Portage Creek** drainage to Lake Clark.

For a longer and more demanding hike through truly spectacular country, consider taking the 50-mile trek from Telaquana Lake east over **Telaquana Pass,** along the **Neacola River** to **Kenibuna Lake.** From there, you can continue your hike to the huge rock spire called **The Tusk.**

INFORMATION & ACTIVITIES

Headquarters
4230 University Dr. #311
Anchorage, AK 99508
907-271-3751
www.nps.gov/lacl

Seasons & Accessibility
There are no roads into or
inside the park. Lake Clark is
accessible year-round by small
aircraft from Anchorage, Kenai,
Homer, and Iliamna (1 to 2
hours flying time). Lake and
Peninsula Air (907-781-2228)
and Lake Clark Air (907-781-
2211) both fly direct from
Anchorage to Port Alsworth.
Other operators include
Iliamna Air Taxi (907-571-
1248), Kenai Fjords Outfitters
(907-235-6066), and Iliamna
Air Guides (907-571-1251).

Be prepared for sudden
changes in weather. Call park
field headquarters (907-781-
2218) for up-to-date conditions. If the weather starts to
close in, stay on the ground.
The best pilots in the world fly
through here, but a few are
overly bold.

Visitor & Information Centers
The park's field headquarters
with visitor center is located
in Port Alsworth, on the south
shore of Lake Clark (1 Park Pl.,
Port Alsworth, AK 99653. 907-
781-2218). For park or visitor
information, contact the
Anchorage or the Port
Alsworth office.

Entrance Fee
None.

Pets
Park recommends that you
leave your pets at home; they
can attract bears.

Facilities for Disabled
All park buildings and lodges
are accessible.

Things to Do
In summer, the park offers
minimal interpretive programs
(June–Sept.). Activities include
hiking, backpacking, climbing,
rafting, kayaking, fishing
(license required), bird-watching
and wildlife viewing, hunting
(in preserve), and flight-seeing.

Call or write headquarters
for a list of concessionaires
offering guide services in the
park, or visit www.nps.gov
/lacl/visiting_the_park.htm.

Special Advisories
■ Bring everything you will
need; no supplies are available
within the park.
■ You must possess excellent
wilderness skills if you intend
to hike, camp, or fish here
without a guide.

Cabin at Twin Lake

■ Do not trespass on or disturb property of local residents.
■ Be sure to bring insect repellent. A head net and insect-proof tent are also advised.

Overnight Backpacking

No permit required, but campers are encouraged to contact park field station before setting out *(907-781-2218)*.

Campgrounds

None. Backcountry camping only. No showers or other visitor amenities except in lodges. Rest rooms at the field headquarters in Port Alsworth.

Hotels, Motels, & Inns

(Unless otherwise noted, rates for two persons in a double room, high season.)

INSIDE THE PARK:
■ **Alaska's Wilderness Lodge** (on southern shore of Lake Clark). *(Summer):* 1 Wilderness Pt., Port Alsworth, AK 99653. *(Rest of year):* P.O. Box 700, Sumner, WA 98390. 800-835-8032. 7 cabins. $5,950 per person, per week. 7-day sport-fishing packages available. All-inclusive, with airfare. Open mid-June to early October.

OUTSIDE THE PARK:
■ **Newhalen Lodge** (on Six Mile Lake near Nondalton). 907-294-2233 *(lodge)* or 907-522-3355 *(all year)*. 9 rooms. $5,800 per person, per week, all inclusive. Sport-fishing packages. Open June to October.

Guides & Outfitters
Alaska Alpine Adventures
(877-525-2577. www.alaska alpineadventures.com) arranges custom-designed backpacking and river-running trips.

See pp. 246–49 or contact park headquarters for additional information on guides and outfitters.

Excursions near Lake Clark

Wood-Tichik State Park

125 miles
west of
Lake Clark

You can't get here from Lake Clark National Park and Preserve. But the detour is worth the extra effort, particularly if fishing happens to be your thing.

Alaska's most remote state park and at 1.6 million acres the largest state park in the United States, Wood-Tichik was created in 1978 to protect the area's fish and wildlife habitat. Named for its two separate drainages, each connecting a series of crystalline lakes, the park contains a landscape of diverse beauty. Mixed stands of white spruce and birch line lowland lakes and waterways, while black spruce sprinkle the open tundra and muskeg. Timberline extends to 900 feet, where alpine tundra, rocky slopes, and meadows take over. In the east, wet tundra, marshlands, and small ponds predominate.

Bordered on the west by the **Wood River Mountains** and on the east by the **Nushagak lowlands,** the park encompasses spired peaks, alpine valleys, and deep, fjordlike arms, as well as gravel beaches and expansive tundra. Fourteen major lakes, some 900 feet deep, vary in length up to 45 miles. The seven **Wood River Lakes** stretch about 30 miles west to east and are drained by the 21-mile-long **Wood River.** In the north lie the seven **Tikchik Lakes,** drained to the east by the **Nuyakuk River.**

Moose and brown bear can be seen almost anywhere in the park. You'll also spot black bear and caribou, and bald eagles, loons, spruce grouse, and myriad waterfowl. Spring and fall bring large flocks of migrating birds such as sandhill cranes and white-fronted geese.

But this is mainly an angler's heaven: All five species of Pacific salmon—king, red, pink, silver, chum—spawn in the park's river systems. Non-anadromous fish (those that do not migrate out to sea) include northern pike, lake trout, arctic char, Dolly Varden, whitefish, and rainbow trout.

What to See and Do
Fishing
These waters act as an enormous fish hatchery, rated by anglers as one of the world's premier fishing destinations. Some years more than three million red salmon return to Wood River Lakes, and over two million to Tikchik Lakes. Annual catches in Bristol Bay vary from 20 million to 25 million fish. Giant rainbow trout can weigh up

to 12 pounds and measure 28 inches long. Take two rods and plenty of flies or lures. Some waters are catch-and-release only; check rules.

Camping & Lodging

You can camp anywhere, but the park has four basic sites plus a first-come, first-served cabin on the Agulukpak River. Five private fishing lodges in the park cater to guests with advance reservations.

On the Water

You can access the area by air or chartered boat from Dillingham *(scheduled air service from Anchorage)* or from Aleknagik *(24 miles N of Dillingham)*. Most visitors are dropped off by aircraft, and depart by floating or paddling to a pick-up point. River trips are offered by Alaska Recreational River Guides *(907-376-8655)* and Tikchik State Park Tours *(907-243-8450 or 888-345-2445)*.

- 1.6 million acres ■ Southwest Alaska ■ Access by aircraft or boat
- Best months June–early Oct. ■ Boating, fishing, wildlife viewing
- Contact the park, 550 W. 7th Ave., Anchorage, AK 99501; 907-269-8698. www.dnr.state.ak.us/parks/units/woodtik.htm

Migrating caribou

Wrangell–St. Elias

E ven in a state famous for its size, Wrangell–St. Elias stands out. By far the largest national park and preserve in the United States—nearly six times the size of Yellowstone—it spans three climactic zones (maritime, continental, and alpine) and encompasses a spectacularly diverse palette of landscapes. Fly over this expanse of wilderness and you see mountains beyond mountains, gargantuan ice fields, endless rivers, miles of open tundra, and tide-scarred coastlines. Hike the tundra slopes in the company of grazing Dall's sheep and mountain goats.

Four major mountain ranges converge here: the volcanic Wrangells, the Alaska, the Chugach, and the St. Elias—the tallest coastal mountains in the world. Together they contain 9 of the nation's 16 highest peaks, 4 of them above 16,000 feet.

Beneath Wrangell–St. Elias, the Pacific plate collides with and slides under the Continental plate, creating faults, earthquakes, and volcanoes. Some of the world's most powerful quakes have jolted the region. And steam continues to vent from the park's active volcanoes, including Mount Wrangell, one of North America's largest.

In contrast with this volcanic heat is the perpetual blanket of ice and snow covering roughly a third of the park. Among the more than 150 glaciers here, the Malaspina, measuring some 850 square miles, is larger than the state of Rhode Island. Ninety-two-mile-long Hubbard Glacier, the continent's longest, is also the most active tidewater glacier.

In 1980, the wilderness protected by Wrangell–St. Elias and Glacier Bay National Parks, and Canada's Tatshenshini–Alsek Provincial and Kluane National Parks became a United Nations World Heritage site.

This vast preserve is not a fortress. Two roads lead to communities born during the gold- and copper-mining boom in the early 1900s. Today it's the prospect of finding pristine wildness, not gold, that beckons present-day travelers to this region.

- South-central Alaska, 189 miles east of Anchorage
- 13.2 million acres
- Established 1980
- Best months June–August
- Camping, hiking, kayaking, fishing, wildlife viewing, river trips
- Information: 907-822-5234. www.nps.gov/wrst

Kennecott, Wrangell–St. Elias National Park

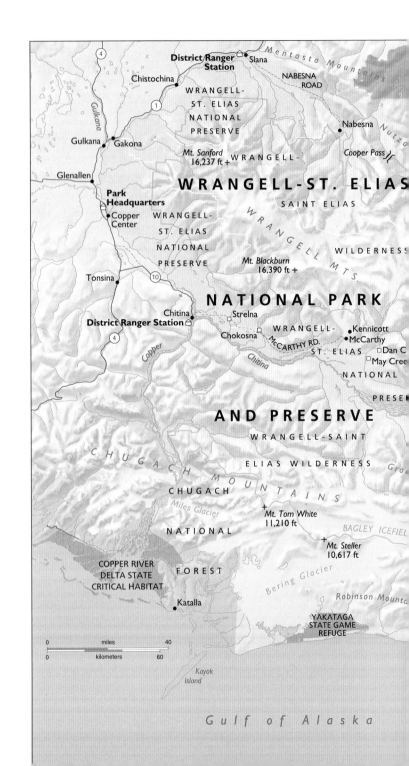

District Ranger Station
Slana
Chistochina
Mentasta Mountains
NABESNA ROAD
WRANGELL-
ST. ELIAS
NATIONAL
PRESERVE
Nabesna
Nutzo
Cooper Pass
Gulkana
Gakona
Mt. Sanford
16,237 ft +
WRANGELL-
Glenallen
WRANGELL-ST. ELIAS
SAINT ELIAS
Park
Headquarters
Copper
Center
WRANGELL-
ST. ELIAS
NATIONAL
PRESERVE
W R A N G E L L   M T S.
WILDERNESS
Mt. Blackburn
16,390 ft +
Tonsina
10
NATIONAL PARK
Chitina
Strelna
District Ranger Station
4
Copper
Chokosna
WRANGELL-
McCARTHY RD.
Kennicott
McCarthy
Dan C
May Cree
Chitina
ST. ELIAS
NATIONAL
PRESE
AND PRESERVE
WRANGELL-SAINT
ELIAS WILDERNESS
Gra
C H U G A C H
M O U N T A I N S
CHUGACH
Miles Glacier
Mt. Tom White
11,210 ft
BAGLEY ICEFIEL
NATIONAL
Mt. Steller
10,617 ft
Bering Glacier
Robinson Mounta
COPPER RIVER
DELTA STATE
CRITICAL HABITAT
FOREST
Katalla
YAKATAGA
STATE GAME
REFUGE
0   miles   40
0   kilometers   60
Kayak
Island
Gulf of Alaska

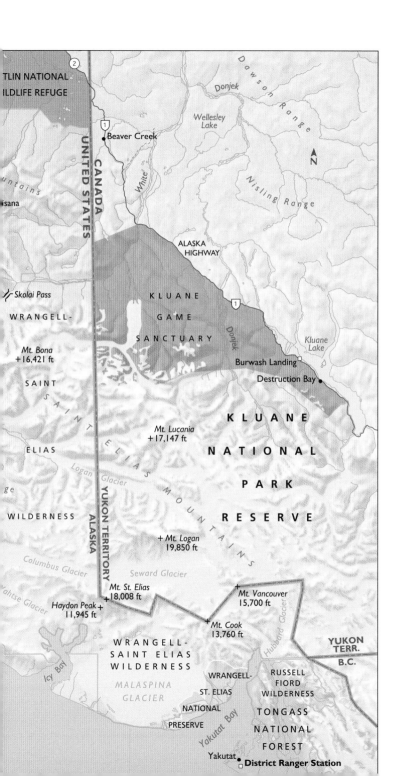

TLIN NATIONAL
ILDLIFE REFUGE

②

Donjek

Dowson Range

Wellesley
Lake

① Beaver Creek

White

CANADA
UNITED STATES

Nisling Range

ALASKA
HIGHWAY

N

Skolai Pass

WRANGELL-

KLUANE

GAME

SANCTUARY

①

Donjek

Kluane
Lake

Mt. Bona
+16,421 ft

Burwash Landing

SAINT

Destruction Bay

S A I N T

ELIAS

Logan

Glacier

YUKON TERRITORY
ALASKA

KLUANE

NATIONAL

PARK

RESERVE

Mt. Lucania
+17,147 ft

ge

WILDERNESS

E L I A S   M O U N T A I N S

+ Mt. Logan
19,850 ft

Columbus Glacier

Seward Glacier

ahtse Glacier

Mt. St. Elias
+18,008 ft

Haydon Peak +
11,945 ft

+ Mt. Vancouver
15,700 ft

Hubbard Glacier

+ Mt. Cook
13,760 ft

YUKON
TERR.

B.C.

Icy Bay

WRANGELL-
SAINT ELIAS
WILDERNESS

MALASPINA
GLACIER

WRANGELL-
ST. ELIAS

NATIONAL

PRESERVE

RUSSELL
FIORD
WILDERNESS

TONGASS

NATIONAL

FOREST

Yakutat Bay

Yakutat

□ District Ranger Station

How to Get There

Charter a plane or drive. By car from Anchorage, take Alas. 1 (Glenn Hwy.) 189 miles northeast to Glennallen; continue northeast for 74 miles along the Copper River and the park's western boundary to Slana, where an unpaved road branches into the park for 42 miles, ending at the town of Nabesna.

Or, head toward the town of McCarthy on Alas. 4 (Richardson Hwy.) from Glennallen 32 miles southeast to the Edgerton cutoff (Alas. 10), then turn left and continue 33 miles to Chitina. There the pavement ends and the road follows an old railroad bed for about 60 miles into the park.

These same roads can be reached from Fairbanks via Delta Junction, and from Haines, Skagway, and Whitehorse (along Alaska–Canada Hwy. in the Yukon) via Haines Junction and Tok. In summer, buses run regularly from Anchorage to Valdez with stops in Glennallen.

Air charters into the park operate out of Anchorage, Fairbanks, Yakutat, Cordova, Glennallen, Gulkana, Tok, Chitina, McCarthy, Nabesna, and Northway. Commercial jets service Yakutat and Cordova year-round.

What Not to Miss

- **Driving the McCarthy Road to historic mining town of McCarthy**
- **Biking or hiking from McCarthy to ghost town of Kennecott, a National Historic Landmark**
- **Driving the scenic Nabesna Road from Slana to old mining town of Nabesna**
- **Rafting or kayaking down one of the park's five rivers**
- **Hiking Trail Creek and Lost Creek Trails to Copper River Basin**

In summer, the Alaska State Ferry serves Valdez from Whittier and Seward (reachable by car from Anchorage).

When to Go

Summer. Lodges and guide services operate in the park from about mid-May through the end of September. June is best for wildflowers, while berries ripen in August. July generally has the warmest daytime temperatures. Be prepared for cloudy skies, although September can be clear and beautiful, with colorful autumn foliage, no mosquitoes, and a dusting of new snow on the mountain peaks. March and April offer excellent cross-country skiing for those of stout heart and strong will.

How to Visit

Take one of the two unpaved roads into the park. The **Mc-Carthy Road** is usually passable in summer; 4WD may be required. Stop at park headquarters in Copper Center for the latest road conditions. The **Slana–Nabesna Road** is also maintained. Both access trail-heads for backcountry hikes.

Or, charter a plane into a remote part of the park and hike or run a river. Several commercial companies offer guided rafting or kayaking trips on the rivers and in the spectacular coastal bays. You can request a full list from the park.

Crossing a stream near McCarthy

EXPLORING THE PARK

McCarthy Road to Kennecott: 61 miles one way; a half day

Two roads penetrate the interior of Wrangell–St. Elias National
Park and Preserve. The McCarthy Road leads to the historic mining town of **Kennecott,** now a virtual ghost town, and to the extant
town of **McCarthy.** This is the only settled area within the park.

There's a mystique about this narrow dirt road, partly because it
winds through prime Alaskan wilderness, but mostly because it is
so bad for a route that can be negotiated without four-wheel drive.
Mostly washboard and pitted with ruts, it becomes slippery during
rainy weather. It also crosses several small streams without benefit
of culverts—and it eats tires. In addition to its crop of pointy
rocks, it runs along the abandoned Copper River and Northwest
Railroad bed, which occasionally produces spikes and other debris.

If you intend to brave the McCarthy on your own, stop at the
Chitina Ranger Station *(907-822-5234. Mem. Day–Labor Day)* and
inquire about current conditions. Allow about three hours one way
(and consider bringing two spare tires).

From the town of Chitina, and the confluence of the Chitina
and Copper Rivers, follow the road into the park. At Mile 17, you'll

Kennicott Glacier Lodge, Wrangell–St. Elias National Park

cross the historic 525-foot-long **Kuskulana River Bridge,** a one-lane span hovering 238 feet above the river. Another abandoned railroad trestle spans the **Gilahina River** at Mile 28.5.

The roads ends at a parking lot and the **Kennicott River**. To reach the old towns of McCarthy and Kennecott, you'll have to park your car and walk across the river on the footbridge. On the east bank, follow the road for about a quarter of a mile. The right fork leads to McCarthy (about a mile), the left to Kennecott (5 miles).

A tiny community of some 35 hardy, year-round residents, McCarthy had a population near 2,000 in its heyday. The town boasts a store, gift shops, a lodge, guides, air taxis, and shuttle service to Kennecott. Stop by the little **Kennecott/McCarthy Historical Museum** *(for information, call McCarthy Lodge, 907-554-4402. Daily Mem. Day–Labor Day),* which brims with intriguing details such as the program for the town's 1929 Fourth of July events.

From McCarthy, a dirt road climbs 500 feet in 5 miles to the decaying town of Kennecott, which was declared a national historic landmark in 1978. If you prefer not to walk, you can take a taxi or rent a bike in McCarthy.

The Kennecott Mines Company operated from 1906 to 1938. (The variation in spelling is due to the fact that the company misspelled the name of the Alaska explorer after whom the valley's glacier was named.) Completion of the railroad in 1911 spurred full-scale copper and silver production here. (Kennecott was once the site of the world's richest copper mine.) Five area mines supplied ore to the 13-story mill, which eventually processed a billion pounds of copper and 10 billion ounces of silver.

Today, the silent mill and dozens of other structures, still covered in mineral-oxide red with white trim, remain reasonably intact. Currently under renovation, they are one of Alaska's most photogenic collections of historic structures.

After exploring Kennecott, you can hike the **trail** north of town for fine views of the **Kennicott** and **Root Glaciers** and **Mount Blackburn.**

Nabesna Road: 45 miles one way; a half day

Travelers who wish to explore the park by car can also drive the Nabesna Road. Except for the first 4 miles, the road is gravel and full of potholes; portions are subject to washouts. Stop at the Slana Ranger Station *(907-822-5238. Early June–early Sept.)* to inquire about conditions before you set out.

From just outside the park's northern boundary in **Slana** *(Mile 59.8 on Glenn Hwy. or Mile 63 on Tok Cutoff),* the road winds into the **Wrangell Mountains** to the old mining town of **Nabesna.** For the first few miles, you pass through dense black-spruce forest, habitat of diurnal northern hawk owls. Pull off at Mile 7 and walk down to **Rufus Creek,** a popular fishing spot for grayling and Dolly Varden trout.

Just past Mile 15, a lovely pond on the road's northeast side offers a great view of the **Mentasta Mountains.** In season, this plateau is rife with lupines, chiming bells, arnica, and other wildflowers. Dwarf birch and willow provide cover for willow ptarmigan and arctic ground squirrels. Blueberries and low-bush cranberries reward late-summer hikers and attract brown bears. In midsummer, watch for moose here and at other ponds. In early spring and late fall, migrating caribou often cross the road. Red foxes are often seen in late evening and early morning.

The road climbs over the watershed divide *(Mile 25)* between the **Copper River,** which drains into the Gulf of Alaska, and the **Nabesna River,** which drains into the Tanana and Yukon Rivers, and finally the Bering Sea. There are excellent views of **Mount Sanford** and the **Copper Glacier** to the southwest.

You can access **Twin Lakes** from the Mile 28 pull-off. Beyond this popular fishing spot, the road starts to deteriorate and a few streams must be forded; the final 4 miles, from Devil's Mountain Lodge to Nabesna, are the most rugged. *(Caution: Don't travel beyond Mile 28 unless you have a high-clearance, 4WD vehicle.)* If you are equipped, and if conditions are right, the drive on to Nabesna town offers unsurpassed mountain views.

At Mile 41, a trail leads to the Nabesna River and to an old airstrip once used by miners to fly out their gold ore. **Devils Mountain** rises to the left of the trail. Look across the river to spot Dall's sheep.

Morning fog at Nabesna

Other Hikes & Water Trips

At Mile 13.5 on the McCarthy Road, the **Nugget Creek–Kotsina Road** branches northeast 2.5 miles to the **Nugget Creek Trail.** Sixteen miles later and a thousand feet higher, the trail arrives at a public-use cabin beneath Mount Blackburn, where you can camp. A dozen good day hikes lead from here. A half-mile-plus past the Nugget Creek Trailhead begins the strenuous **Dixie Pass Trail,** which climbs 3,600 feet in 10 miles; if the weather is clear, it's worth the effort.

Off the Nabesna Road, look for **Trail Creek** *(Mile 30)* and **Lost Creek** *(Mile 30.8).* There are no defined trails; simply follow the creek beds north as far as you like. The hiking is not generally difficult, but you may have to hop or wade creeks. Excellent views of the upper Copper River basin await. If you plan to overnight, talk to a ranger.

Commercial outfitters offer rafting trips of varying difficulty down the Nabesna, Kennicott, Copper, Chitina, and Nizina Rivers. Short trips last 3 hours, extended ones 2 weeks. Contact the park for a listing of outfitters that operate there, or see pp. 246-49.

INFORMATION & ACTIVITIES

Headquarters
P.O. Box 439, Copper Center, AK 99573; 907-822-5234. www.nps.gov/wrst

Seasons & Accessibility
Park open year-round; best time to visit is mid-May through September. Snow limits winter access. Call park headquarters to ascertain road conditions before attempting to drive into the park.

Visitor & Information Centers
Park headquarters is located at Mile 106.8 on Old Richardson Highway at western edge of the park (daily Mem. Day–Labor Day, weekdays rest of year). Information also available outside the park at Yakutat, Slana, and Chitina Ranger Stations (Chitina closed Oct.–May.)

Entrance Fee
None.

Pets
Permitted on leash except in public buildings and off leash in the backcountry.

Facilities for Disabled
None.

Things to Do
The park offers no organized activities, but the following are available to visitors: hiking, horseback riding (rentals in McCarthy) and pack trips, river running, kayaking, jet boating, lake fishing, mountain climbing, flight-seeing, and cross-country skiing.

Contact park headquarters for a list of companies that offer guide and outfitting services, or visit the park's website at www.nps.gov/wrst/wrstcommercialservices.htm

Special Advisories
■ This is a wilderness park; hikers and backpackers must be completely self-sufficient. Do not attempt to enter the backcountry without a guide unless you have extensive wilderness experience and proper gear.
■ Exercise caution when and where you cross rivers; many are impassable.
■ Be respectful of native camps, fishnets, and other private property.
■ Mosquitoes can be brutal in June, July, and August; bring repellent, a head net, and an insect-proof tent.

Overnight Backpacking
Permit not required, but it's best to register before going into the backcountry.

Alaskan malamute

Campgrounds

There are two private campgrounds within the park: Tram Station Campground *(907-554-4401)* and Glacier View Campground *(907-554-4490)* are located at the end of McCarthy Road. You can also camp at several roadside pull-outs along Nabesna Road; first come, first served. No fee.

Outside the park, Silver Lake Campground *(Mile 9.3 on McCarthy Rd.)* offers camping and limited services.

The park maintains 12 public-use cabins. Fees $15 per night. Contact park headquarters for information.

Hotels, Motels, & Inns

(Unless otherwise noted, rates are for two persons in a double room, high season.)

INSIDE THE PARK:

■ **Kennicott Glacier Lodge** (in Kennecott) P.O. Box 103940, Anchorage, AK 99510. 907-258-2350 or 800-582-5128. 25 rooms, shared baths. $179 per person, including meals.

■ **Ma Johnson's Hotel** (in McCarthy, part of historic McCarthy Lodge) P.O. Box MXY, McCarthy, AK 99588. 907-554-4402. 20 rooms, semiprivate baths; amenities package available. $159, including full breakfast and shuttle service. www.mccarthy lodge.com

OUTSIDE THE PARK:

■ **Copper Center Lodge** (Mile 101.5 on Old Richardson Hwy.) Drawer J, Copper Center, AK 99573. 907-822-3245. 21 rooms, 11 with private baths. $109–$129. Restaurant.

■ **Gakona Lodge** (Mile 2 on Tok Cutoff) P.O. Box 285, Gakona, AK 99586. 907-822-3482. 1 cabin, private bath $100; 8 rooms, shared baths $80. Restaurant. Open May through September.

Contact headquarters for additional accommodations in and near the park.

Excursions from Wrangell

Glenn Highway

Between Glennallen and Anchorage

189 miles long, 1 day This drive angles across south-central Alaska, starting at the foot of the wild Wrangell Mountains and following glacier-carved river valleys, framed by the towering peaks of the Chugach and Talkeetna Mountains, to Cook Inlet and Anchorage.

The Wrangell peaks, among the highest in Wrangell–St. Elias, dominate easterly vistas as you leave Glennallen and the junction with Alas. 4, the **Richardson Highway** *(see pp. 230–33).* At Mile 176.6, a turnout affords a fine view east across **Copper River Valley** to the Wrangells. An interpretive sign identifies 14,163-foot **Mount Wrangell,** a steaming, semidormant volcano.

A side road at Mile 159.8 leads 20 miles to **Lake Louise,** a good spot for fishing and boating. The so-called "drunken forests" seen in this area are the result of trees growing in soil too soggy to hold them upright. **Tazlina Glacier** and 20-mile-long **Tazlina Lake** appear near Mile 156.

Abundant meltwater keeps hundreds of lakes and ponds filled to the brim.

Looking east from Mile 131, you'll see the **Wrangell Mountains,** whose highest elevations exceed 16,000 feet. This is caribou country; watch for migrating herds in autumn. The views are splendid from 3,322-foot **Eureka Summit** *(Mile 129.3),* the Glenn's loftiest pass and the divide of the Matanuska, Susitna, and Copper river systems.

Around 3,000-foot-high **Tahneta Pass** *(Mile 122),* sparse stands of stunted black spruce struggle to survive in sodden muskeg.

Between Miles 118 and 107, look for Dall's sheep on **Sheep Mountain** (6,300 feet) to the north. Wildflowers bloom profusely along this stretch, including pink fireweed (named for its quick reappearance after fires) and yellow-eyed, blue-petaled alpine forget-me-not, the state flower. Turnouts at Miles 107.8 and 102.8 offer great photo ops.

Trails from **Matanuska Glacier State Recreation Site** *(Mile 101)* lead to unobstructed views of 1,000-foot-thick **Matanuska Glacier**. *(Access to base is via private road from Mile 102; contact*

Moose crossing Glenn Highway

Matanuska Visitor Bureau, 907-745-2534. Adm. fee.) Striated by broken rock, the glacier flows 27 miles from 13,000-foot-high Chugach ice fields. It once reached Knik Arm, flowing through what is now the Matanuska Valley.

At Mile 93, you can see **Monument Glacier,** a rock glacier formed from the stony debris carried by an ice glacier. Turnouts at Miles 71 and 70.6 offer river access.

Heading west, the highway follows the **Matanuska River.** Aspen and cottonwood provide beautiful autumn color along this stretch, and there's an impressive view of 4,541-foot **Pinnacle Mountain** at Mile 66.5, where the clear **Kings River** joins the muddy Matanuska.

Just outside Palmer, visit the **Musk Ox Farm** *(907-745-4151. www.muskoxfarm.org. Early May–late Sept.; adm. fee)* breeds the hoofed, shaggy survivors of the Ice Age that were hunted nearly to extinction in the 19th century. Their ultralight underwool, called qiviut, is worked by an Eskimo knitting cooperative.

About a mile farther on is the **Independence Mine State Historical Park** *(see pp. 228–29, 907-745-2827. www.dnr.state.ak.us/parks/ units/indmine.htm. June–Labor Day; fee for tours),* a relic from gold-mining days.

About 17 miles east, you reach **Palmer,** a pleasant town of 3,000 people in the Matanuska Valley named for the river that irrigates its rich farmlands. Here the old and new roads split. Take the **Old Glenn Highway** and loop 18.6 miles through the **Matanuska Valley Colony,** a Depression-era agricultural project that relocated some 200 impoverished Great Lakes farm families.

Back on the main highway, Alaska's Athapaskan and Russian heritage live on at the **Eklutna Historical Park** *(Mile 26 exit. 907-688-6026. www.eklutna.com. Adm. fee),* where Orthodox churches and colorful cemetery "spirit houses" combine Russian-Slavic and Tanaina Athapaskan design.

Downtown Anchorage

As you drive toward Anchorage, the highway skirts Knik Arm, a fjord off Cook Inlet, and the western reach of the Chugach Mountains. Great views and the possibility of seeing moose, bear, and Dall's sheep justify a 13-mile side trip to **Eagle River Nature Center** in **Chugach State Park** *(see pp. 160–66; Eagle River exit at Mile 12. 907-694-2108. www.ernc.org. May–Labor Day).*

■ **Glennallen to Anchorage on Alas. 1** ■ **Be aware of heavy traffic, winter frost heaves and bumps, and many dangerously narrow stretches.** ■ **June–mid-Sept.** ■ **Hiking, wildlife viewing, auto tour**

Independence Mine State Historical Park

130 miles west of Wrangell   Nestled in a beautiful bowl of meadows and wild-flowers—bluebells and wild geraniums and arctic sandworts—and surrounded by jagged peaks and terrific ridges for hiking, Independence Mine offers a fascinating journey through one of Alaska's hard-rock gold-mining operations.

Independence Mine in the Willow Creek Mining District was one of Alaska's greatest gold producers in the 1930s. The old mine buildings and equipment are preserved today in this historical park, which is located in the Hatcher Pass area. You can see dilapidated shafts high above on the mountainsides and ruins of gold mines drilled or blasted deep into the mountains.

A narrow, dirt road twists along **Willow Creek** and leads you up to Hatcher Pass. The river flows down from **Mint Glacier** and still carries traces of that elusive, glittering pay dirt that lured so many hardy souls into this country. In winter, Hatcher Pass gets generous amounts of snow, making it a great destination for early and late cross-country skiing. (It's also suspectible to avalanches of serious proportions).

To reach the park, drive past Palmer on the **Glenn Highway.** At

Independence Mine, Hatcher Pass

WRANGELL–ST. ELIAS NATIONAL PARK

Mile 49.1, take **Fishhook-Willow Road,** which becomes the **Hatcher Pass Road** as it winds along Little Susitna River up the canyon into the mountains. At Mile 17, continue straight on to the access road to Independence Mine, another 1.2 miles.

The visitor center, located in the old mine manager's house, is open daily in summer *(usually June–mid-Sept.)*. Have a look at the center's interpretive displays, then head out to explore the park along the self-guided **Hard Rock Trail.** A guided tour *(fee)* will get you inside the mine buildings.

Hiking

Located above tree line, the area offers wonderful alpine hiking in virtually all directions. There are no established trails here so just pick a ridge and head for it. *(Caution: road to the pass is steep, narrow, and often muddy, making it unsafe for campers or trailers.)* In summer, you can save yourself some effort by driving to the highest point, 3,886-foot-high **Hatcher Pass,** and then walking up from there to the top of a ridge.

If you're more inclined toward a real trail, try the popular day outing to **Reed Lake** (6 to 8 miles). There you can hop boulders, relax by a waterfall, and look for ptarmigan, marmots, and eagles.

Backcountry Skiing

In winter, skiers flock to Hatcher Pass because it usually has skiable snow long before (and after) most other places near Anchorage. You can cross-country ski on groomed trails or carve your own route up the mountains with cross-country, mountaineering, or telemark skis.

Always use caution. As the experts say, pay attention to the clues Mother Nature is giving you. Avalanches are common and several backcountry travelers have been buried here in past years.

■ 761 acres ■ 67 miles northeast of Anchorage ■ Avalanches can close Hatcher Pass Rd. in winter. Chains or 4WD advisable ■ Year-round; road over Hatcher Pass from Independence Mine to Willow side usually closed by snow Oct.–July ■ Hiking, cross-country skiing, sledding, snowboarding, paragliding, berry picking, tours ■ Fee for use of groomed cross-country ski trails ■ Contact the visitor center (open seasonally); 907-745-2827. Or Alaska Division of Parks, HC 32, Box 6706, Wasilla, AK 99654; 907-745-3975. www.dnr.state.ak.us/parks/parks.htm

Richardson Highway

115 miles long, one-half day The Richardson Highway got its start as a treacherous gold-rush trail leading to the Klondike. This portion of the historic route travels through south-central Alaska, skirting volcano country, passing through tundra and forest, and arcing over barren ridges where glaciers slide from ice fields.

Begin east of Glennallen by driving south on the Richardson Highway from its junction with the **Glenn Highway** *(see pp. 224–27).* Stop at the viewpoint near Mile 112 for a long vista across the Copper River to a quartet of snowcapped peaks. These are the highest peaks in the **Wrangell Mountains.** The tallest two, **Mount Sanford** and **Mount Blackburn,** exceed 16,000 feet.

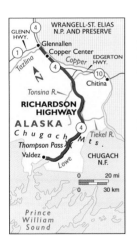

Near Mile 111 you'll cross the **Tazlina River,** where there's a perfect spot for a picnic. The Tazlina (which means "swift river" in Athapaskan) flows from the **Tazlina Glacier,** north of Valdez, into the Copper River at Glennallen.

From Mile 106, a 6.5-mile loop road leads to **Copper Center,** a gold rush-era refuge for snowbound tenderfeet. The vintage log Copper Center Lodge *(907-822-3245)* offers rustic rooms and sourdough-style fare.

Two adjoining, old log bunkhouses contain the **George Ashby Memorial Museum** *(June–Aug. Mon.–Sat.),* an eclectic display of artifacts, including items from early Russian settlements.

At Mile 105 *(between Copper Center loop road turnoffs),* you come to the Wrangell–St. Elias National Park and Preserve Visitor Center *(907-822-5234. www.nps.gov/wrst. Daily Mem. Day–Labor Day, Mon.–Fri. rest of year).*

Heading south from here, you'll cross rolling hills covered with paper birch, black spruce, and willow. This area was favored by homesteaders who arrived here in the early 20th century. The **Willow Lake Turnoff** *(Mile 87.7)* offers an excellent view of the Wrangell Mountains' ice fields.

A mile farther on, you'll pass the roaring trans-Alaska pipeline system's **Pump Station 11.** Two or three pumps move about 1.8

million barrels of oil a day a distance of 800 miles, from Prudhoe Bay to Port Valdez.

At Mile 82.6, the **Edgerton Highway** offers an easy, 33-mile-long side trip to **Chitina,** a former railroad stop and supply center on the Copper River. In the summer, hordes of dip-netters gather here for the annual salmon runs.

Back on the Richardson, across from **Tonsina Lodge** *(Mile 79)* you'll see layers of silt, sediments, and cobbles left by melting icebergs, evidence of the deep glacial lake that once covered the area. As you travel through the **Tiekel River Valley,** watch for moose grazing along the 20-mile stretch beginning at the **Little Tonsina River State Recreation Area** *(Mile 65.1. 907-762-2261).* There's an interpretive viewpoint nearby at **Pump Station 12.**

Silence prevails again along the **Tiekel River,** where, beginning around Mile 60, you'll see beaver dams and lodges. In summer, deep red dwarf fireweed and blue arctic lupine decorate the roadside. The riverside rest area at Mile 47.9 lets you gaze up at 7,217-foot **Mount Billy Mitchell.** A couple of miles beyond, **Stuart Creek** attracts nesting trumpeter swans in spring and summer.

As the highway angles through the **Tsina River Valley,** notice the sheer cliffs rising from the moraines, worn smooth by passing glaciers. When the valley narrows, stop to listen to the murmur of rushing streams and take in the nearly 360-degree panorama of soaring peaks. From here the highway climbs to **Worthington Glacier** *(Mile 28.7).*

Fishing from a floatplane, Willow Lake

Columbia Glacier, Valdez Arm

Continue on to barren 2,678-foot **Thompson Pass** *(Mile 26; see pp. 234–35),* which holds Alaska's seasonal snowfall record: 81 feet! Snow patches on the pass often last through summer. Push your hand into one: Its density suggests how the weight of accumulating snow layers compacts the underlayers into ice so dense that its crystals absorb all but the blue spectrum of light, thus giving glaciers their distinctive blue color.

The stone ramparts of the Chugach Mountains loom as you descend to **Heiden Canyon** and **Blueberry Lake State Recreation Site** *(907-762-2261),* considered one of Alaska's most idyllic alpine settings. Around Mile 16, you'll enter precipitous **Keystone Canyon.** White-water enthusiasts relish the challenges of the **Lowe River,** which tumbles through the gorge. Look above the highway for terraced remnants of the original **Valdez–Eagle Trail,** built for horse-drawn sleds and wagons. Violent feuds among competing early railroaders left the roadside tunnel *(Mile 14.9)* unfinished. Along this stretch, waterfalls cascade into the canyon.

You'll emerge from Keystone Canyon beside the gravel plain of the Lowe River Delta and cross the moraine of **Valdez Glacier** *(Mile 0.9).* **Valdez Arm,** an 11-mile-long fjord, is America's northernmost ice-free harbor. The old Valdez townsite was abandoned after its waterfront was submerged during the devastating 1964 earthquake.

As you approach **Valdez,** watch for **Duck Flat,** a migratory water-fowl sanctuary. Also near here is **Crooked Creek,** where spawning salmon converge in midsummer and fall. An observation platform

The Great Alaska Quake of '64

On the evening of March 27, 1964, the strongest earthquake ever recorded in the history of North America struck Alaska. From its epicenter in Prince William Sound, the earthquake sent shock waves over an area 500 miles wide, releasing twice as much energy as the San Francisco Earthquake of 1906 and moving more earth horizontally and vertically than previous quakes. In the month that followed, residents suffered through some 9,000 aftershocks, registering more than 6.0 on the Richter scale.

The earthquake, which measured 8.6 on the Richter scale (9.2 on the revised moment-magnitude scale used today), led to the deaths of 131 people. But it wasn't the quake itself that claimed 90 percent of those lives; it was the tsunamis, or ocean waves, generated by it. So powerful were these tsunamis that their effects were felt as far away as Antarctica.

The word "tsunami" is Japanese for "harbor wave," though the more scientific definition is "seismic wave." In the 1970s, the United Nations officially adopted the Japanese term to describe the phenomenon of ocean waves created by an earthquake, a large landslide, a volcanic eruption, or a man-made nuclear explosion.

In the open ocean, a tsunami can travel up to 600 miles per hour. The tsunamis created by the 1964 earthquake rushed into Prince William Sound in enormous waves; some reached a height of 90 feet at the point where they crashed onto the shore. The tsunamis savaged the Alaska coast from Cordova all the way to Kodiak, destroying entire towns.

allows visitors to get an up-close look at the fish.

In town, don't miss the superb **Valdez Museum** *(907-835-2764. www.alaska.net/~vldzmuse. Daily in summer, Mon.–Sat. fall–spring; adm. fee)*, which celebrates the region's human and geologic history. Also stop by the **Alyeska Pipeline Visitor Center** *(Tatitlek St. 907-835-2686)* for information about the history and construction of the pipeline.

■ **Glennallen to Valdez on Alaska 4** ■ **June–mid-Sept.** ■ **Mileposts show mileages in reverse, from Valdez to Glennallen** ■ **Wildlife viewing, auto tour**

Thompson Pass

80 miles southwest of Wrangell

Helicopter skiing in Thompson Pass, a former site of the World Extreme Skiing Championships, has boomed as word of the area's exceptional skiing conditions has gotten around.

The location of the pass—one of the highest points on the Richardson Highway, where it crosses the Chugach mountain range—has proved ideal. Winter storms roll in from the Gulf of Alaska, piling clouds heavy with precipitation up against the mountains. These create snowfalls favorable for good powder conditions on the steep-angled slopes cherished by daredevil skiers.

In fact, snowfalls in Thompson Pass are legendary: The pass holds the record in Alaska for the most snow in a single season (81 feet in 1953), the most snow in a month (29 feet in February of 1964), and the most snow in a single day (more than 5 feet on December 29, 1955).

Helicopter guiding services, such as Alaska Backcountry Adventures *(907-835-5608 or 888-283-9354. March–April)* deliver skiers to the tops of mountains for a day of schussing down breathtakingly precipitous slopes. Local guides are knowledgeable about avalanche risks; before you attempt helicopter skiing, you too should be trained to assess dangers, understand precautions, and know what gear to take with you.

A third of Alaska's major ice fields lie in south-central Alaska. If you're into ice climbing, the area around **Valdez** has one of the largest concentrations of ice routes in the world. Among these are the intriguingly named Wowie-Zowie, Hung Jury, and Bridal Veil Falls, all of which are located in **Keystone Canyon,** right off the Richardson Highway. The **Valdez Ice Climbing Festival** *(907-835-5182)* draws the top national and international climbers every February to compete on the frozen waterfalls of Keystone Canyon en route to Thompson Pass.

If you prefer summer activities, you'll find the meadows and mountains here perfect for summer walking. The pass, which lies above tree line, is covered with beautiful alpine wildflowers, such as fireweed, lupine, and mountain harebell.

In **Worthington Glacier State Recreation Area** *(907-262-5581)* at Mile 28.7 on the Richardson Highway, look for the mile-long **Worthington Glacier View Trail.** The path will take you right to the edge of this picture-postcard glacier.

From here you can pick any ridge, meadow, or hill as your destination and set out on your own path. For those who prefer the company of an expert, there are a variety of guided hikes along the ridges of Thompson Pass. Contact **Thompson Pass Treks,** the guiding service of the **Thompson Pass Chalet** *(907-835-4817. www.alaskagold.com/tpass/scenic.htm).* Along with the exercise, you'll benefit from your guides' knowledge about the area's history and natural history.

Bikers can tour the Thompson Pass along the Richardson Highway. There are no formal off-road trails, but the vistas from the road are spectacular.

■ **2,678 feet** ■ **30 miles from Valdez at Mile 26 on Richardson Hwy.**
■ **Best months March–April and June–Sept.** ■ **Hiking, biking, downhill and cross-country skiing, snowshoeing, snowboarding** ■ **Contact Valdez Visitor Information Center, 200 Fairbanks Dr., Valdez, AK 99686; 907-835-2984. www.valdezalaska.org**

Viewing Thompson Pass

Prince William Sound

100 miles southwest of Wrangell

In 1899, America's crème de la crème of scientists and artists boarded a luxury steamship, the *George W. Elder,* in Seattle and headed north for wild Alaska. The allure? Hundreds of miles of uncharted glaciers and coasts, a bevy of new fauna and flora, and the thrilling promise of scientific discoveries. Railroad tycoon Edward Harriman had originally conceived this voyage as a hunting expedition in pursuit of the colossal Kodiak brown bear. But in the sweeping style of 19th-century tycoon-philanthropists, he couldn't resist transforming the undertaking into a grand gesture to the world of science. Loaded on board, along with live turkeys, cows, chickens, and cases of champagne, were the tools of the artists' and scientists' trade: tents, canoes, traps, surveying instruments, and painters' canvases.

Like a scientific Noah's Ark, Harriman's expedition included two men from every possible discipline: geologists, botanists, foresters, mining engineers, photographers, artists, and preservationists. Among them was an old Alaska hand, John Muir, whose words

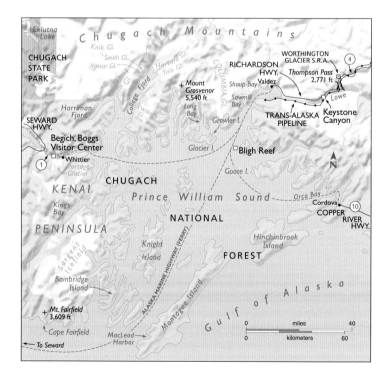

Kayaking near Columbia Glacier

"do something for wildness and make the mountains glad," would inspire the creation of national parks.

At the northern reaches of the Gulf of Alaska, the *George W. Elder* sailed past Hinchinbrook and Montague Islands and into Prince William Sound. Sailing to the western side of the sound, the expedition soon found itself, in the words of one member, in a "great ice chest." It held a magnificent treasure of beautiful fjords and breathtaking glaciers for the scientists to examine and record.

As Harriman and his companions approached the Barry Glacier, an uncharted fjord sparkled before them. Known today as **Harriman Fjord,** this exquisite corner of Prince William Sound is filled with tidewater glaciers laced with waterfalls. A little farther north, amid rafts of sea otters and seals, lay another fjord. Harriman named its plunging glaciers after some of the East Coast's Ivy League and Seven Sister colleges: Harvard, Yale, Bryn Mawr, Vassar, and Smith. Not surprisingly, the inlet itself became known as College Fjord.

Harriman's expedition was not the first to have explored the sound. More than a hundred years earlier in May 1778, English explorer Capt. James Cook sailed into the sound and christened it Sandwich Sound after the earl of Sandwich. By the time Cook's ship returned to England, however, the earl had fallen from grace. The name was changed to Prince William Sound to honor the king's third son (who would become King William IV).

Ode to the Ice Worm

At the turn of the 20th century, Robert W. Service, the famous poet who immortalized the Klondike gold rush era, wrote a poem entitled "The Ballad of the Ice-Worm Cocktail." In it, a brash "cheechako" (a newcomer to Alaska) is challenged by old-timers to swallow an ice worm at the bottom of his drink at the Malamute Saloon. Although he chokes it down, the man soon makes a speedy exit. The old-timers roar with laughter at the joke: The worm they slipped into his drink was only a spaghetti noodle inked with two big red eyes.

Like the saloon's mocking patrons, many people believe the ice worm to be a myth. But the joke's on them: There really is an ice worm. True to its name, this tiny black worm lives on coastal glaciers and ice fields in Alaska. Not built to withstand much heat, the ice worm's body hovers around the freezing point of water. How does it survive? On windblown dirt, pollen, and algae. Cocktails at the Malamute Saloon are not part of its diet.

Other events that have transpired in the sound have proved less benign. In March 1964, the largest earthquake ever recorded in North America struck Alaska *(see p. 233)*; its epicenter was here in Prince William Sound. In all, 131 people died and entire towns and villages at the edge of the sea were destroyed by the quake-generated tsunamis.

Twenty-five years later, on the evening of March 23, the loaded oil tanker *Exxon Valdez,* sailing south through the sound from the port of Valdez, requested permission from the U.S. Coast Guard to change sea lanes to avoid icebergs coming off the Columbia Glacier. Shortly after midnight, the ship radioed the Coast Guard again. In what would become one of the great understatements of the day, the captain reported, "We've fetched up hard aground, north of Goose Island off Bligh Reef, and evidently we're leaking some oil."

Approximately 11.3 million barrels of North Slope crude spilled into the pristine waters of Prince William Sound. The oil slick swept out into the gulf and from there into lower Cook Inlet, devastating populations of marine wildlife and hundreds of miles of coastal habitats. Thousands of creatures died in the largest oil spill in U.S. history.

The scientific jury on the long-term consequences to the habitat is still out. But after more than a decade of winter storms and massive environmental cleanup efforts, the effects of the oil spill cannot readily be seen with the naked eye. When the sun shines and the seas are calm, there's no place else on Earth you'd rather be than Prince William Sound. Its hundreds of miles of coastline, blue waters, emerald islands, fjords, and rivers of ice tumbling into the sea entrance visitors.

What to See and Do

There are many sights to see in Prince William Sound. If you'd like to spend more than a day here, plenty of accommodations are available. Throughout the area, you'll find dozens of public-use cabins managed by the Forest Service, available for $25 to $45 per night *(877-444-6777. www.reserveusa.com)*. For more information call Chugach National Forest and ask for "Public Recreation Cabins: Chugach National Forest Alaska," a 30-page booklet that describes each cabin and how to reach it.

You can also overnight at Growler Island Wilderness Camp *(907-835-4731 or 800-992-1297)*, a rustic retreat with cabins and heated tent-cabins. There are no established campgrounds here, but primitive camping is possible on the islands that dot the sound.

Ferries & Driving Tour

The state ferry system, the **Alaska Marine Highway** *(800-642-0066. www.dot.state.ak.us/amhs/)*, can take you from Whittier, or from Seward on Resurrection Bay, to Valdez and Cordova, and back.

The ferry provides much more than transportation; it's festive, communal, and a great way to get out on the water and appreciate the remoteness of the sound. The crossing from Whittier to Valdez takes about 7 hours. You can walk or drive onto the ferry.

If you take your car, extend your marine excursion by driving the 350-mile circular route that begins (or ends) in Anchorage: Traveling counterclockwise, for example, you would follow the **Seward Highway** to Whittier, take the ferry to Valdez, and then take the **Richardson** *(see pp. 230–31)* and **Glenn Highways** *(see pp. 224-27)* back to Anchorage—a circuit that can take you several days.

Boat Cruises

From the west and the east sides of the sound, 1-day boat trips can be arranged to view glaciers and whales. Prince William Sound Cruises and Tours *(800-922-1297)* offers boat cruises from Valdez and Whittier.

From Whittier on the western side, you are likely to cruise into **Blackstone Bay, Harriman Fjord,** or **College Fjord.** If you are interested in whales, scan the horizon for the plumes of humpback whales, which can shoot 15 feet high. Or look for the black, triangular dorsal fins of orcas as they slice through the water.

Traveling out of Valdez on the sound's eastern side, you can see the spectacular **Columbia Glacier.** One of North America's largest tidewater glaciers, it rumbles down to the sea from high in the Chugach Mountains. Until 20 years ago, Columbia Glacier lay in almost the same position as when Capt. George Vancouver of the British Royal Navy mapped it in 1794. Around 1980, however, its 300-foot-high face imploded, kicking out massive quantities of ice (and now preventing you from boating close to the glacier). Since then, the glacier has retreated about 7.5 miles. Scientists predict that within this century, the movement will open up a whole new fjord about 25 miles in length.

Facing Columbia Glacier are **Glacier** and little **Growler Islands.** You can explore the islands' basalt sea caves by air or boat charter.

Sea Kayaking, Sailing & Rafting

Alaskans like to explore the sound by kayak. Compared with a larger boat, the small, easily maneuverable craft allows them to experience more intimately the area's waters, coast, and wildlife. Outfitters such as Wilderness Alaska *(907-345-3567)* or Alaska Sea Kayakers *(907-472-2534 or 877-472-2534)* can set you up with a kayak or take you on half-day or week-long trips. Novice paddlers should hire a guide.

If you are experienced and choose to kayak without a guide, be aware that the weather here is mercurial; expect sudden changes. Though the sound is sheltered from the wild storms of the Gulf of Alaska, winds can come up out of nowhere and leave you bucking 7-foot seas.

Be prepared for other hazards as well: flipping your boat and cold-water immersion, hypothermia, calving tidewater glaciers, rolling icebergs, strong currents, rough water, and the intrusion of bears (which love peanut butter, salmon, toothpaste, and everything else you might have stuffed in your food bags). Anadyr

Alaska's "Soft Gold"

With no blubber to keep it warm, the sea otter depends on its luxurious coat for protection against icy waters. Fortunately, it has the densest fur of any mammal. Yet more than 250 years ago, this fur touched off a series of events that nearly wiped out this creature.

In the early 18th century, Russia's Peter the Great commissioned a Danish sea captain named Vitus Bering to explore whether land connected Siberia and North America.

On his second voyage, Bering reached an island off the Alaskan coast. While sailing back to Russia with news of his discoveries, Bering and his crew fetched up on the shores of an uninhabited island in what is known today as the Bering Sea.

Suffering from scurvy and weakened by cold and hunger, the captain and many of his men died. Sea otters saved the others, who ate the creatures' flesh and kept themselves warm with the fur.

When the bedraggled crew finally made it home, they found people were less excited by Bering's discoveries than by the otter pelts the sailors had brought back.

The creature's fur became known as "soft gold." So prized was it that it inspired a stampede of hunters who, in their rush to get rich, nearly decimated the sea otter population along the Aleutian Chain and into the Gulf of Alaska.

In 1911, with the sea otter population on the brink of extinction, an international treaty was drawn up to provide the animal some protection, the first effort to save it.

Sea otter, Kachemak Bay

Adventures *(907-835-2814 or 800-865-2925)* offers day trips on small sailboats in the sound.

Just outside Valdez, Keystone Raft and Kayak Adventures *(907-835-2606)* runs a popular half-day white-water rafting trip on the **Lowe River** through **Keystone Canyon.**

■ 90-100 miles across ■ Northern edge of Gulf of Alaska, east of Kenai Peninsula ■ Best months June–Aug. ■ Camping, kayaking, sailing, fishing, bird–watching, whale–watching, boat tours ■ Fishing license required
■ Contact Chugach National Forest, 3301 C St., Suite 300, Anchorage, AK 99503; 907-271-2500. Glacier Ranger District, Girdwood, 907-783-3242. Cordova Ranger District, 907-424-7761. Seward Ranger District, 907-224-3374. www.fs.fed.us/r10/chugach

Prince William Sound at sunset

Tetlin National Wildlife Refuge

150 miles northeast of Wrangell

Thousands of lakes and ponds play host to dense concentrations of nesting waterfowl drawn to Tetlin National Wildlife Refuge. The spring thaw arrives earlier here than at sites to the north, so Tetlin is an important rest stop for migrating birds, among them sizable spring and fall migrations of sandhill cranes.

The glacier-fed **Chisana** and **Nabesna Rivers** merge near the center of the refuge to create the **Tanana River.** Extensive stands of deciduous trees shelter wildlife, while spindly black spruce, some almost two centuries old, sprout from muskeg underlain with permafrost.

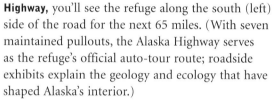

Driving into Alaska from Canada via the historic **Alaska Highway,** you'll see the refuge along the south (left) side of the road for the next 65 miles. (With seven maintained pullouts, the Alaska Highway serves as the refuge's official auto-tour route; roadside exhibits explain the geology and ecology that have shaped Alaska's interior.)

In the summer, consider stopping at the visitor center *(Mile 1229)* to pick up an interpretive auto-tour cassette; you can listen (and learn) as you drive, then drop it off at the Alaska Public Lands Information Center *(on the main street in town of Tok).*

If you camp at **Deadman Lake Campground** *(Mile 1249),* take time to walk the quarter-mile **Taiga Trail** or fish for pike from the handicap-accessible pier.

The refuge ends at Mile 1284, but the highway continues on to **Tok,** a tenuous beachhead in the interior wilderness.

■ 730,000 acres ■ Southeast of Tok on Alaska Hwy.
■ Year-round ■ Camping, hiking, hunting, fishing, bird-watching, auto tour ■ Contact the refuge, P.O. Box 779, Tok, AK 99780; 907-883-5312. Or Alaska Public Lands Information Center (APLIC), P.O. Box 359, Milepost 1314, Alaska Hwy., Tok, AK 99780; 907-883-5667. http://tetlin .fws.gov/index.htm

Resources

The following is a select list of resources for Alaska. Contact the national parks and other sites for additional outfitter and lodging options.

Current information about road conditions is available at 907-586-8751.

Federal and State Agencies

Alaska Department of Fish and Game
P.O. Box 25526
Juneau, AK 99802
907-465-4100

Wildlife Information Center
333 Raspberry Rd.
Anchorage, AK 99518
907-267-2344
www.state.ak.us/adfg/
Hunting and fishing licenses, and site information.

Alaska Marine Highway System
P.O. Box 25535
Juneau, AK 99802
800-642-0066

605 W. 4th Ave.
Anchorage, AK 99501
907-272-7116
www.ferryalaska.com
Providing access to 32 Alaskan communities, the AMHS is an essential resource for exploring the inside passage. Complete schedule and fare information.

Alaska's National Parks
(See Alaska Public Lands Information Centers)

Alaska Public Lands
Information Centers
605 W. 4th Ave., Ste. 105
Anchorage, AK 99501
907-271-2737

250 Cushman St., Ste. 1A
Fairbanks, AK 99701
907-456-0527

Southeast Alaska Discovery Center
50 Main St
Ketchikan, AK 99901
907-228-6220

P.O. Box 359
Tok, AK 99780
907-883-5667
www.nps.gov/aplic/
These inter-agency offices allow visitors one-stop shopping for information on state and federally managed public lands. Recreation permits and reservations for backcountry cabins may also be made here.The Alaska Natural History Association has outlets in each of these locations selling natural history books, maps, and guides to all areas of Alaska. Fee for Ketchikan office during summer only.

Alaska State Parks
Department of Natural Resources
Public Information Center
550 W. 7th Ave., Ste. 1260
Anchorage, AK 99501
907-269-8400

3700 Airport Way
Fairbanks, AK 99709
907-451-2705

400 Willoughby Ave.
Juneau, AK 99801
907-465-4563
www.dnr.state.ak.us/parks
Information on Alaska parks, including camping and cabin rentals.

Alaska State Tourism
Alaska Travel Industry Association
2600 Cordova St., Ste. 201
Anchorage, AK 99503
907-276-4118 or 800-478-1255
www.travelaska.com/
General resource for statewide travel, including accommodations, activities, and attractions.

U.S.D.A. Forest Service
Chugach National Forest
    Public Information
    3301 C St., Ste. 300
    Anchorage, AK 99503
    907-743-9500
    www.fs.fed.us/r10/chugach
Source for maps, as well as recreational
information in the forest—located
along the Gulf of Alaska—including
cabins and camping.

U.S.D.A. Forest Service
Tongass National Forest
    Forest Service Information Center
    Federal building
    648 Mission St.
    Ketchikan, AK 99901
    907-225-3101
    www.fs.fed.us/r10/tongass
Source for maps, as well as recreational
information in the forest—located
along the Southeastern Coast of Alaska
—including cabins and camping.

U.S. Fish and Wildlife Service
    Public Information
    Division of Refuges
    1011 E. Tudor Rd.
    Anchorage, AK 99503
    907-786-3309
    www.r7.fws.gov
Indepth information on Alaska's
national wildlife refuges.

United States Geological Survey
    Earth Science Information Center
    4230 University Dr., Ste. 101
    Anchorage, AK 99508
    907-786-7011
    www.usgs.gov
Topographic maps to the state of
Alaska.

Lodging

    (See Alaska Tourism Marketing
    Council)

Bed & Breakfast Association of Alaska
    P.O. Box 202663
    Anchorage, AK 99520
    www.alaskabba.com

Alaska Travel Adventures
    888-778-7700
    www.alaskarv.com
Recreational Vehicle campground
information as well as rentals.

American Youth Hostel, Inc.
    700 H St.
    Anchorage AK 99501
    907-276-3635
    www.anchorageinternational
    hostel.org

Katmailand, Inc.
    4125 Aircraft Dr.
    Anchorage, AK 99502
    907-243-5448 or
    800-544-0551
Premier fishing lodges in Katmai.

Camping

For a listing of private campgrounds,
contact the Alaska Tourism Marketing
Council. Alaska State Parks, the
U.S.D.A. Forest Service, the National
Park Service, and the U.S. Fish and
Wildlife Service also operate camp-
grounds throughout the state. Addi-
tional information is available through
the Alaska Public Lands Information
Centers or online at www.gorp.com.

Hotel and Motel Chains

Best Western International
    800-528-1234
Choice Hotels
    800-4-CHOICE
Comfort Inns
    800-228 5150
Days Inn
    800-325-2525
Hilton Hotels
    800-Hiltons
Holiday Inns
    800-HOLIDAY

Hyatt Hotels and Resorts
    800-223-1234
Marriott Hotels Resorts Suites
    800-228-9290
Quality Inns
    800-228-5151
Ramada Inns
    800-2-RAMADA
Sheraton Hotels
    800-325-3535
Westin Hotels and Resorts
    800-325-3000

Outfitters and Activities

The following is a select list. For additional recommendations on licensed outfitters, contact the Alaska Public Lands Information Centers (see p. 244).

ABEC's Alaska Adventures
    1550 Alpine Vista Ct.
    Fairbanks, AK 99712
    907-457-8907 or 877-424-8907
    www.abecalaska.com
Options include exploring Gates of the Arctic NP, Arctic NWR, and the Brooks Range

Alaska Air Taxi, LLC
    4501 Aircraft Dr.
    Anchorage, AK 99502
    907-243-3944
    Fax: 907-248-2993
    airtaxi@arctic.net
    www.alaskaairtaxi.com
Provides charter services to Denali, Katmai, Kenai Fjords

Alaska Alpine Adventures
    General Delivery
    Port Alsworth, AK 99653
    877-525-2577
    www.alaskaalpineadventures.com
Arranges small custom backpacking and river-running trips in Lake Clark NP

Alaska Discovery
    5310 Glacier Highway
    Juneau, AK 99801
    907-780-6226 or 800-586-1911
    www.akdiscovery.com
Guided kayak tours of Glacier Bay and Wrangell-St. Elias NPs

Alaska Fishing and Raft Adventures
    269 Topside Rd.
    Fairbanks, AK 99712
    907-455-7238 or 800-890-3229
    www.aktours.net
Single and multi-day tours showcase the interior's fishing, hiking, and wildlife

Alaska Mountaineering School
    P.O. Box 566, 3rd St.
    Talkeetna, AK 99676
    907-733-1016
    Fax: 907-733-1362
    info@climbalaska.org
    www.climbalaska.org
Offers courses and climbing expeditions in Denali NP

Alaska Seaplane Service
    1873 Shell Simmions Dr., Ste. 110
    Juneau, AK 99801
    907-789-3331
    www.akseaplanes.com
Flight-seeing and charters in southeast Alaska

Alaska Troutfitters
    Mile 48.2 Sterling Hwy.
    P.O. Box 570
    Cooper Landing, AK 99572
    907 457-8907 or 877-424-8907
    www.aktroutfitters.com
Experienced fly-fishing service on the headwaters of the Kenai River

Alaska Waters, Inc.
    P.O. Box 1978
    Wrangell, AK 99929
    907-874-2378 or 800-347-4462
    www.alaskawaters.com
Adventure tours and guided trips of the Inside Passage and Tongass NF

Alaska Wildland Adventures
P.O. Box 389
Girdwood, AK 99587
907-783-2928
Fax: 907-783-2130
kirkawa@aol.com
www.alaskawildland.com
Offers trips in Denali and Kenai Fjords

Alaskan Mountain Safaris
HC 60 Box 299C
Copper Center, AK 99573
907-822-3410
www.akmountainsafaris.com
Half-day to multi-day horseback and
fishing trips in Wrangell-St. Elias NP

Alpine Air, Inc.
P.O. Box 1047
Girdwood, AK, 99587
907-783-2360
Fax: 907-754-1504
info@alpineairalaska.net
www.alaska.net/~alpineair

Anadyr Adventures
P.O. Box 1821
Valdez, AK 99686
907-835-2814 or 800-865-2925
anadyr@anadyradventures.com
www.anadyradventures.com
Sailing, kayaking, and hiking tours of
Prince William Sound

Camp Alaska Tours
P.O. Box 872247
Wasilla, AK 99687
907-376-9438
Fax: 907-376-2353
info@campalaska.net
www.campalaska.com
Offers camping, hiking, kayaking, and
rafting in Denali, Kenai Fjords NPs

Chilkat Guides, Ltd.
P.O. Box 170
Haines, AK 99827
907-766-2491
www.raftalaska.com
Eagle tours in the Chilkat Valley

Copper Valley Air Service
Milepost 118 Richardson Hwy.
P.O. Box 234
Glennallen, AK 99588
907-822-4200
Fax: 907-376-0777
cvas@alaska.net
www.coppervalleyair.com
Offers flight-seeing tours of Wrangell–
St. Elias, Lake Clark, and Denali NPs

Denali Backcountry Lodge, Inc.
410 Denali St.
Anchorage, AK 99501
907-644-9980 ext. 204 or
800-841-0692
Fax: 907-644-9981
info@denalilodge.com
www.denalilodge.com
Lodge offers all-inclusive Denali
NP stays

Denali Park Resorts
Aramark Sports & Entertainment
241 W. Ship Creek Rd.
Anchorage, AK 99501
907-264-4600
www.denaliparkresorts.com
Offers vacation packages to Denali NP

Denali West Lodge, Inc.
P.O. Box 40, AC
Lake Minchumina, AK 99757
907-674-3112 or 888-607-5566
Fax: 907-674-3112
info@denaliwest.com
www.denaliwest.com
Offers dog sledding and other activities

Denali Wilderness Centers, Ltd.
(Camp Denali)
P.O. Box 67
Denali Park, AK 99755
907-683-2290
FAX: 907-683-1568
info@campdenali.com
www.campdenali.com
Lodge in Denali with view of Mount
McKinley

Doug Geeting Aviation
P.O. Box 42
Talkeetna, AK 99676
907-733-2366 or 800-770-2366
Fax: 907-733-1000
airtours@alaska.net
www.alaskaairtours.com
Offers scenic flights and glacier
landings in Denali NP

Earthsong Lodge Dog Sled Adventures
P.O. Box 89
Healy, AK 99743-0089
907-683-2863
Fax: 907-683-2868
koala@mtaonline.net
www.earthsonglodge.com
Lodge offers overnight camping trips in
Denali NP

Equinox Wilderness Expeditions
2440 E. Tudor Rd., #1102
Anchorage, AK 99507
604-222-1219 or 877-615-9087
www.equinoxexpeditions.com
State-wide trips, specializing in custom
and women-only trips

Great Alaska Adventure Lodge
33881 Sterling Highway
Sterling, AK 99672
907-262-4515 or 800-544-2261
Fax: 907-262-8797
greatalaska@greatalaska.com
www.greatalaska.com
All-inclusive lodge offers sport fishing,
nature safaris, and bear viewing in
Kenai Fjords NP

Hudson Air Service, Inc.
P.O. Box 648
Talkeetna, AK 99676
907-733-2321 or 800-478-2321
Fax: 907-733-2333
hudson@mtaonline.net
www.hudsonair.com
Offers flight-seeing tours, charters, and
wildlife tours

Kantishna Air Taxi
P.O. Box 46
Denali Park, AK 99755
907-683-1223
info@katair.com
www.katair.com
Custom charters and flight-seeing tours
of Denali and other Alaska destinations.

Lake Clark Air Inc.
Port Alsworth, AK 99653
907-781-2208 or 888-440-2281
www.lakeclarkair.com
Located within the national park, provides air services, lodging, and guiding

Lifetime Adventures
P.O. Box 1205
Palmer, AK 99645
907-746-4644 or 800-952-8624
www.lifetimeadventures.net
Tours and rentals for exploring Katmai
NP and Chugach SP

National Outdoor Leadership School
284 Lincoln St.
Lander, WY 82520
307-332-5300 or 800-710-6657
www.nols.edu
With a campus in Palmer, NOLS offers
courses in canoeing, kayaking, backpacking, and mountaineering

Pangaea Adventures
P.O. Box 775
Valdez, AK 99686
907-835-8442 or 800-660-9637
www.pangaeaadventures.com
Sailing and boat tours of Prince William
Sound. Multi-activity tours combine
kayaking, rafting, and backpacking

Prince William Sound Cruises and
Tours
2525 C St., Ste. 405
Anchorage, AK 99503
907-277-2131 or 800-992-1297
www.princewilliamsound.com
Cruises and guided expeditions in
Prince William Sound area

River Wrangellers
  P.O. Box 146
  Gakona, AK 99586
  907-822-3967 or 888-822-3967
  www.alaskariverwrangellers.com
White-water rafting in south central
Alaska

Royal Coachman Lodge
  P.O. Box 450
  Dillingham, AK 99576
  888-347-4286
  www.royalcoachmanlodge.com
Fishing and lodging in Wood-Tickchik
State Park

Rust's Flying Service
  P.O. Box 190867
  Anchorage, AK 99519
  907-243-1595 or 800-544-2299
  www.flyrusts.com
Fishing and flight-seeing tours in
Prince William Sound

Sea Otter Kayak
  P.O. Box 228
  Gustavus, AK 99826
  907-697-3007
  www.he.net/~seaotter
Kayak rentals and day cruises of
Glacier Bay

Sourdough Outfitters
  P.O. Box 26066
  Bettles Field, AK 99726
  907-692-5252
  www.sourdough.com
Dog-sledding on the North Slope.
Summer activities include hiking, fish-
ing, and rafting in the Brooks Range

Spirit Walker Expeditions
  P.O. Box 240
  Gustavus, AK 99826
  907-697-2266 or 800-529-2537
  www.seakayakalaska.com
Hiking and kayaking throughout the
southeast

St. Elias Alpine Guides
  P.O. Box 111241
  Anchorage, AK 99511
  907-345-9048 or 888-933-5427
  www.steliasguides.com
Hiking, ice climbing, mountaineering,
and rafting in Wrangell-St. Elias NP

Stan Stephens' Cruises
  P.O. Box 1297
  Valdez, AK 99686
  907-835-4731 or 866-867-1297
  www.stanstephenscruises.com
Cruises and guided kayaking and
sailing from Valdez and Whittier

Stickeen Wilderness Adventures
  P.O. Box 934
  Wrangell, AK 99929
  907-874-2085 or 800-874-2085
  www.akgetaway.com/wildside/
  swa.htm/
Guided bear-watching trips to Anan
Wildlife Observatory

Wilderness Alaska
  P.O. Box 113063
  Anchorage, AK 99511
  907-345-3567
  www.wildernessalaska.com
Offering 4- to 8-day hiking trips in
Prince William Sound

Wood River Lodge
  P.O. Box 1369
  Dillingham, AK 99576
  800-842-5205
  www.woodriverlodge.com
All inclusive fishing lodge in Wood-
Tickchik SP

Wrangell Mountain Air
  #25 P.O. Box MXY
  McCarthy, AK 99588
  907-544-4411 or 800-478-1160
  www.wrangellmountainair.com/
Flight-seeing tours and charters to
Wrangell-St. Elias NP

INDEX

One of the world's largest nonprofit scientific and educational organizations, the National Geographic Society was founded in 1888 "for the increase and diffusion of geographic knowledge." Fulfilling this mission, the Society educates and inspires millions every day through its magazines, books, television programs, videos, maps and atlases, research grants, the National Geographic Bee, teacher workshops, and innovative classroom materials. The Society is supported through membership dues, charitable gifts, and income from the sale of its educational products. This support is vital to National Geographic's mission to increase global understanding and promote conservation of our planet through exploration, research, and education.

For more information, please call 1-800-NGS LINE (647-5463) or write to the following address:

National Geographic Society
1145 17th Street N.W.
Washington, D.C. 20036-4688
U.S.A.

Illustration Credits

All photographs by Michael Melford, except as noted:

9 Joel Sartore/www.joelsartore.com. 81 Rich Reid/Colors of Nature. 92 Karen Kasmauski.
98 Barbara Brundege/AccentAlaska.com. 114 Joel Sartore/www.joelsartore.com. 138 RichReid/NGS
Image Collection. 147 Steve Raymer. 157 Rich Reid/Colors of Nature. 186 Tim Thompson. 191
Michio Hoshino/ Minden Pictures. 200 Jim Brandenburg/Minden Pictures. 212 George F. Mobley.
220-221 George F. Mobley. 225 Ken Graham/AccentAlaska.com. 231 Steven C. Kaufman.
232 Steve Raymer.

Staff Credits

National Geographic Guide to the National Parks Alaska
Published by the National Geographic Society

John M. Fahey, Jr., *President and Chief Executive Officer*
Gilbert M. Grosvenor, *Chairman of the Board*
Nina D. Hoffman, *Executive Vice President, President, Books and School Publishing*
Kevin Mulroy, *Vice President and Editor-in-Chief*
Marianne Koszorus, *Design Director*
Elizabeth L. Newhouse, *Director of Travel Publishing* & *Project Manager*
Alison Kahn, *Editor*
Cinda Rose, *Art Director*
Carl Mehler, *Director of Maps*
Ruth Ann Thompson, *Designer*
Lise Sajewski, *Style/Copy Editor*
Gregory Ugiansky, The M Factory, *Map Production*
Lewis Bassford, *Production Project Manager*
Meredith Wilcox, *Illustrations Assistant*
Robert Swanson, *Indexer*
Ben Archambault, Ben Bodurian, Cindy Kittner, Larry Porges, Simon Williams,
Jordan Zappala, *Contributors*

Library of Congress Cataloging-in-Publication Data

National Geographic guide to the national parks Alaska / [prepared by the Book Division].
    p. cm.
Includes bibliographical references and index.
ISBN 0-7922-9540-4
1. National parks and reserves--Alaska--Guidebooks. 2. Parks--Alaska--Guidebooks. 3. Alaska--Guidebooks.
I. Title: Guide to the national parks Alaska. II. National Geographic Society (U.S.). Book Division.
F902.3.N38 2005
917.9804'52--dc22   2004022871

NATIONAL GEOGRAPHIC
Guides to the National Parks

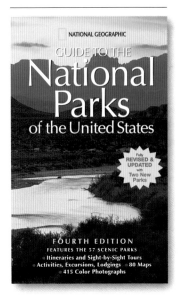

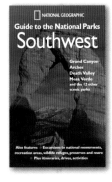

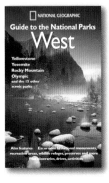

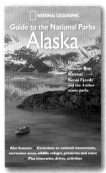

- **National Geographic Guide to the National Parks of the U.S.** *(4th Edition)* ISBN: 0-7922-6972-1

- **National Geographic Guide to the National Parks: Alaska** ISBN: 0-7922-9540-4

- **National Geographic Guide to the National Parks: East & Midwest** ISBN: 0-7922-9537-4

- **National Geographic Guide to the National Parks: Southwest** ISBN: 0-7922-9539-0

- **National Geographic Guide to the National Parks: West** ISBN: 0-7922-9538-2

- **Glacier and Waterton Lakes National Parks Road Guide** ISBN: 0-7922-6637-4

- **Grand Canyon National Park Road Guide** ISBN: 0-7922-6642-0

- **Rocky Mountain National Park Road Guide** ISBN: 0-7922-6641-2

- **Yellowstone and Grand Teton National Parks Road Guide** ISBN: 0-7922-6639-0

- **National Geographic Park Profiles: Canyon Country Parklands** ISBN: 0-7922-7353-2

- **National Geographic Park Profiles: Grand Canyon Country** ISBN: 0-7922-7032-0

- **National Geographic Park Profiles: Yellowstone Country** ISBN: 0-7922-7031-2

- **National Geographic Park Profiles: Yosemite** ISBN: 0-7922-7030-4

- **ALSO: National Geographic Guide to the State Parks of the U.S.** *(2nd Edition)* ISBN: 0-7922-6628-5

AVAILABLE WHEREVER BOOKS ARE SOLD